As the Workforce Ages

Frank W. Pierce Memorial Lectureship and Conference Series
Number 9

As the Workforce Ages

Costs, Benefits, and Policy Challenges

Olivia S. Mitchell, Editor

ILR Press
Ithaca, New York

Library of Congress Cataloging-in-Publication Data

As the workforce ages : costs, benefits, and policy challenges /
Olivia S. Mitchell, editor.
p.   cm. — (Frank W. Pierce memorial lectureship and
conference series ; no. 9)
Includes bibliographical references and index.
ISBN 0-87546-195-6 (alk. paper). — ISBN 0-87546-196-4 (pbk. :
alk. paper)
1. Aged—Employment—United States.   2. Aged–Government policy—
United States.   3. Aged—Employment—Cross-cultural studies.
I. Mitchell, Olivia S.   II. Series.
HD6280.A8   1993

331.3'98'0973—dc20   92-31402

Copies may be ordered through bookstores or directly from

ILR Press
School of Industrial and Labor Relations
Cornell University
Ithaca, NY 14853–3901

Printed on acid-free paper in the United States of America

5 4 3 2 1

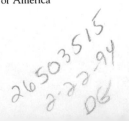

For Gene, Erica, and Hilary

Contents

TABLES

FIGURES

PREFACE

THIS VOLUME CONSISTS of papers presented at a conference in late 1991 at Cornell University's School of Industrial and Labor Relations. More than fifty experts participated, including U.S. government officials from the Department of Labor and the Department of Health and Human Services, visitors from the Japan Institute of Labor, social scientists from Cornell and elsewhere, and members of the labor and business communities. As the start-up activity of the school's new Institute for Labor Market Policy, the conference focused attention on the institute's labor market policy research, training, and extension activities both at home and abroad.

The conference was organized and hosted by Olivia S. Mitchell, professor of labor economics in the school and the director of the Program on Labor Force Demographics for the Institute for Labor Market Policy. Funding for the conference was provided by Cornell University's Pierce Lecture Series and by the School of Industrial and Labor Relations. Additional funding came from the U.S. Department of Labor's Pension and Welfare Benefits Administration.

Excellent assistance in conducting the conference was provided by Pat Dickerson, Brenda Lapp, and Dick Shore. Ronald Ehrenberg, Gary Fields, Robert Gibbons, Maria Hanratty, Richard Hinz, Silvana Pozzebon, Albert Rees, and Timothy Smeeding all offered extremely useful comments on the papers. Additional comments from Donald Parsons and Dallas Salisbury were also valuable.

Production of this volume was facilitated by Alison Pennell and the superbly professional staff of ILR Press, under the direction of Frances Benson. Their participation was instrumental in making this book better, and we thank them.

INTRODUCTION

Chapter 1.
AS THE WORKFORCE AGES

Olivia S. Mitchell

E ACH OF US IS an aging worker, and each of us has a stake in the
ways aging is changing the form and structure of jobs, pay, and
retirement. This volume discusses the challenges confronting the
United States and other countries as their workforces age. Clearly, the
older-worker labor market differs in many ways from the lower-paid,
more mobile, less career-oriented youth labor market of the 1970s and
1980s. As employees age, they want to be paid and rewarded in different
ways, including with ever-more costly health insurance. These changes
must be recognized and met by businesses and their employees over the
next few decades. Government and private retirement programs, particularly pension plans and social security, must also be prepared to meet
the new demands.

In this volume, we review the key labor market causes and consequences of this massive demographic transition. Our goal is to make
accessible key insights generated by social scientists over the last few
years about how the labor market and labor market policies function
for older workers. Included are contributions from demographers, economists, human resource specialists, and government policy analysts.
Accomplishments of the past are enumerated, along with shortfalls and
areas where progress still needs to be made. We hope that this work
will serve as a springboard for further discussion and future research on
how the labor market must change to meet the demands of an aging
workforce.

This book is divided into three sections, each reflecting a different
focus on the aging workforce. The first section examines aging workers
around the world. The second section explores jobs and pay, including

benefit plans, that seem to suit older workers. The last section addresses policy challenges of an aging population and an increasingly older workforce.

AGING WORKERS AROUND THE WORLD

A provocative and insightful report and interpretation of key demographic trends is offered in the first chapter, by Martha Farnsworth Riche. Her work focuses on population aging in the United States.

Riche makes several important points. She shows that seemingly tiny and quite believable differences in forecasts about fertility, mortality, and immigration imply hugely different projected population patterns. As a result, depending on whether one uses one or a second set of fertility and mortality assumptions, the U.S. population in ninety years is projected to be either 330 million or 500 million. Forecast ranges of this magnitude highlight the almost impossible task of predicting the future. Furthermore, although most demographers agree that the rates of immigration, both legal and illegal, will be high and increasing in the next several decades, the exact magnitudes are as yet unknown, making population forecasts by age groups extremely imprecise.

Despite the wide confidence bands that must be placed around population forecasts, Riche makes the important point that, whatever the range of births, deaths, and migratory flows (within reason), the population will definitely age, along with the labor force, over the next several years. The U.S. labor force is predicted to hit its all-time peak over the next ten to fifteen years as the baby boomers swell its ranks. Indeed, the front-runners of the baby-boom generation will hit the "age 55 wall" in the year 2001 and age 65 in 2011.

Though the millennium is nearly upon us, it remains difficult to think clearly about the years beyond 2000. For this reason, it is useful to convert a life expectancy table to calendar time, as in table 1-1. This table illustrates when people of different birth years will attain the age of 65 and their consequent life expectancies. Certainly many will live longer than the table predicts, while others will not. Nonetheless, the table makes more palpable the impact of many statistics presented both in Riche's paper and later in the volume. When we speak of the labor force peaking between the years 2000 and 2010, the reader can now place himself or herself on the correct side of the divide.

Another point that Riche's chapter makes is that there is a growing ethnic gap between the old and the young in the United States. She

TABLE 1-1. LIFE EXPECTANCY OF AMERICANS

Age in 1990	Birth Year	Year of 65th Birthday	Year Life Expectancy Is Attained	
			Women	Men
65	1925	1990	2009	2005
50	1940	2005	2021	2016
40	1950	2015	2030	2025
20	1970	2035	2049	2043
0	1990	2055	2068	2061

Source: Derived from U.S. Bureau of the Census 1990.

points out that by the year 2010, the average white person will be 41, while the average black will be 31, and the average Hispanic 29. This is partly a result of the higher fertility rates among young migrants and partly a result of the lower life expectancies of nonwhites. Riche intimates that this growing difference between the age structure of different ethnic groups will exacerbate the sometimes already strident debate between the young and the old over the economic pie. Along similar lines is her observation that older women, both married and not, will play an increasingly important role in the labor market of the next two decades and that their labor force attachment patterns as they approach retirement deserve more attention from analysts and policy makers alike.

Building on Riche's population forecasts, Phillip B. Levine counsels caution in pondering labor force trends. As Levine points out, like it or not, labor force projections are a necessary part of everyday life. They are used by company managers making training and investment decisions, young people making college choices, older employees who are planning their retirements, and, certainly not least, policy makers charged with making budgets and determining benefit payouts from social security, medicare, and other social programs.

Though we need labor force forecasts, Levine recommends that we be wary of them, particularly very long-term forecasts. He also warns us that policies based on these forecasts are vulnerable to error, especially when they are derived from extrapolations of past demographic trends. Levine arrives at this conclusion by first replicating forecasts prepared by the U.S. Department of Labor's Bureau of Labor Statistics (BLS). He demonstrates that a simple straight-line trend projection has been the primary approach used to date, with adjustments when forecasts seemed either impossible (e.g., when more than 100 percent of the population was projected to be working) or unreasonable (e.g., when women were projected to be working at greater rates than men). He then goes on to demonstrate that these simple straight-line extrapolations are inevitably wrong, since behavior is influenced by economic and other factors and a straight-line trend projection is not. These errors prove to be most serious when there are sharp changes in participation trends over time, as occurs with both younger and older women. Levine's graphical depiction of the degree of under- and overshooting is a striking reminder that behavioral analysts need to be involved in forecasting, if only to provide evidence that forecasting is an imperfect art.

Levine then offers his own first pass at a behavioral model, which seems to work remarkably well. He relates changes in the work rates of older men to benefit levels from social security and notes that they correlate quite highly. He concludes that the hazard rates of retiring seem to respond to changes in social security benefit patterns. Based on these initial findings, it appears that an economic model offers substantial promise for forecasters. There is much that remains to be done, however. One serious question is whether the correlation between older men's work rates and social security benefits is spurious or real. Several authors have recently sought to link time-series changes in older men's market attachment to social security and have not been very optimistic about disentangling these effects. A top-notch Ph.D. dissertation could be done in this area, explaining the time-series patterns in the labor force participation rates (LFPR) of older workers.

Another question Levine's work raises concerns the changing nature of work for people age 55 and older. Some allege that retirement is still the process of withdrawing altogether from one main job at some specified age (say, 62). If we term this "the 1980s definition of retirement," it may be contrasted with "the 1990s definition of retirement." The latter has been characterized by some as the process whereby people withdraw gradually from full-time and go on to take part-time or "bridge" jobs in occupations and industries different from those in which they pursued their full-time careers.

Though recent data are not yet available, it is important to point out that the so-called 1980s definition of retirement did not hold for most people in the past. As the data in table 1-2 show, the vast majority of U.S. workers did not hold only one job until age 55; indeed, the average 55-year-old male held ten jobs over his lifetime, and the pattern for women was not too different. For many people, then, the characterization of retirement popularized in the 1980s may have been inaccurate.

TABLE 1-2. NUMBER OF JOBS HELD BY AMERICANS OVER THEIR LIFETIMES

Age	Jobs Held	
	Women	Men
20–24	3.8	4.1
25–29	5.2	5.8
30–34	6.4	7.0
35–39	7.4	7.9
40–44	8.3	8.7
45–49	9.0	9.3
50–54	9.4	9.8
55–59	9.8	10.2
60–64	10.0	10.5
65–69	12.2	10.7
70+	10.2	10.8
Fraction with Tenure of Twenty-plus Years		
Women	15.1%	
Men	37.3	

Source: Derived from Hall 1982, using 1979 Current Population Survey data.

The patterns may have changed relatively little, or they may have changed a great deal. Updating these trends, both in the United States and internationally, is a first priority if we are to understand the aging of the labor force.

Robert L. Clark's chapter rounds out the first section of the volume by providing comparative evidence on international trends in workforce aging. Many Westerners are unaware that most developed countries had post–World War II baby booms, as the United States did. Equally surprising, the baby boom in the United States lasted relatively long— fifteen years—compared with other nations—Japan's fertility boom lasted only three years, for example. In both countries, a sharp drop in fertility followed the boom, accompanied by a more gradual increase in life expectancy over time. These sharper swings in the fertility rates in Japan imply that aging is taking place more quickly in the Japanese workforce than anywhere else in the world. As a consequence, many Western economists, demographers, and others are eagerly studying relevant Japanese labor and social policy in an effort to determine what lessons, if any, can be applied in other nations.

Looking beyond Japan, Clark shows that population aging is proceeding apace in other countries as well. In many of the developed nations, one-quarter of the population will be 65 or older by the year 2025. As these populations age and fertility rates remain below replacement levels, the absolute size of the population in many of these nations will shrink for the first time since the plagues of the Middle Ages. The populations of the developing countries are still much more youthful than those of the developed nations: their median age was 19 years in 1970, ten years less than the median age in the developed nations, and it will remain about ten years lower in 2025—30 years of age versus 40 in the developed world. But here too the trend is similar to that in the United States, Japan, and Europe. This is primarily because of declines in population growth in Latin America, Asia, and Oceania, so that only Africa will experience net population increases though 2025.

Accompanying this aging around the world is a parallel aging of the workforce. Clark notes that many factors will affect older people's willingness to work and their need to remain employed at older ages. Several important effects of workforce aging are highlighted, including the view that fewer new jobs must be created when the labor force shrinks, which in turn could mean reduced unemployment around the world. Though this change must be seen as beneficial, other changes may not be quite so welcome. In particular, Clark forecasts a growing tension between older workers' desire to retire early, on the one hand, and governments' desire to get people to work longer, on the other. This tension, expressed most clearly in the U.S. policy debate, will most likely be restated in other nations as the ripple effects of the aging workforce grow and multiply.

New Jobs for an Older Workforce

The second section focuses on the labor market for older workers. Specific topics include job opportunities, unemployment patterns, and pay and benefits both in the United States and abroad. Several themes are repeated across these studies. The first is that the labor market for older workers is as complex, if not more so, than that for younger workers. While this may not come as a surprise to experienced labor market analysts, it bears repeating and certainly makes labor market policy evermore complex. A second theme, linked to the first, is that pay and benefits patterns change in important and systematic ways as workers age. The evidence shows that these changes occur both as a result of employers' wishes and because they reflect employees' desires as well. Finally, postretirement schemes, such as those that are common in Japan, offer reemployment opportunities for older workers who have the potential to become popular in the United States if the legal environment can be made more flexible.

Robert M. Hutchens reports that job opportunities for older workers are somewhat different than for younger employees. Hutchens contends that, because some jobs require large investments in training, employers may be reluctant to hire older workers when younger ones are available. In particular, an employer who foots the bill for on-the-job training will not want to hire an older worker who might retire soon, for fear of not recouping the investment. Using an economic job search model, Hutchens predicts that newly hired older workers will receive less pay, if they are hired, in recognition that their training costs will probably be spread over a shorter time. He also contends that younger workers seeking to change jobs will be more likely to remain in the same industry, where the value of their industry-specific skills can be recouped, but that many older workers seeking a new job will be forced to change industry and may have to accept jobs requiring less training than would comparably qualified younger workers.

Hutchens tests these predictions using data on workers displaced as a result of a plant closing who were interviewed by the Current Population Survey. Hutchens finds several interesting results, many of which support his theory. Older persons who lost their jobs through displacement had a more difficult time finding new employment than did younger workers. For instance, among the workers aged 50 to 59, more than 25 percent never found a job, while the figure for the younger workers was around 16 percent. More of the older persons dropped out of the labor force or were unemployed—upwards of 35 percent, compared with around 25 percent of the younger employees. Those older workers who did find jobs were less likely to find jobs with pay as high as they earned previously, whereas younger workers did better. Further, older workers who moved out of their previous industry and occupation category tended to move into jobs where shorter-duration employment was the norm.

While Hutchens's results support his job search model in several ways, some of the findings are perplexing. He found that older workers after being displaced were somewhat more likely than their younger counterparts to remain in the same industry or occupation. As he notes, this may indicate that younger workers are more ready to move to greener pastures, while older workers remain unemployed, waiting for jobs similar to the ones they lost. This study certainly demonstrates that the job market for older workers in the United States is very complex and that employment opportunities differ markedly from those available to younger workers. A great deal remains to be learned about this topic. Hutchens outlines several directions in which research can fruitfully proceed.

The ways in which the United States is responding to the aging workforce can be compared with the ways in which other nations are responding to the same phenomenon. For instance, succeeding waves of legislation in the United States have limited and finally barred the use of age as a criterion for retirement, pay, and many aspects of benefits accrual and payment. In contrast, older workers in Japan face seemingly more impermeable institutional barriers to employment. Mandatory retirement at age 60 is commonly accepted, for example, as are wage cuts for those older than 60. Nevertheless, Japanese workers over age 60 have one of the highest labor force participation rates in the world.

Why so many older people in Japan work, given that they tend to be forced out of their "career jobs" via mandatory retirement policy, is one of the more fascinating puzzles in labor economics. Marcus Rebick's chapter tries to fashion an answer to this puzzle by describing the job market for older workers and then evaluating what factors encourage older people in Japan to work. He finds that a very important element of the explanation lies in the formalized lifetime employment contract system, which guarantees Japanese workers job security in exchange for a promise to leave the firm at a given age. Rebick notes that this rigid labor contract can enhance productivity, and then he goes on to explore what happens at the termination point of this long-term contract. Most workers appear to renegotiate the terms and conditions of employment, in stark contrast to the United States, where retirees generally go home and stay there. In Japan an employer may agree to retire a worker on a Friday and then rehire the very same employee for a lower-paying job beginning the following Monday. Frequently, the worker reports to the very individuals he once supervised. This phenomenon has not become widespread in North America partly because laws prohibit mandatory retirement and age discrimination in pay. This is not the entire explanation for the differences in work patterns postretirement, however, insofar as these differences existed well before the U.S. laws were passed.

It may be that cultural rather that economic features explain why older Japanese continue to work. Many other explanations merit attention, however, before giving up on what economics has to offer. For instance, Rebick points out that in many cases pensions are much lower for Japanese workers than for North Americans, forcing the Japanese to continue working after age 60. In addition, the social security rules in Japan penalize those who work less than they do elsewhere, making the payoff from work greater. These and other institutional features specific to the Japanese legal system deserve additional analysis.

One factor that differentiates the labor market in the United States from that in other nations is that workers in the United States still rely on their employers to provide health insurance, whereas many Asian and European countries have national health schemes. As the workforce ages, employer-provided health insurance will become increasingly costly for U.S. firms with older workforces. The chapter by Melissa W. Barringer and Olivia Mitchell examines how the demand for health insurance changes with age when a firm offers employees choice in their health coverage via a flexible-benefits or so-called cafeteria plan. This system, which is increasingly being instituted by large U.S. firms, allows workers to opt for plans that meet their health-care needs and preferences, while at the same time requiring high-end users to pay more for their coverage.

The chapter provides statistical evidence on plan-selection behavior in a large firm where employees are permitted to select from six different health-care coverage options, three of which are traditional indemnity fee-for-service plans and three are prepaid plans. The firm offering these choices priced each option differently, reflecting the expected utilization rates for each. Workers were identified according to salary, age, marital status, and sex; plan information, including price (premium) and other features, was also modeled. The results showed that, as expected, charging more for a plan reduced employee demand and that the response pattern was similar for different age groups. Older workers proved to prefer high-coverage fee-for-service plans more than did younger workers, however, which suggests that as the workforce ages we should anticipate increases in the market share of such plans. The authors also explore other age-related differences in the demand for health-care plans that might occur in the future.

Another key element of the compensation package is pension benefits, which are the subject of the chapter by Alan L. Gustman and Thomas

L. Steinmeier. Their particular concern is pension cost-of-living ad-justments (COLAs), which are sometimes used to offset the effects of inflation in eroding retirees' financial well-being. Many retirees presum-ably desire such cost-of-living protection, and it turns out that pension COLAs account for a substantial portion of retirees' benefits when they are provided. Many pension plans do not offer anywhere near full-inflation indexation, however, and the ones that do tend not to advance-fund their cost-of-living protection. The message is that pensions are much more complex than most people probably realize.

On the basis of their investigations, Gustman and Steinmeier suggest that some aspects of pensions strongly influence worker behavior. This is true, for example, of such institutional features as benefit vesting delays, which induce young workers to stay with a firm, and benefit incentive devices, structured to induce retirement at a particular age. By contrast, pension benefit indexation (or the lack thereof) plays a relatively small role in regulating worker turnover, retirement, and effort on the job. In general, the authors conclude that a great deal remains to be learned about the ways in which pension plans fit into the lifetime compensation package and that pension policy, if it is to be properly designed, must also be a high priority for future investigations.

POLICY CHALLENGES OF AN AGING WORKFORCE

The last section of this volume examines some important policy chal-lenges associated with an aging workforce. One problem is that gov-ernment and private sector retirement policy and philosophy in the United States are increasingly in conflict. On the one hand, many in Congress would like older workers to remain employed at later ages, which would raise tax revenue, reduce the burden on social security and medicare, and perhaps diminish reliance on welfare and other transfer programs. On the other hand, much private sector policy is headed in precisely the opposite direction—toward encouraging ever-earlier re-tirement. The last decade has seen a great deal of corporate downsizing and early-out retirement windows, both of which help cushion com-panies' reductions in force. Unions have also negotiated early-retirement supplements to open up jobs for workers seeking advancement in a shrinking job market. People have increasingly accepted social security benefits at younger ages, instead of waiting until age 65, which used to be the norm.

One explanation for why people are retiring early is the availability of social security payments and the benefit reductions that occur when an older person returns to paid employment. This is the subject of Michael V. Leonesio's study, which presents a thorough and up-to-date survey of economic retirement studies. Leonesio concludes that social security benefits have a strong influence on retirement patterns but not in the manner in which many people seem to think. In recent years, for example, policy makers have been subjected to intense lobbying by those who wish to eliminate the social security benefit cutbacks people experience if they earn more than the legislated threshold. Leonesio's study finds, however, that eliminating the retirement earnings test would not induce many more people to work, while increasing social security payouts would most benefit the upper-middle class and would cost a great deal.

Far less is known about policy in a related area, disability and employers' accommodations to it. Richard V. Burkhauser explores cross-national data on how handicapped workers fare in the labor market in Europe and the United States, concluding that research is desperately needed. In 1990, the U.S. Congress passed the Americans with Disabilities Act (ADA), which was intended to ensure that, without undue hardship for firms, employers would adapt the workplace so that handicapped workers could be employed. Cross-national comparisons show that other nations have not been very successful in achieving this end, even when substantial subsidies are offered. In the United States, no direct subsidies have been offered, which will probably reduce the impact of the law.

Burkhauser also contends that the "doubly handicapped"—older workers who are somewhat disabled—are left behind in the United States during periods of economic retrenchment. One of the most interesting findings of his study has to do with the differences in disability rates across developed nations: in 1989, the United States supported 250 disabled workers per 1,000 active workers aged 60 to 64, while Germany (before the Berlin Wall fell) supported 1,309 per 1,000 for the same age and the Netherlands 1,987 per 1,000. Differences in disability transfer policy must account for some of the differences across nations, but the specific effects remain to be pinpointed. This chapter, perhaps more than any other in the volume, points the way to an exciting and as yet undeveloped body of research.

Instead of focusing on the trees, in the final chapter of the volume Gary Burtless identifies the contours of the forest by examining how the costs of an aging population will place new demands on taxes and transfers. Burtless's models indicate that the United States currently devotes about 8 percent of its gross national product (GNP) to public spending on the elderly and projects that by 2035 the figure will rise to almost 17 percent if promised benefits are maintained. This claim on resources is not moderated much even if benefit promises are curtailed somewhat. His policy recommendation is to raise taxes now to prefund this future claim, a proposal that is currently subject to raging debate in the economics profession. Burtless analyzes the counterproposals and concludes that his assumptions about key variables conform better to his expectations than do the alternatives. Whatever the right assumptions, all the results show that the aging workforce will require workers in succeeding cohorts to pay for ever-increasing numbers of aged and disabled. Burtless's tax reform proposal is one approach; others include encouraging older people to continue working.

CONCLUSIONS

This volume contains several messages for analysts and policy makers concerned with the aging workforce. A great deal still needs to be learned about older workers' pay and employment needs, as well as their employability. There is also a powerful and unresolved tension among those in the U.S. government who want to defer retirement and those workers and employers who want early retirement to be encouraged.

Both in the United States and abroad, labor market analysts and policy makers need a greater understanding of how the older workforce is changing the labor market. Unfortunately, data sources on this subject are few and far between. During the 1980s, for instance, no survey was undertaken generating the information needed to examine the causes and consequences of labor force aging. This problem will begin to be remedied with the new longitudinal Health and Retirement Survey undertaken by the University of Michigan. It promises to provide some of the much-needed evidence required to follow older workers as they near and move into retirement. It will enable researchers to see what drives decisions, what health and income consequences follow, and what impact government policies have. This survey will open new windows into understanding the labor market for older workers.

This volume should speak to us all. Better policy requires further discussion and further research, including more carefully measured estimates of how firms, workers, and the government respond to workforce aging. Without such policy and research, we run the risk of losing opportunities for innovative ways to meet labor market challenges as the workforce ages.

PART I.
AGING WORKERS AROUND THE WORLD

Chapter 2.
DEMOGRAPHIC CHANGE AND THE DESTINY OF THE WORKING-AGE POPULATION

Martha Farnsworth Riche

EVEN THOUGH THEY involve only three variables—births, deaths, and net migration—projections of the size and composition of the population vary widely according to the assumptions that are selected. The variation is becoming wider as human decisions increasingly determine the rate of change in these fundamental human outcomes. The four most likely official projections come up with a total population in 2080 ranging from 333 million to 501 million, and current trends suggest the total may be even higher. In any case, the working-age population will be older. More working-age adults will be older, fewer younger—evening out the potential labor force shares of young, mid-life, and mature workers. At the same time, changes in the racial, geographic, and household distribution of the population will enhance the differences among these cohorts.

The size and nature of our population, and hence of our labor force, is a product of human decisions. For thirty years now, technology has allowed women to control their fertility, as the small size of today's youth workforce attests. Improved medical care for major causes of death can now postpone mortality, as can people's choices about health-related behavior. Finally, immigration continues to be regulated, though imperfectly, by legislation.

Many of these decisions could be reversed, or at least attenuated. The country may intensify its focus on children, leading to an increase in the fertility rate. The electorate may decide that we are receiving too many immigrants and close the gates again. And scientists continue to debate whether there are natural limits to life. Thus, our future population could be larger—or smaller—than we now expect. But whether our population grows, stagnates, or declines, it will still become an increasingly older one because older people will account for a larger share of it. This chapter explores some of these patterns and their implications for population projections.

ASSESSING THE CURRENT PROJECTIONS

The current official projections, prepared by the U.S. Bureau of the Census in 1987, are the first to estimate an eventual decline in the size of the population (U.S. Bureau of the Census 1989). According to the middle, "most likely" projection series (of thirty series), the U.S. population will peak at just under 302 million in 2038 and then decline. According to this series, the rate of population growth between 1987 and 1995 will be smaller than during any previous period except the Depression—0.81 percent a year, compared with 0.70 percent a year during the 1930s. After 1995, the growth rate will decline below even the Depression rate, turning negative toward the middle of the next century.

Like all projections, these series are based on a range of assumptions, and the different series allow users to select assumptions they believe are most likely to occur. It is already clear that our population is growing more rapidly than the official, "most likely" scenario. All of the assumptions that underlie that projection series were too conservative relative to what has happened since, and demographers have now abandoned them.

From the beginning, most demographers faulted the current projections for underestimating net immigration. The middle series assumed a continuation of recent annual totals of 600,000, dropping to 500,000 by 1998. As a government agency, the Census Bureau was probably constrained to assume that the Immigration Reform and Control Act of 1986 would reduce illegal immigration—from an estimated 200,000 a year to 100,000 a year. Demographers who considered this outcome unlikely could select a series that assumed "high" immigration—800,000 a year. Changing to this assumption eliminates the estimate of an eventual population decline—at least by 2080, the last year projected. According to projection series 17 (middle assumptions for fertility and mortality, high assumption for immigration), the population will number 324 million in 2040, compared with 302 million according to the middle series, and will reach 333 million by 2080, compared with a diminished 292 million according to the middle series.

Before reviewing all the assumptions in the light of current trends, it is important to note that even though assuming high rates of immigration significantly increases the likely size of the population, it does not make much of a difference in the aging of the population. According to the middle series, the median age of the population will increase more than ten years between 1990 and 2080—from 33.0 in 1990 to 43.9 in 1990. Under the high-immigration scenario, it will still increase more than ten years—to 43.2—which makes the prospect of an aging workforce equally likely.

Since the official projections appeared, the immigration law has been revised upwards. The provisions of the Immigration Act of 1990 took effect in November 1991, and the Immigration and Naturalization Service has projected an immediate jump in immigration, to 744,900. The service projects fewer immigrants in subsequent years, but in almost every year of the decade it still expects at least 700,000 per year (Hoefer 1991). This figure does not include refugees, who have totaled about 100,000 a year in recent years. Given what seems to be a renewed inflow of illegal immigrants, even the high-immigration assumption of the official projections is now too low, unless emigration increases significantly. Until the Census Bureau issues a new set of projections, most demographers will use the high series or make their own projections. Based on current expectations, the Population Reference Bureau is assuming net immigration of 900,000 a year.

The demographic turnaround that might seriously distort the current projections—in the long, not the short, term—is a turnaround in fertility. Dramatic and abrupt changes in fertility made earlier projections ludicrous. For example, according to projections made during the midst of the baby boom, the U.S. population would have reached its current size during the latter part of the 1970s (U.S. Bureau of the Census 1957). In the few years since the current projections were made, fertility has increased significantly and demographers disagree as to whether this increase represents a short-lived phenomenon or a new long-term trend.

Americans had more than 4 million babies in 1990, more than in any year since 1961 (U.S. National Center for Health Statistics 1991a). This is not unexpected since, thanks to the baby boom, so many women are of childbearing age. According to the previous set of government projections, however, births to baby boomers should have peaked in 1988 (U.S. Bureau of the Census 1984). Some demographers say that women just postponed having babies longer than expected (a change in timing); others say that women are having more children (a change in volume).

Certainly starting in mid–1987, the fertility rate began to move upward, and provisional data indicate that in 1990 it exceeded the level projected under the high-fertility assumption. Will the rate continue to rise? Will it stabilize? Or will it fall again?

The answer lies on the interface between social and economic behavior, which may be why there are so many persuasively argued yet widely differing scenarios. Some social scientists hold that the birth rate of the baby boomers has been constrained because there were so many of them—they crowded first the labor market, then the housing market (see, for example, Easterlin 1980 and Preston 1991). This is the view expressed most often in the popular press, and it is generally accompanied by the prediction that the baby-bust generation will have a higher fertility rate than the baby-boom generation because its small size will grant it superior economic opportunities.

Others point to the relative stability in birth expectations—surveys still report that Americans want, on average, two children—and assert that the upturn in the fertility rate simply represents the end of the transition to delayed childbearing, a delay that began with the widespread dissemination of the birth control pill. These demographers (for example, Bumpass 1990) expect that the fertility rate will not continue to rise, or even stabilize, at this new higher rate. Instead, they think the rate will resume its long-term downward trend.

The latter view seems far more likely in that the proponents of the former fail to account for a significant trend: more women are having and/or raising children on their own. Almost all of the recent increase in fertility has occurred among women who were not currently married (U.S. National Center for Health Statistics 1991c). Moreover, although the divorce rate seems to have stabilized overall, it is actually higher for new marriages—Bumpass estimates that six in ten new marriages will fail, based on current age-specific rates. As a result, women are making decisions about their childbearing conscious that they may have to raise their child or children on their own (*Self* 1990 is one of many surveys).

But if the economy improves, will that not reduce the economic strains on marriage and make divorce less frequent? Probably not. One of the greatest economic strains on a marriage seems to be a shift after marriage in the relative incomes of husband and wife in favor of the wife (Tzeng and Mare 1990). During the 1980s, income grew for women relative to men at almost every age and educational level (U.S. Bureau of the Census 1991a). Most predictions are that this shift will continue, given the occupational evolution of the economy and women's increasing investment in education and job tenure (see, for example, O'Neill 1990). At the same time, women's and men's daily activities are becoming more alike—more competing, less completing (Goldscheider and Waite 1991).

If we think of current fertility and birth rates as the result of decisions made by women rather than by couples, and view them in the context of current labor force participation rates for mothers of small children, it is telling that the rates are so high. They suggest a demographic universal: that American women will have an average of close to two children, no matter how arduous raising them may be. If this is true, it puts a floor on the likely fertility rate. What about a ceiling?

The economics of childbearing are not likely to change; if anything, children will become even more costly as women's earnings continue to approach men's. The psychology of childbearing may have shifted into a new phase, however. To a certain extent, people's decisions about childbearing are influenced by what others are doing. This is undoubtedly one cause of the baby boom, although it was probably much less important than the gap between husbands' and wives' relative earning power occasioned by government-paid college education for veterans.[1]

Starting in the mid–1960s and continuing through the 1970s, children and parenthood were out of style. A goodly share of the baby boom pursued what had to have been the longest adolescence on record, and women postponed having children to take advantage of new opportunities outside the home. Now the pendulum has swung in the opposite direction. Most baby boomers now have children, and this generation,

---

1. The share of college enrollment accounted for by men was higher in 1950 than it had been since 1870, which is as far back as the U.S. data go. This sharp reversal of a long-term trend toward a proportionately greater share accounted for by women was undoubtedly an artifact of the G.I. bill, as well as of the prevailing desire for "normalcy" after the Depression and then World War II. The increase in men's enrollment occasioned by government-provided funds meant that men who otherwise would have finished their education with a high school diploma started their careers with a college degree. The difference between what they could earn and what their future wives could earn was so great that in most cases it made little economic sense for the women to work. Thus, more men and women married, and they married earlier, had children earlier, and had more of them. By 1960, women's share of college enrollment was on its way up again, climbing steadily until it surpassed men's share in the late 1980s.

which continues to dominate our culture, has shifted its priorities to family. Moreover, Americans are beginning to perceive that the combination of increased life expectancy and smaller families is making childrearing a shrinking share of adult life for both men and women. Women *can* "have it all," sequentially if not simultaneously.

It is vexing to see decades labeled according to a single mood—the swinging sixties, the greedy eighties. The shift of a digit on the calendar year can hardly cause such a profound swing in the national psyche, and to the extent that such swings really occur, they generally touch only a fraction of the population. Nevertheless, the 1990s will be dedicated in a major way to children and family because family life will be at its peak for the most influential generation in the population—influential by virtue of its size and now aging into positions of influence. This shift cannot help but influence fertility decisions at the margin. Thus, other things being equal, we will probably see a somewhat higher fertility rate. How high cannot be predicted, but it will probably not be very much higher than the 2.2 in the high-fertility projection series, since the opportunity costs of having children are more likely to increase than to decrease.[2]

In the longer term, fertility will probably decrease again. Whether it will go below the replacement rate will depend on too many considerations—many of them having to do with how people perceive population growth as affecting the physical environment—to estimate with any certainty. In any case, the fertility rate is not likely to increase enough to halt the aging of the labor force. Given the increase in life expectancy, let alone the aging of the baby boomers, it would take far too many children to bring the proportion of younger to older workers back to where it was in recent years.

Table 2-1 shows that assuming a high rather than a middle rate of fertility would not make much difference in the aging of the labor force. The median age of the population would continue to rise—it would just rise more slowly. The share of the population in the prime working years—ages 18 to 64—would change slightly. It would be nearly 1 percentage point smaller in 2000, because of the higher share of young

---

2. It is probably time to consider the possibility of a reversal in the long-term decline in unintended births, insofar as the legal status of abortion remains unsettled. Given the near halt in birth control research, limiting access to abortions might result in an increase in the fertility rate, at least temporarily.

people. It would be more than 2 percentage points smaller in 2020. Then the gap would start to close, as the new, larger generations of children joined the labor force. By 2080, the latest year projected, under the higher-fertility scenario, the share of the working-age population would actually increase—by 0.1 of a percentage point.

Even assuming a high fertility rate, the share of the population under age 18 is projected to decline, albeit slowly, while the share of the population aged 65 and older will grow significantly—from 12.6 percent in 1990 to 19.8 percent in 2030, when the last of the baby boomers reach 65. By 2050, the share will decline slightly, as deaths among baby boomers deplete it, but it will rise again once the baby boomers are dead.

Mortality is the least controversial of the assumptions, although some demographers are currently disputing whether or not there are natural limits to the life span. Those who assert that there are (see Olshansky, Carnes, and Cassel 1990 for a persuasive account) would opt for the middle mortality rate in the official projections; those who do not (see, for example, Preston 1991 for an equally persuasive account) would choose the lower rate. If the current trend toward healthier lifestyles continues, the latter may be correct. The people who have made significant changes in their health habits by not smoking, using seatbelts, and exercising are middle-aged. We do not yet know the impact on life expectancy if they pursue their healthful habits into old age. We can expect, however, that the difference between women's and men's life expectancy will continue to narrow as their risk-taking behaviors (e.g., smoking) become more similar.

Table 2-1 shows that choosing the middle versus the low mortality rate has only an infinitesimal effect on the share of the population in the usual working ages until 2020, when roughly half the baby boomers will be 65 or older. With the low mortality rate, 60.1 percent of the population would be 18 to 64 in 2020; with the middle rate, the share would be 60.9 percent. The gap would be greater in 2030, when all the baby boomers will be 65 or older, and would widen greatly thereafter.

In sum, based on current trends, it is safest to use the set known as the "highest" of the current official series of projections because it will produce the highest population levels—low mortality, high immigration, and high fertility assumptions. (The Population Reference Bureau is currently using more generous assumptions for all three components

TABLE 2-1.   U.S. POPULATION AGE DISTRIBUTIONS ASSUMING
DIFFERENT RATES OF FERTILITY AND MORTALITY, 1990–2020

	≤ 17	18–64	≥ 65
Middle fertility, middle mortality (series 14)			
1990	25.6	61.8	12.6
2000	24.5	62.5	13.0
2010	22.2	63.9	13.9
2020	21.4	60.9	17.7
2030	20.7	57.5	21.8
2050	19.9	57.2	22.9
2080	19.3	56.2	24.5
High fertility (series 15)			
1990	25.7	61.7	12.6
2000	25.6	61.6	12.8
2010	24.5	62.1	13.4
2020	24.6	58.8	16.6
2030	22.6	55.6	19.8
2050	24.7	56.4	18.9
2080	24.3	56.3	19.4
Low mortality (series 5)			
1990	25.6	61.8	12.6
2000	24.4	62.3	13.3
2010	21.9	63.4	14.7
2020	20.9	60.1	19.0
2030	20.0	56.2	23.8
2050	19.0	54.8	26.2
2080	18.0	52.7	29.3

Source: U.S. Bureau of the Census 1989.

of change.) In 2080, the population will total 501 million if these
assumptions are met. The lowest likely population, again based on current trends, is the one produced if one assumes middle rates of mortality,
high rates of immigration, and middle rates of fertility: the "high-
immigration" set. In 2080, the population will total nearly 333 million
if these assumptions are met.

AGE STRUCTURE OF THE WORKING-AGE POPULATION

Table 2-2 shows the age distribution of the working-age population
based on these two projections as well as two other plausible series. In
all of these series, the population, and hence the labor force, will continue to grow. Based on the higher fertility rates, it will grow by nearly
three-quarters. If the middle fertility rate occurs, it will grow by 21.5

or 23.8 percent (assuming middle or low rates of mortality). But under all of these scenarios, it will age, because the age structure of our population is undergoing a profound change.

Traditionally, a population has been distributed by age in the form of a pyramid—with a relatively small group of older people at the top, a middling number of middle-aged people in the middle, and many young adults, teenagers, and children at the bottom. As recently as 1970, this was a good representation of our population, but several trends have transformed this historic pattern (see fig. 2-1).

◆ Between 1946 and 1964, birth rates rose markedly. Starting in 1965, women began to postpone having children and the birth rate dropped dramatically.
◆ Now the baby boomers are having children, but because they are having them later, at best they will only replace themselves.
◆ More people are living to a ripe old age.

When we put these trends together, the American age structure now resembles not a pyramid but a pillar: it features three roughly equal age groups—youth, the middle-aged, and the mature (Riche 1990a).

Under all the projection scenarios currently deemed likely, the population will continue to age, leaving proportionately fewer working-age women in their childbearing years. (This should encourage labor economists to look beyond women's preferences for staying home with young children when they assess female labor force participation rates.) As Samuel H. Preston has pointed out, the population will continue to age because, even at a fertility rate of 2.2—the high-fertility assumption— women will have fewer children in the future than women have borne, on average, in the past. Even with high rates of immigration, higher life expectancy will offset the influx of younger people into the population. So the replacement of the traditional pyramid by the pillar is a good long-term image for the age structure of the population and, by extension, of the labor force.

Because the baby boom will continue to be our largest generation, over the next few decades it will determine precisely where in the age cycle the labor force will age: first among the middle-aged, then among older workers. Over the next twenty years, the baby boom will move steadily into the upper reaches of the labor force. In 2001, the first baby boomers will reach age 55; in 2011, they will reach age 65. Assuming that they wait until age 65 to retire, the size of the working-age pop-

Martha Farnsworth Riche

United States, 1970

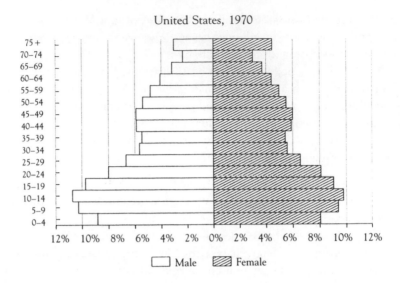

☐ Male   ▨ Female

United States, 2020

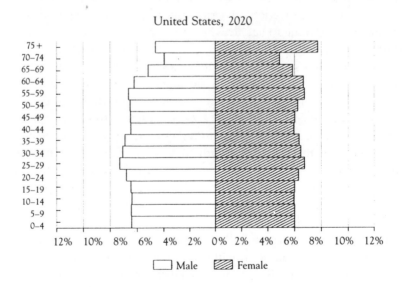

☐ Male   ▨ Female

Source: Population Reference Bureau

FIGURE 2-1.   U.S. POPULATION BY AGE AND SEX, 1970 AND 2020

TABLE 2-2.   AGE STRUCTURE OF THE WORKING-AGE POPULATION
UNDER THE MOST LIKELY CENSUS BUREAU PROJECTION SCENARIOS

	Percentage of Total Population		
	18–34	35–49	50–64
Series 9 (low mortality, high immigration, high fertility)			
1990	28.0	20.6	13.1
2000	23.1	23.2	15.1
2010	22.5	20.0	19.2
2020	21.9	17.6	18.8
2030	21.3	17.9	15.7
2050	21.7	17.5	15.8
2080	21.0	17.3	15.8
Series 8 (low mortality, high immigration, middle fertility)			
1990	28.1	20.7	13.1
2000	23.4	23.6	15.3
2010	22.9	20.7	19.9
2020	21.7	18.7	20.0
2030	20.4	19.1	17.3
2050	19.9	17.8	17.8
2080	18.9	17.3	17.2
Series 18 (middle mortality, high immigration, high fertility)			
1990	28.0	20.6	13.1
2000	23.2	23.3	15.1
2010	22.8	20.2	19.2
2020	22.4	17.9	18.8
2030	21.9	18.3	15.8
2050	22.6	18.1	16.1
2080	22.1	18.2	16.3
Series 17 (middle mortality, high immigration, middle fertility)			
1990	28.1	20.7	13.1
2000	23.6	23.7	15.3
2010	23.3	20.9	19.8
2020	22.2	19.1	20.0
2030	21.0	19.6	17.4
2050	20.9	18.6	18.3
2080	20.3	18.5	18.0

ulation relative to the population as a whole will peak then. By 2050,
just slightly more than half of the population will be aged 20 to 64. But
even then, as table 2-2 shows, the working-age population will be significantly older, on average, than it is today.

OTHER CHANGES IN THE WORKING-AGE POPULATION

The older cast to the population represents an important change from
the past. But three other important changes in the population will also

affect the labor force: the change in its racial composition, the change in its geographic distribution, and the change in its household composition.

The racial and ethnic structure of the population, particularly that of its younger members, is changing rapidly. The 1990 census found that whites accounted for eight in ten Americans, down from nine in ten as recently as 1960. Subtracting white Hispanics, non-Hispanic whites accounted for only three out of four Americans in 1990.

During the 1980s, the U.S. received 6 million immigrants, up from 4.5 million during the 1970s and 3.3 million during the 1960s. Few immigrants today are of European origin. Moreover, immigrants, as well as native Hispanics and blacks, generally have more children than native whites. Together, these two factors are boosting the share of minorities in the population (Riche 1991).

These trends are also creating diversity within the minority population. According to preliminary estimates, the 1990 census missed at least one in twenty blacks and almost as many Hispanics (U.S. Bureau of the Census 1991b). Nevertheless, it clearly delineates the rapid growth in their numbers. Twelve percent of Americans identified themselves as black, 9 percent as Hispanic in origin (some were also black), 3 percent as Asian or from the Pacific Islands, 1 percent as Native Americans, and 4 percent as "other."[3]

Because of continuing trends in immigration and fertility, the first three groups will continue to grow faster than the white population. By 2000, non-Hispanic whites will most likely represent less than 71 percent of the population, blacks nearly 13 percent, Hispanics more than 11 percent, and Asians more than 4 percent. The proportions will change even more for younger age groups.

Thanks to both high immigration and higher fertility rates, minority group members are now younger than the white population. According to preliminary census tabulations, in 1990, whites, with a median age of 34.4 years, were far older than members of minority groups. Hispanics were youngest, with a median age of 25.5 years. Native Americans and Alaskans were second youngest, at 26.3 years, while blacks had a median

3. In this context, "other" almost universally refers to Hispanics who chose to give that response to the question about race rather than list themselves as white or black. (Hispanic is a category in the ethnicity question, not the race question.)

age of 28.1 years and Asians and Pacific Islanders had a median age of 29.8 years.

All racial and ethnic groups are aging, but non-Hispanic whites are aging most rapidly. According to Census Bureau projections, in 2010, for example, the average non-Hispanic white will be 41.4 years, fully ten years older than the average black, who will be 31.4 years. Hispanics will be even younger, averaging 29.3 years, while "other" races will average 35.6 years (U.S. Bureau of the Census 1986).

As a result, different age groups are becoming multicultural at different rates. According to Population Reference Bureau projections, although nearly 71 percent of Americans will be white in 2000, fewer than two in three children will be—63 percent of children under age 8, 65 percent of children aged 8 to 13, and 66 percent of children aged 14 to 17. In contrast, nearly 80 percent of Americans aged 45 and older will be white.

These projections call for an assessment of the educational and occupational preparedness of the labor force. On the one hand, high school dropout rates are significantly higher for Hispanics than for other groups. On the other hand, Asian-Americans have very high levels of educational attainment. Moreover, the Immigration Act of 1990 for the first time gave preference to people with high skill levels. The demographic problem of work readiness may stem as much if not more from the inadequate educational performance of non-Hispanic whites, as measured by scores on standardized educational tests, as from the shift to a multicultural workforce.

The serious workforce issues these trends suggest are more subtle. For consumer businesses, one issue is the growing cultural gap between workers and customers. In some parts of the country, they may not even speak the same language. And in all businesses, more women and minorities are entering the upper ranks of management because of their increasing presence in the workforce. This broadens the challenge of managing the interface between women and men, between Asians, Hispanics, blacks, and whites, and between differently constituted generations.

Another demographic feature of the aging workforce arises from the differential effects of migration. The continuing flow of Americans from the North and the East toward the West and the South has contributed to a younger age structure in most of the receiving states. Interstate migrants tend to be young adults seeking new opportunities. As a result, states that suffer a net loss of migrants will lose those migrants' children as well.

Already the median age varies among states. According to the 1990 census, New Hampshire is the only northeastern state with a population that is younger—barely—than that of the nation as a whole. The median age for the United States was 32.9 years; for New Hampshire, it was 32.8. Not coincidentally, New Hampshire was the only northeastern state with a large net gain from migration during the 1980s. In contrast, the inhabitants of most western states were younger than those of the nation as a whole.

Most of the states that gained significantly from migration—notably California, Arizona, and Texas—had younger populations, on average, while states with significant net outmigration—such as Iowa and West Virginia—had older populations. Table 2-3 shows the distribution of the U.S. working-age population by age and state, as measured by the 1990 census. Unless migration flows change direction, the opportunities and challenges of an aging workforce will be experienced unevenly across the nation.

Within states, migration flows also affect the age structure of the population. On the one hand, international migration tends to swell the population of metropolitan areas. According to recent estimates, 94 percent of immigrants choose metropolitan areas, mostly on the East or West coasts (Speare 1987). On the other hand, as the 1990 census data demonstrate, Americans continue to move from the cities to the suburbs (U.S. Bureau of the Census 1991c).

Moreover, Americans have been saying that, given a choice, they would prefer to live in smaller cities, and the growth trends of the 1980s suggest that they may be starting to act on those preferences. We do not know how such a movement, were it to accelerate, would change the age structure of the workforce. Traditionally, migrants are young; however, older workers readying themselves for retirement might appreciate the opportunity to relocate to a smaller city. In the end, the nature and numbers of jobs will, as always, be determining factors.

Finally, a demographic characteristic that is often overlooked in evaluating workforce issues is the household composition of the population. This characteristic has changed dramatically over the last two decades.

Historically, households composed of married couples with children have been the nation's most common household type. Early in the 1980s,

TABLE 2-3. DISTRIBUTION OF U.S. POPULATION BY AGE FOR STATES, APRIL 1, 1990

State	≤ 17	18–64	≥ 65
United States	25.6%	61.9%	12.6%
Alabama	26.2	60.9	12.9
Alaska	31.3	64.6	4.1
Arizona	26.8	60.2	13.1
Arkansas	26.4	58.7	14.9
California	26.0	63.4	10.5
Colorado	26.1	63.9	10.0
Connecticut	22.8	63.6	13.6
Delaware	24.5	63.4	12.1
District of Columbia	19.3	67.9	12.8
Florida	22.2	59.5	18.3
Georgia	26.7	63.2	10.1
Hawaii	25.3	63.4	11.3
Idaho	30.6	57.3	12.0
Illinois	25.8	61.7	12.6
Indiana	26.3	61.2	12.6
Iowa	25.9	58.8	15.3
Kansas	26.7	59.5	13.8
Kentucky	25.9	61.4	12.7
Louisiana	29.1	59.8	11.1
Maine	25.2	61.5	13.3
Maryland	24.3	64.9	10.8
Massachusetts	22.5	63.9	13.6
Michigan	26.5	61.6	11.9
Minnesota	26.7	60.8	12.5
Mississippi	29.0	58.5	12.5
Missouri	25.7	60.3	14.0
Montana	27.8	58.9	13.3
Nebraska	27.2	58.7	14.1
Nevada	24.7	64.7	10.6
New Hampshire	25.1	63.6	11.3
New Jersey	23.3	63.4	13.4
New Mexico	29.5	59.8	10.8
New York	23.7	63.2	13.1
North Carolina	24.2	63.6	12.1
North Dakota	27.5	58.3	14.3
Ohio	25.8	61.2	13.0
Oklahoma	26.6	59.9	13.5
Oregon	25.5	60.8	13.8
Pennsylvania	23.5	61.1	15.4
Rhode Island	22.5	62.5	15.0
South Carolina	26.4	62.2	11.4
South Dakota	28.5	56.8	14.7
Tennessee	24.9	62.4	12.7
Texas	28.5	61.4	10.1

(continues)

TABLE 2-3. *(continued)*

State	≤ 17	18–64	≥ 65
Utah	36.4	54.9	8.7
Vermont	25.4	62.8	11.8
Virginia	24.3	64.9	10.7
Washington	25.9	62.3	11.8
West Virginia	24.7	60.3	15.0
Wisconsin	26.4	60.3	13.3
Wyoming	29.9	59.7	10.4

Source: 1990 census.

however, households composed of married couples without children became more numerous (in official parlance, "married couples without children under age 18 living in the home," i.e., empty or crowded nesters as well as childless couples and couples with children from other marriages living elsewhere). In large part, this is a reflection of two trends—the increase in life expectancy and the decrease in family size. Put simply, Americans are spending a smaller share of their adult lives in families (Espenshade 1985).

Continued high divorce rates along with delayed first marriages have increased the number and share of single-person households. If these trends continue, and most demographers expect that they will, single-person households will come to outnumber married-couple-with-children households during this decade. Moreover, the bulk of these singles will be older, not younger. One of the most interesting demographic trends of the 1980s was a precipitous decline in the remarriage rate for men (U.S. National Center for Health Statistics 1991b). At the beginning of the decade, divorced men remarried at about three times the rate of divorced women. By the end of the decade, they remarried at only twice that rate.

Many demographers expect this rate to fall even further (Goldscheider 1990). As men's and women's lives (and financial resources) become more similar, particularly after the childrearing stage, the advantages of remarriage (for women in particular) decline relative to the costs. The result will be a larger share of older single people and consequently potentially higher labor force participation rates among older workers.

The Population Reference Bureau projects that the number of households composed of mature single people (never-marrieds aged 35 and older and divorced, widowed, or separated people aged 18 to 49) will increase by 40 percent over the 1990s, compared with an increase of 3 percent among households made up of never-married singles aged 18 to 34. Households of single persons aged 50 and older should increase by 18 percent. At the same time, the share of households made up of married couples with children under age 6 should decline slightly (by 5 percent), while empty-nest households should grow significantly (by 20 percent).

In sum, the aging of the population is producing a larger share of households that are postchildrearing. It is also producing a larger share that are postmarital. In both cases, the likelihood of workforce participation increases for these people as they age.

One further demographic change is occurring, and that is a gradual inflation in the ages at which people undertake major life-course activities. At the entry end of adulthood, there is in effect a new life stage— one that lasts from the age of 18 to 24. This is a stage of experimentation, of boomeranging between an array of living arrangements, educational activities, and occupational and locational choices (Riche 1990b). In general, this stage occurs among high school dropouts as well as college graduates.

The popular media are interpreting this delay in adult behavior as a cohort effect (i.e., a phenomenon peculiar to the current generation of young adults). People are attributing their slowness to attach themselves to adult activities as the result of the small size of their generation following the flood of baby boomers and the economic conditions prevailing as they reach adulthood. It is far more likely that activities such as dropping in and out of school, moving in and out of living arrangements (including occasional returns to the parents' home), and delayed marriage are an age effect (i.e., a permanent life stage). They are a response to the increased need for information-gathering given the increased range of life choices.

This delay in the onset of adulthood results in a series of postponements: of marriage, childbearing, and home buying, as well as of permanent attachment to the workforce. As these activities interact with one another, they interrupt the order as well as the ages at which they traditionally take place. As a result, one requirement for effectively managing an aging workforce is to abandon stereotypes that link specific activities to specific ages. Both individuals and workforce managers need to take a fresh look at work-life planning. With a gradually aging population, both productivity improvement and career enhancement demand more flexibility in relating workers to jobs at given ages.

CONCLUSION

The demographic present and future represent a combination of change and permanence. Where people are concerned, some things do not change. Under the heading of demographic universals, the most notable, given the rapid changes in women's lives over the last quarter-century, is the persistence of their desire to have and raise children. Currently, a record-high number of American women are in their child-bearing years, and a record-high share of childbearing women are working. Furthermore, a record-high share of these women are not married. The combination of all these trends means that an unprecedented number of women are experiencing work-family conflicts, yet we *still* have a fertility rate of approximately replacement level.

Another demographic universal is that people migrate in search of better lives. Immigration is currently running at levels not seen since the beginning of this century, and may well increase. Similarly, domestic migration continues to reshape our population geography.

Current trends suggest that other demographic characteristics are not universal, however. Households and living arrangements are becoming increasingly diverse, and the traditional family has become just that— a tradition. Men's and women's lives are becoming more similar, though their differences pinch in new ways. Even racial identities are shifting as our culturally diverse society countenances an increasing amount of intermarriage.

As a result of these trends, the demographics of the workforce, as well as its wage and experience levels, or tenure in an industry or occupation, are becoming more heterogeneous. Understanding such economic decisions as retirement thus becomes more difficult. Obvious differences such as marital status—two-earner couples versus single-earner couples or single people—must be taken into account in any serious analysis.

Finally, the continuing rise in life expectancy calls into question the whole range of age-related activities, such as the ages at which people enter and leave the labor force. The transition of young people into the labor force (and other adult activities) is increasingly less predictable as a broader array of choices lengthens the trial-and-error stage of information gathering. Similarly, the transition of older adults out of the labor force is likely to become less predictable as the range of individual circumstances widens.

More fundamentally, the rise in life expectancy is transforming the shape of the population from the traditional pyramid to something more closely resembling a pillar. Even with higher-than-expected rates of fertility and immigration, we will still have an aging population, and an aging working-age population as well.

Chapter 3.
EXAMINING LABOR FORCE PROJECTIONS FOR THE TWENTY-FIRST CENTURY

Phillip B. Levine

W HAT WILL THE COMPOSITION of the labor force be in the year 2020? The correct answer, of course, is that it is impossible to tell. In 1960, who would have predicted that the labor force participation rate (LFPR, defined as the ratio of the number of people in the labor market to the total population) of men over age 60 would fall from 45 to 28 percent by 1990 and that the LFPR of prime-age women (aged 25 to 54) would increase from 48 to 74 percent? (See Ransom and Sutch 1988 and U.S. Department of Labor 1961 and 1991.)

Labor force projections are necessary, however. Consider, for example, the Social Security Administration's (SSA) need to set payroll tax rates. In anticipation of the huge burden that baby boomers will place on the social security system when the majority of them reach retirement age around 2020, the SSA has planned to accumulate adequate reserves in advance. But the amount of reserves that need to be accumulated depends on future events. Less money needs to be saved if older workers reverse their trend toward early retirement or if women continue to enter the labor force in increasing numbers. Tax rates need to be set today without knowing the outcome of these labor force trends. It is therefore impossible to retreat from the task of predicting the future size of the labor force.

The need for shorter-term projections is even more acute, as indicated

I would like to thank Missy Walsh for research assistance, Olivia Mitchell and Ann Velenchik for helpful discussions and comments, and John Stinson of the Bureau of Labor Statistics for graciously providing unpublished data. Some of the material in this chapter appeared in Levine and Mitchell 1992 and is reprinted with permission.

by the business community's response to *Workforce 2000* (Johnston and Packer 1987). Consider the firm that decides to make a capital investment in a labor-saving machine with a life expectancy of, say, fifteen years. Even if the investment is cost-efficient given current wage rates, suppose future wage rates fall because of an increase in the labor supply. Similarly, if the new machine requires skilled workers, it is important to know if these workers will be available over the life of the machine. While projections over a shorter time frame seem more likely to hit their target, historically they have often strayed dramatically from observed behavior (Fullerton 1982, 1988).

The purpose of this chapter is twofold. First, I argue that the existing methodology for projecting the labor force is significantly flawed. While criticizing past projections because they are often incorrect seems unjust, analyzing the reasons for error is certainly legitimate. The standard technique currently employed extrapolates past trends in labor force behavior into the future, with minor ad hoc modifications. I contend that inherent problems in this methodology doom it to failure whenever change occurs.

Second, I argue for the development of an economic model of labor force behavior to project changes in the labor force. Rather than present a formal model directly, I sketch its likely components. While an economic model would almost surely result in substantial projection errors as well, I believe that it would be more accurate. In support of this position, I use time-series data to show that changes in LFPRs among older men, which were unanticipated by past projections, are quite consistent with the predictions an economic model would have made.

PAST LABOR FORCE PROJECTIONS

The projected size of the labor force is a function of both the size of the population and the LFPR. Since the chapter by Martha Riche explores projected changes in the size and composition of the population, I focus solely on projections of LFPRs.

There are at least three major sources of labor force projections. The SSA and the Bureau of Economic Analysis (BEA) both provide projections reaching well into the twenty-first century. SSA projections extend until the year 2060 and were reported only once just before the debate over the 1983 amendments to the Social Security Act. By contrast, the BEA provides projections every five years of the size of the labor force over the following fifty years. The Bureau of Labor Statistics

(BLS) regularly provides shorter-range projections, typically extending fifteen years into the future.

The methodology employed by these agencies in projecting LFPRs is quite similar.[1] In fact, there is a direct connection between the BEA's projections and those reported by the BLS since the BEA uses the endpoint of the BLS's projections as its starting point. The foundation of the projections is a linear extrapolation technique. Historical LFPRs are used to estimate the trend over time, and the trend is simply extended into the future. Ad hoc adjustments to these estimates are made to account for impossible or unlikely predictions. For example, LFPRs of any group cannot exceed 100 percent or fall below 0 percent, and they assume that female LFPRs will not rise above male LFPRs.

A sample of these projections along with current participation rates is reported in table 3-1. The similarity in technique is indicated by the similarity in projected participation rates. For example, the projected LFPR for all men in 2015 and 2020 by the BEA and SSA, respectively, are identical and indicate a drop in the rate among men of about 4 percent. The projected decrease is a result of reduced labor market activity among older men and the heavier weights placed on the older segment of the population in the future.

Comparing the projected rates for all women shows that they are also very similar. Both the BLS's and the SSA's projections suggest that an additional small percentage of women will be in the labor force by the year 2000, while the SSA's and the BEA's projections indicate that this trend will moderate by 2020. In this case, the increasing entry of 25- to 44-year-old women over time will be slowly offset by the reweighting toward older women.

Comparisons of the projections for specific demographic groups show discrepancies, however. For example, the BEA and the BLS both project that women between the ages of 25 and 44 will increase their labor force participation considerably, but the SSA predicts only a small increase. Among men aged 55 to 64, the BLS and the SSA project very little change in retirement behavior, whereas the BEA predicts that the trend toward increasing withdrawal from the labor force will continue for this group. Understandably, discrepancies are more common among the groups whose work patterns have changed the most over the recent past—women and older men.

1. Flaim and Fullerton (1978) provide a detailed description of the BLS methodology.

TABLE 3-1. CURRENT AND PROJECTED CIVILIAN LABOR FORCE
PARTICIPATION RATES IN THE UNITED STATES BY AGE AND SEX

Age Group	(1) Observed 1990	(2) BLS 2000	(3) SSA 2000	(4) BEA 2015	(5) SSA 2020
Men					
All	76.1%	75.9%	77.5%	72.0%	72.0%
16–24	71.5	—	—	74.8	—
16–19	55.7	59.0	66.9	63.9	67.7
20–24	84.3	86.5	86.9	84.0	87.4
25–54	93.4	—	—	92.4	—
25–34	94.2	94.1	—	92.5	—
25–29	93.8	—	95.0	—	95.3
30–34	94.6	—	95.2	—	95.4
35–44	94.4	94.3	—	94.9	—
35–39	94.9	—	95.1	—	95.4
40–44	93.9	—	94.1	—	94.4
45–54	90.7	90.5	—	90.2	—
45–49	92.3	—	92.0	—	92.0
50–54	88.8	—	87.7	—	86.4
55–64	67.7	68.1	—	62.9	—
55–59	79.8	—	79.5	—	75.3
60–64	55.5	—	62.1	—	57.3
65 +	16.4	14.7	—	13.0	—
65–69	26.0	—	27.0	—	26.3
70 +	10.8	—	10.6	—	10.7

(continues)

Since the accuracy of labor force projections cannot be gauged until the projected date, it is impossible to evaluate long-range projections. For some time, however, the BLS has been providing forecasts for periods up to fifteen years into the future, and the accuracy of its projections to date can be established. If shorter-range projections are shown to be considerably different from observed behavior, the reliability of longer-range projections should be seriously questioned.

A comparison of BLS projected and observed LFPRs for three dates for several demographic groups appears in table 3-2. Projections for the years 1980, 1985, and 1990 made seven to eight years and fourteen to fifteen years before these years along with observed LFPRs are reported. Table 3-2 shows that fifteen-year projections and observed LFPRs often differ greatly; in some instances projected LFPRs are in error by 50 percent or more. For example, in 1985, the LFPR for men over age 65 was 18.6 percent. In 1970, however, the BLS projected that the cor-

TABLE 3-1.   (continued)

Age Group	(1) Observed 1990	(2) BLS 2000	(3) SSA 2000	(4) BEA 2015	(5) SSA 2020
Women					
All	57.5	62.6	59.0	57.5	54.6
16–24	63.1	—	—	—	—
16–19	51.8	59.6	62.4	59.1	63.4
20–24	71.6	77.9	76.9	84.5	76.7
25–54	74.1	—	—	79.9	—
25–34	73.6	82.4	—	84.3	—
25–29	73.8	—	75.1	—	75.8
30–34	73.4	—	74.4	—	75.4
35–44	76.5	84.9	—	85.6	—
35–39	75.5	—	76.3	—	77.0
40–44	77.6	—	78.0	—	78.4
45–54	71.2	76.5	—	70.7	—
45–49	74.8	—	76.4	—	76.3
50–54	66.9	—	71.6	—	71.7
55–64	45.3	49.0	—	43.0	—
55–59	55.3	—	56.5	—	55.0
60–64	35.5	—	38.8	—	36.7
65 +	8.7	7.6	—	7.3	—
65–69	17.0	—	17.6	—	18.0
70 +	4.8	—	5.4	—	5.5

Sources: Column 1, U.S. Department of Labor, Bureau of Labor Statistics 1991; column 2, Fullerton 1989; column 3, U.S. Department of Health and Human Services, Social Security Administration 1983; column 4, U.S. Department of Commerce, Bureau of Economic Analysis 1985; column 5, U.S. Department of Health and Human Services, Social Security Administration 1983.

responding figure would be 27.3 percent. Similarly, in 1965, 40.3 percent of the women between the ages of 25 and 34 were projected to be in the labor force in 1980, while the actual value was 65.3 percent.

Although the projections made seven to eight years in advance are more accurate, the errors are still substantial. Again, for women aged 25 to 34, the observed LFPR in 1980 of 65.3 percent is still 30 percent higher than the rate projected in 1973, 50.2 percent.

As one might expect, the projections seven to eight years into the future tend to lie between the observed values and the fifteen-year projections. This is not always true, however. In some instances projections made at different dates for the same year are substantially different, and the size of an underestimate in one projection is sometimes matched by an overestimate of similar magnitude in the other projec-

TABLE 3-2. PROJECTED AND OBSERVED LABOR FORCE PARTICIPATION RATES IN THE UNITED STATES, BY AGE AND SEX

Age	Projections for 1980		Actual	Projections for 1985		Actual	Projections for 1990		Actual
	1965	1973	1980	1970	1978	1985	1976	1983	1990
Men									
16–19	56.7%	56.0%	61.2%	55.1%	65.2%	59.3%	61.3%	62.3%	55.7%
20–24	87.2	83.0	85.7	82.3	85.7	85.5	82.1	84.4	84.3
25–34	96.2	94.6	94.2	97.4	94.3	94.7	94.7	93.7	94.2
35–44	96.7	95.1	94.6	97.4	95.2	95.0	94.8	95.6	94.4
45–54	95.0	91.6	90.3	95.3	89.9	91.0	90.2	91.3	90.7
55–64	83.7	79.1	71.4	81.9	70.1	70.0	69.9	65.5	67.7
65 +	21.8	21.2	18.3	27.3	18.4	18.6	16.8	14.9	16.4
Women									
16–19	46.6	45.5	53.0	43.5	61.3	53.9	55.2	56.8	51.8
20–24	52.6	63.4	69.0	57.9	76.8	71.8	75.2	78.1	71.6
25–34	40.3	50.2	65.3	46.7	73.2	70.9	63.5	78.1	73.6
35–44	50.0	53.2	65.2	53.6	69.5	71.8	63.0	78.6	76.5
45–54	59.5	56.2	59.6	55.6	58.7	64.4	60.3	67.1	71.2
55–64	47.3	44.7	41.1	46.5	42.2	43.6	42.3	41.5	45.3
65 +	9.9	8.6	7.6	12.1	9.6	9.8	7.6	7.4	8.7

Sources: Flaim and Fullerton 1976; Fullerton 1982, 1988; Fullerton and Tschetter 1983; and U.S. Department of Labor, Bureau of Labor Statistics 1991.

tion.[2] For example, in 1970, the BLS projected that in 1985 the LFPR for teenage males would be 55.1 percent, and in 1978 it projected the rate would be 65.2 percent. The observed value was 59.3 percent.

Although predicting the future is a risky endeavor and the observation that some of the projections miss their target is not surprising, there is a systematic pattern. Among demographic groups whose labor market participation has been growing at an increasing rate, such as prime-age women, projections consistently underestimate observed rates. Similarly, among those groups withdrawing from the market at increasing rates, such as older men, projections consistently overestimate observed rates.

This pattern of error appears to be a direct result of the linear extrapolation methodology employed. The underlying problem with this methodology is that change over time is not constrained to be linear. Any nonlinear change in behavior will lead to potentially large projection errors. If LFPRs are increasing at an increasing rate, a linear extrapolation will always provide underestimates, whereas if LFPRs are increasing at a decreasing rate, a linear extrapolation will always lead to overestimates. Similar problems are apparent when LFPRs are decreasing at a nonconstant rate.

Three examples are provided to illustrate this point. I consider the labor force history of women between the ages of 20 and 24, men between the ages of 55 and 64, and women between the ages of 55 and 64 and project participation rates for 1980, 1985, and 1990 using data available in 1965, 1970, and 1976 (the "projection dates"), respectively, applying the linear extrapolation technique. The slope of a trend line is first estimated using data for the twenty years before each projection date for each demographic group. The projected LFPRs are then obtained by extending the trend line fifteen years into the future, beginning at the actual LFPR for each group at each projection date.

The results of this exercise are presented in table 3-3. The LFPRs predicted here are similar to those reported by the BLS; many are nearly identical.[3] For example, projected LFPRs for 1990 for 20- to 24-year-old women are 80.4 percent and 81.6 percent as the BLS reports and as I have estimated, respectively. Similarly, the simple linear extrapo-

---

2. Quinn (1992) also points out that projections for the same date made two years apart can vary tremendously.
3. The difference between the two sets of projections most likely indicate the ad hoc adjustments made by the BLS.

TABLE 3-3. COMPARISON OF PROJECTION ERRORS USING THE
LINEAR EXTRAPOLATION AND THE BLS TECHNIQUE

LFPR	1980	1985	1990
20- to 24-Year-Old Women			
Observed	69.0%	71.8%	71.6%
BLS projection	52.6	57.9	80.4
Linear extrapolation	52.1	65.2	81.6
55- to 64-Year-Old Men			
Observed	71.4	67.9	67.7
BLS projection	83.7	81.3	65.0
Linear extrapolation	83.6	77.9	62.7
55- to 64-Year-Old Women			
Observed	41.1	42.0	45.3
BLS projection	47.3	45.5	39.8
Linear extrapolation	56.6	56.6	43.8

lation technique and the BLS projection for 1980 participation rates among 55- to 64-year-old men are within 0.1 percent of each other.

A graphical representation of this exercise, shown in figures 3-1, 3-2, and 3-3, clearly displays the problems inherent in the technique. Figure 3-1 shows observed LFPRs and the three linear extrapolations for women between the ages of 20 and 24. This demographic group provides the best example of projection errors because participation rates first increased rapidly beginning in the 1960s and then proceeded to increase at a slower rate over the 1980s. Initially, the rapid growth in labor market attachment led to projections that were considerably lower than reality, as expected based on the previous discussion. Projections for 1980 and 1985 were 24 percent and 9 percent below the observed LFPR, respectively. Yet by 1990, after the slowdown in growth, the extrapolation technique provided the anticipated overestimate of labor force participation by 14 percent.

Similar patterns are observed in figures 3-2 and 3-3. Figure 3-2 shows that the observed trend in labor force participation among 55- to 64-year-old men declined at an increasing rate in the 1960s and then declined close to linearly after that. Therefore, as might be expected, projections made in 1965 and 1970 for labor force behavior in 1980 and 1985 are substantially overstated. Projections for 1990, following the largely linear decline in rates over the 1970s and 1980s, are relatively close to the observed value. LFPRs of women aged 55 to 64 increased linearly until the mid–1960s and then leveled off, as shown in figure 3-

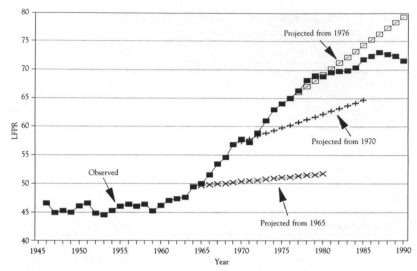

FIGURE 3-1.   PROJECTION ERRORS USING LINEAR EXTRAPOLATION:
LFPRS OF WOMEN AGES 20 TO 24

3. Again, consistent with the inherent flaw in the extrapolation methodology, projected LFPRs for 1980 and 1985 are overstated but projections for 1990 are close to the mark.

My purpose has not been to indict current methods but rather to
indicate that there are problems associated with them. In the next two

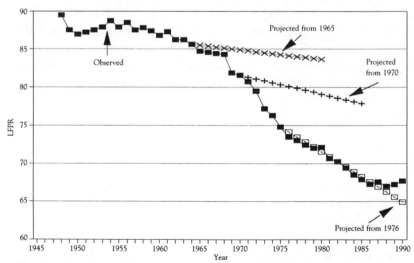

FIGURE 3-2.   PROJECTION ERRORS USING LINEAR EXTRAPOLATION:
LFPRS OF MEN AGES 55 TO 64

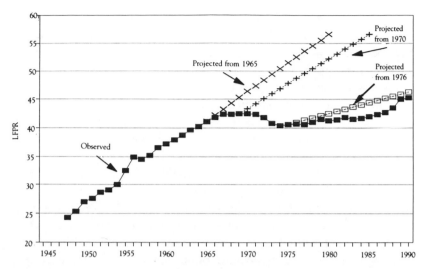

FIGURE 3-3.   PROJECTION ERRORS USING LINEAR EXTRAPOLATION:
LFPRs OF WOMEN AGES 55 TO 64

sections I propose that labor force projections be based on an economic
model so as to avoid some of these problems and potentially to provide
more accurate projections.

ECONOMIC MODEL

A considerable amount of empirical research has examined the factors
that affect the decision to work, particularly among women and the
elderly. From this literature, several important components of a structural model of labor market activity can be identified. Although I do
not present a formal model, this section will briefly outline these factors,
focusing on the behavior of older workers and the decision to retire.
The ability of these factors to explain the observed pattern of labor force
withdrawal among older workers over time is also considered.

Gary Fields and Olivia Mitchell (1984) outline the components of a
model of retirement behavior, and several recent literature reviews assess
the potential contribution of each component (Quinn, Burkhauser, and
Myers 1990; Burkhauser and Quinn 1990; Levine and Mitchell 1992).[4]
Factors associated with the retirement decision can be broken down

---

4. The brief survey that is presented here will largely be drawn from these more
extensive reviews. The reader is directed to these sources for additional detail.

into two categories: economic and noneconomic determinants. Among the noneconomic determinants, poor health and mandatory retirement have been used in the past as potential explanations of retirement behavior. Economic factors include the availability of social security, private pensions, and private wealth.

Health limitations would certainly contribute to the decision to withdraw from the labor force. The extent to which this variable influences the decision to retire is hard to measure, however, because of the difficulty in accurately measuring health status. Sources of data providing self-reported health status may be unreliable. Those who retire early may be more likely to report poor health because it is a more socially acceptable explanation for their behavior. Nonetheless, evidence from this literature has led to some consensus. For the most part, researchers have found that while health is a factor in the retirement decision of some workers, it is a relatively minor one overall. Furthermore, it must be an even smaller component of a model trying to explain changes in labor force participation over time. The increasing trend toward early retirement would require that the health status of older workers be deteriorating. There is little convincing evidence that this is the case.[5]

Historically, mandatory retirement also might have been a noneconomic component in a model of the retirement decision. The number of workers who actually were constrained by mandatory retirement has been shown to be very small, however, even when the mandatory retirement age was as low as 65. In fact, the age at which mandatory retirement could be imposed was first increased to age 70 in 1978 under the Age Discrimination in Employment Act, and it has since been banned outright for all but a few workers. Clearly, this pattern is inconsistent with the time-series trend toward early retirement.

Since noneconomic factors would appear to play a small role in this hypothetical model of labor force behavior, I now turn to economic components. Each economic factor is simply a different measure of the same theoretical concept, the current discounted value of lifetime income. Fields and Mitchell (1984) present a formal theoretical model of the retirement decision in which workers choose their retirement date to maximize their lifetime utility, which is a function of additional years worked and consumption and earnings. The decision is constrained by

5. There is some controversy over this point, however. See Berkowitz 1988 for a recent review of the literature.

a budget set that indicates the amount of income that an individual would receive over his or her remaining lifetime as a function of the retirement date. In an empirical model of labor force behavior, some of the operational components of the budget set include social security (SS) benefits, private pension benefits, and private wealth.

A large empirical literature supports the notion that higher social security benefits will lower the average retirement age. Furthermore, institutional changes in the SS system itself are consistent with the observed trend toward earlier retirement. Over the 1970s, SS benefits became considerably more generous, increasing by close to 50 percent on average. Furthermore, workers have been eligible for benefits at age 62, three years before the regular retirement age, since 1956 and 1961 for women and men, respectively.[6] The fraction of workers covered by the SS system has also increased, from 60 percent to more than 90 percent since the 1950s.

Institutional changes in employer-provided pensions are also consistent with the trend toward earlier retirement. Pension coverage has more than doubled in the last forty years, and many of these pensions provide financial incentives for workers to retire early. A considerable amount of evidence indicates that workers respond strongly to these incentives.

Increases in individual wealth over time also help explain the trend toward early retirement. As workers acquire additional wealth, nonlabor income will increase and the amount of leisure consumed (i.e., years of retirement) will increase correspondingly, assuming leisure is a normal good. It is very difficult to obtain information on this variable, however, so there is little evidence of its effect on retirement behavior.

ADVANTAGE OF AN ECONOMIC MODEL

Unlike the linear extrapolation technique, an economic model could incorporate many of the changes in the factors underlying the retirement decision in projecting future labor force participation rates. Projections could be made by statistically estimating the historical relationship between the components of the model and labor force behavior. This

---

6. Since the benefit reduction for early retirement is actuarially fair, this institutional change would not be predicted to affect behavior according to economic theory if capital markets were perfect. It will be maintained throughout the rest of this chapter that this condition is not true.

relationship could then be used to predict the effect of changes in the components on future LFPRs.

Projections made from an economic model apparently would have outperformed linear extrapolation in predicting the recent trend toward early retirement. This trend, which was missed by the linear extrapolation method, seems quite consistent with changes in the components of an economic model. Given the broad support in the literature that SS and pension benefits strongly affect retirement behavior, the increasing generosity of both forms of retirement income would have led to the prediction that people would retire earlier.

Before a strong endorsement of an economic model can be made, however, two caveats must be raised. While researchers have shown that pension and SS benefits are strongly correlated with the retirement decision, most use cross-sectional data or relatively short panels in their empirical work.[7] These data allow the researcher to test whether differences in the explanatory variable across people are correlated with retirement behavior, all else being equal. For example, the hypothesis that higher SS benefits leads to earlier retirement is supported if two workers are identical except that one is eligible for higher SS benefits and retires earlier.

The ability of an economic model to project labor force participation accurately over time requires that the model explain a different relationship, however. It requires that variation in retirement behavior over time be consistent with changes in the explanatory variable over time. For example, the hypothesis that higher SS benefits lead to earlier retirement is supported if SS benefits are increased between one year and the next and more people decide to retire in the second year. Very little of the research on determinants of retirement uses such variation in the data.[8]

In addition, the alleged success of an economic model is based on the increasing generosity of SS and private pensions and increases in wealth, all of which are consistent with the increasing trend toward early retirement. In an operational model used to project future labor

7. See Moffitt 1987 and Quinn 1987 for a detailed discussion of this issue.
8. Of course, if the statistical model were properly specified, the same results would be obtained by using either type of data. It is possible, however, that some unforeseen relationship exists between workers who will receive high SS benefits and the propensity to retire which would bias results from cross-sectional data and lead to different conclusions.

behavior, however, measures of wealth would be hard to obtain and even harder to predict. If changes in wealth over time were the main force behind observed trends in retirement, then an economic model would be hard-pressed to predict future trends accurately. In practical terms, the success of an economic model requires that the predictive power of SS benefits and pensions, which may be more easily forecast, be stronger than that of wealth.

To address both of these issues, I have compiled two sets of data. The first consists of the labor force participation rates of men ages 60 to 61 and 62 to 64 and the social security average primary insurance amount (PIA) for men between 1963 and 1988.[9] The second set contains LFPRs by exact age for the years 1970–74 and 1985–89 estimated from the relevant March Current Population Surveys.

The hypothesis that I would like to test is whether social security and pension benefits are related to changes in LFPRs over time, abstracting from changes in wealth. The analysis that is performed here is intended to correspond to the following thought experiment. Suppose a group of people with identical wealth were assigned to treatment and control groups and members of the treatment group were given SS and/or pension benefits that increased between one year and the next. Support for the hypothesis would be observed if the difference in LFPRs between the two groups increased between the two years.

I conduct analyses similar in spirit by assuming that, on average, two workers who are very similar in age should have roughly the same amount of wealth. Using time-series data on those workers aged 60 to 61 and 62 to 64, I take the difference in their LFPRs and show how the difference changes as the average PIA, an indicator of social security generosity, changes. Since the younger group is not eligible for social security retirement benefits, an increase in benefits should increase the gap in the LFPRs.[10]

Table 3-4 and figure 3-4 provide results that quite clearly support the hypothesis that increases in social security benefits reduce LFPRs, abstracting from wealth changes. Figure 3-4 shows that increases in real retirement benefits began around 1970 and continued through the late 1970s. Correspondingly, it shows that the difference in labor force par-

---

9. The primary insurance amount is the benefit a worker without a spouse would receive if he or she retired at the normal retirement age of 65.

10. Again, the assumption of imperfect capital markets is implicit in this statement.

TABLE 3-4.   LABOR FORCE PARTICIPATION RATES AND AVERAGE
SOCIAL SECURITY BENEFITS IN THE UNITED STATES AMONG NARROW
AGE GROUPS, 1963–88

(1) Year	(2) LFPR 60–61	(3) LFPR 62–64	(4) Difference (2)–(3)	(5) Average SS Benefits (1988 $s)
1963	85.9%	75.8%	10.1%	$310.16
1964	85.1	74.6	10.5	309.74
1965	84.8	73.2	11.6	318.06
1966	84.7	73.0	11.7	341.62
1967	84.0	72.7	11.3	317.85
1968	83.7	72.6	11.1	352.93
1969	83.3	70.2	13.1	342.10
1970	82.6	69.4	13.2	377.52
1971	81.7	68.4	13.3	403.94
1972	80.8	66.3	14.5	423.76
1973	78.0	62.4	15.6	452.42
1974	77.5	60.8	16.7	448.60
1975	75.2	58.6	16.6	454.05
1976	74.3	56.1	18.2	472.66
1977	74.5	54.6	19.9	485.11
1978	72.9	54.0	18.9	492.89
1979	71.9	54.3	17.6	497.74
1980	71.8	52.6	19.2	493.41
1981	70.8	49.4	21.4	500.91
1982	69.7	48.0	21.7	490.58
1983	69.7	47.7	22.0	485.04
1984	68.1	47.5	20.6	473.58
1985	68.9	46.1	22.8	475.98
1986	67.7	45.8	21.9	489.41
1987	67.6	46.0	21.6	486.94
1988	67.0	45.4	21.6	489.23

Sources: Columns 2 and 3, unpublished tables provided by John Stinson of the Bureau of Labor Statistics; column 5, *Social Security Bulletin,* Annual Statistical Supplement, 1990.

ticipation rates between the two age groups diverged and then stabilized at approximately the same dates. The difference in LFPRs between those 60 to 61 and 62 to 64 was relatively constant at about 11 percent before 1969 but increased steadily to about 21 percent by about 1981 and has remained roughly constant since. The correlation between the two series is 0.91.

A similar exercise can be conducted using the data on LFPRs by exact

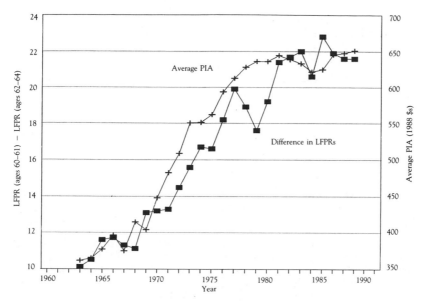

FIGURE 3-4.   DIFFERENCE IN LFPRS BETWEEN MEN AGES 60–61 AND
62–64 AND AVERAGE PRIMARY INSURANCE AMOUNT FOR MEN,
BY YEAR

age in the periods 1970–74 and 1985–89.[11] Comparing two average
workers at, say, exact age 61 and exact age 62, the older worker's current
discounted value of lifetime income will take a discrete jump because
of social security eligibility, even though the two workers will have
roughly equal wealth. Therefore, a discrete jump should be observed in
the number of workers who decide to retire (defined here as withdrawing
from the labor force) at exact age 62. Furthermore, since social security
became more generous between the two periods, the jump in retirement
at exact age 62 should be higher in the later period.[12] Similar arguments
can be made at exact ages 55 and 60, the two most common ages at
which private pensions allow early retirement (Kotlikoff and Smith
1983).

To measure the number of workers withdrawing at any given age, I
estimate the retirement hazard rate, the probability of withdrawing from
the labor force conditional on participating in the previous period (equal

11. I group the years into two periods because there are not enough people in a
Current Population Survey at every age to produce stable estimates of the LFPR.
12. Ippolito (1990) uses a similar identification strategy.

TABLE 3-5.   LABOR FORCE PARTICIPATION RATES AND RETIREMENT
HAZARD RATES OF U.S. MEN BY EXACT AGE, 1970–74 AND 1985–89

Age	1970–74		Standard Error of Hazard	1985–89		Standard Error of Hazard
	LFPR	Hazard	Hazard	LFPR	Hazard	Hazard
50	0.934	0.019	0.005	0.910	0.005	0.003
51	0.930	0.005	0.003	0.900	0.011	0.004
52	0.924	0.006	0.003	0.889	0.012	0.004
53	0.917	0.008	0.003	0.877	0.013	0.004
54	0.909	0.009	0.003	0.867	0.011	0.004
55	0.900	0.010	0.004	0.844	0.027	0.006
56	0.889	0.012	0.004	0.817	0.032	0.007
57	0.878	0.012	0.004	0.787	0.036	0.007
58	0.866	0.014	0.004	0.778	0.012	0.004
59	0.855	0.013	0.004	0.746	0.042	0.008
60	0.822	0.038	0.007	0.678	0.091	0.011
61	0.798	0.029	0.006	0.653	0.037	0.008
62	0.725	0.092	0.011	0.530	0.188	0.016
63	0.657	0.094	0.012	0.455	0.142	0.016
64	0.618	0.060	0.010	0.407	0.105	0.015
65	0.453	0.267	0.019	0.310	0.237	0.021
66	0.389	0.140	0.017	0.293	0.056	0.012
67	0.378	0.029	0.009	0.239	0.184	0.021
68	0.335	0.113	0.017	0.203	0.152	0.021
69	0.306	0.089	0.016	0.212	−0.045	0.012
70	0.283	0.074	0.015	0.189	0.108	0.020
71	0.240	0.151	0.021	0.162	0.141	0.023
72	0.219	0.088	0.018	0.151	0.073	0.018
73	0.196	0.106	0.020	0.142	0.056	0.015
74	0.190	0.031	0.012	0.126	0.117	0.022
75	0.170	0.105	0.021	0.110	0.127	0.024

Source: Author's calculations from several March Current Population Surveys.

to the ratio of withdrawals from the labor force at exact age x to the
ratio of participants at exact age $x - 1$). The results of this analysis,
reported in table 3-5 and figure 3-5, support the hypothesis that retirement patterns over time are related to changes in pension and SS benefits
after controlling for differences in wealth. As predicted, retirement
hazard rates did increase at exact ages 55, 60, and 62 between the earlier
and later periods.

Both of these tests provide support that an economic model may have
some success at projecting future trends. Historical patterns of change

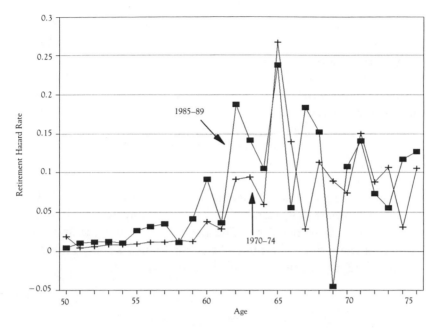

FIGURE 3-5.   RETIREMENT HAZARD RATES FOR MEN BY EXACT AGE, 1970–74 AND 1985–89

in labor force behavior are shown to be related to changes in SS and pension benefits over time, abstracting from changes in wealth. Since these two factors are more easily observed and forecasted, an economic model may provide some predictive power.

CONCLUSION

Regardless of the technique used, predicting the future is a risky business. I make no claim that projections based on an economic model of behavior will accurately predict labor force participation rates or even that it would necessarily provide more accurate predictions than the current technology of linear extrapolation. For example, both techniques would have had difficulty predicting the trend toward increased female labor force participation.

In a changing environment, however, the economic model provides some hope of correctly forecasting changes in behavior; the linear extrapolation technique will always provide inaccurate projections under such circumstances. I have discussed in this paper an example of labor force participation among older workers in which an economic model would have predicted an observed decline that was completely missed by the extrapolation technique.

A complication of the economic model, of course, is that to project future labor force behavior the forecaster has to know the changes that will occur in the underlying variables of the model. While it will often be difficult or impossible to project these changes, changes in the components of the model will often be known well in advance. For example, legislation passed in 1983 spells out changes in the SS system well into the next century.

While this chapter has not explicitly presented a formal model of labor force participation useful for projecting future trends, I believe that such a model is necessary. The need to know the size and composition of the future labor force is too important an issue. Future research should investigate such models more deeply.

Chapter 4.
POPULATION AGING AND WORK RATES OF OLDER PERSONS: AN INTERNATIONAL COMPARISON

Robert L. Clark

T HIS CHAPTER PRESENTS an overview of worldwide population trends with an emphasis on the differences between developed and developing regions. Against this backdrop, the implications of demographic changes on the labor force are examined. Specific attention is given to the propensity of older workers to remain in the labor force and to how the participation rates of older persons have changed over time and across stages of economic development.

Reductions in fertility and mortality rates over the last thirty years have led to a rapid aging of the population in most developed nations. Projections by the United Nations (1989) indicate that in the first quarter of the twenty-first century these countries will continue to experience significant population aging.

Developing countries have much higher rates of population growth than developed countries, but the rate of population growth in most developing countries has also begun to decline. The slowing of population growth in these countries is producing a gradual population aging. Despite this reduction in the rate of population growth, however, the absolute size of the populations in developing regions continues to increase.

Table 4-1 shows that the rate of population growth for the world increased from 1.8 percent per year between 1950 and 1955, to 1.99 percent per year between 1960 and 1965 before beginning to decline. By the 1980s, the rate had fallen to 1.74 percent. Current projections by the United Nations are that the rate will continue to decline and will fall below 1.0 percent by 2020.

Declines in the rate of population growth mean that the proportion of the younger-age population declines relative to that of the older-age population, leading to an increase in the median age of the population. In addition, the aging of the population influences the growth rate of the labor force. These changes can have important economic effects.

Table 4-1 also shows that there are considerable differences in the rate of population growth across regions. Europe, North America, and the former USSR have much lower rates of population growth than other regions, and the rates in these areas have been declining since 1950. Based on this pattern, the absolute size of the population of Europe is expected to begin declining around 2020. Extremely high rates of population growth in Africa and some other areas have kept the demographic focus on the absolute size and growth in the numbers of people in these areas, but even Africa is beginning to show the preliminary signs of a slowdown in the rate of its growth.

EFFECTS OF POPULATION AGING IN DEVELOPED COUNTRIES

In the years following World War II, most developed countries experienced an increase in their rates of population growth because of sharp increases in their national fertility rates. These national baby booms varied in length from only three years in Japan to more than fifteen years in the United States. After the baby booms, fertility rates declined to the point where they dropped below the replacement level in many countries. These swings in fertility rates have created large fluctuations in the rates of population growth and have dramatically altered the age structure of populations.

Concomitantly, declines in mortality rates have increased life expectancy. Recent reductions in mortality rates in developed countries have occurred primarily among older persons, thereby increasing the momentum of population aging. Thus, the median age of the population in the developed regions increased from 28.2 years in 1950 to 32.5 in 1985 and is expected to reach 40.7 by 2025 (see table 4-2). Europe's population is aging more rapidly than North America's while Japan's is the most rapidly aging in the world.

Several population ratios can be used to indicate the extent of population aging in the developed regions. The proportion of the population aged 0 to 14 has dropped sharply as fertility rates have fallen from 27.8 percent in 1950 to 21.4 percent in 1990 (see table 4-3). This figure is expected to decline to 17.9 percent in 2025. The decline in the proportion of children in the population implies that a lower proportion of

TABLE 4-1. AVERAGE ANNUAL RATE OF POPULATION INCREASE WORLDWIDE

Year	World	Africa	Latin America	Northern America	Asia	Europe	Oceania	Former USSR
1950–55	1.80%	2.18%	2.74%	1.80%	1.90%	0.79%	2.25%	1.71%
1960–65	1.99	2.48	2.80	1.49	2.19	0.91	2.09	1.49
1970–75	1.96	2.69	2.48	1.06	2.27	0.58	1.78	0.96
1980–85	1.74	2.95	2.19	1.00	1.86	0.32	1.55	0.84
1990–95	1.71	3.01	1.94	0.71	1.82	0.22	1.34	0.68
2000–5	1.47	2.84	1.63	0.56	1.44	0.13	1.18	0.61
2010–15	1.21	2.42	1.37	0.52	1.09	0.02	1.04	0.52
2020–25	0.98	1.85	1.12	0.35	0.87	−0.06	0.85	0.47

Source: United Nations 1989:37, table 25.

TABLE 4-2.   MEDIAN AGE OF PEOPLE IN MAJOR AREAS OF THE WORLD

Year	World	More Developed Regions	Less Developed Regions	Africa	Latin America	Northern America	Asia	Europe	Oceania	Former USSR
1950	23.4	28.2	21.2	18.7	19.7	30.0	21.8	30.5	27.9	24.7
1970	21.6	30.1	19.0	17.6	18.6	27.7	19.7	32.2	25.1	28.7
1985	23.4	32.5	21.0	17.3	20.9	31.5	22.2	33.9	27.6	30.0
2000	26.0	36.3	23.8	17.7	24.1	36.5	25.8	37.5	30.5	33.0
2025	31.1	40.7	29.7	22.6	30.2	40.8	32.5	42.9	34.5	36.4

Source: United Nations, 1989:53, table 2.14.

TABLE 4-3.   POPULATION RATIOS: ESTIMATES AND PROJECTIONS

	1950	1970	1985	1990	2000	2025
World						
Children (0–14)	34.6	37.5	33.5	32.3	31.3	24.4
Youth (15–24)	18.3	18.0	19.4	19.1	17.1	16.0
Elderly (≥ 60)	8.6	8.3	8.9	9.2	9.8	14.8
Dependency ratio[a]	65.7		65.3	62.7	61.5	51.8
Urbanization	29.1	37.2	41.2	42.7	46.7	60.5
Developed regions						
Children	27.8	26.6	22.2	21.4	20.1	17.9
Youth	17.0	17.0	15.9	14.9	13.7	12.3
Elderly	11.4	14.2	16.1	17.1	18.7	25.3
Dependency ratio[a]	54.8		50.6	50.2	50.9	58.3
Urbanization	53.8	66.6	71.5	72.7	74.8	79.0
Less developed regions						
Children	37.9	41.8	37.2	35.6	34.2	25.6
Youth	18.8	18.6	20.5	20.4	18.0	16.8
Elderly	6.3	6.0	6.6	6.9	7.6	12.1
Dependency ratio[a]	71.7		70.6	66.7	64.4	50.6
Urbanization	16.9	25.5	31.5	33.9	39.5	56.9

Source: United Nations 1989.
Projections are based on medium variant assumptions.
[a]Population 0 to 14 and 65 and older divide population 15 to 64.

total national income needs to be devoted to this relatively dependent component of the population.

Potential new entrants into the labor force can be viewed as the population 15 to 24. The proportion of the population composed of these potential new workers declined from 17.0 to 14.9 percent between 1950 and 1990 and is expected to drop to 12.3 percent by 2025. Reductions in the size of the population aged 15 to 24 slows the rate of growth of the labor force and thus also affects labor force mobility, productivity, measured unemployment, and the rate of introduction of new technology and knowledge into the labor force.

In contrast, the proportion of the population 60 and older rose from 11.4 to 17.1 percent during the same period and is expected to increase to 25.3 percent by 2025. Such increases lead to increases in the cost of providing retirement income and of national health expenditures. Having a higher proportion of older workers in the labor force thus has important implications for firms' labor costs and hence the willingness of employers to provide jobs to older persons.

A detailed examination of the data for individual countries indicates

62   *Robert L. Clark*

TABLE 4-4.   ACTUAL AND PROJECTED PERCENTAGE OF POPULATION
65 AND OLDER

Year	France	West Germany	Japan	Netherlands	United Kingdom	United States
1950	11.4%	9.4%	4.9%	7.7%	10.7%	8.1%
1960	11.6	10.8	5.7	9.0	11.7	9.2
1970	12.9	13.2	7.1	10.2	12.9	9.8
1980	14.0	15.5	9.0	11.5	15.1	11.3
1990	13.8	15.4	11.7	12.7	15.4	12.6
2000	15.4	17.0	15.9	13.6	15.2	12.8
2010	15.7	20.4	19.6	15.2	15.7	13.6
2020	19.3	22.2	23.7	19.4	18.2	17.5
2025	20.8	24.1	23.9	21.3	19.4	19.8

Source: United Nations 1991.
Population projections are based on medium variant projections of the United Nations.

that the populations of Japan and of some European countries is aging more rapidly than that of other developed nations. Table 4-4 shows that the proportion of the population 65 and older in Japan more than doubled between 1950 and 1990 and is expected to increase from 11.7 percent in 1990 to 23.9 percent in 2025. While the pace of aging is somewhat slower in the other countries shown in table 4-4, people 65 and older are expected to represent between one-fifth and one-quarter of their populations by 2025.

The proportion of the population 65 and older in France and the United Kingdom is expected to about double between 1950 and 2025. These two nations had among the oldest populations in the world in 1950. The proportion of the elderly is expected to increase threefold in Germany and the Netherlands; Japan is likely to experience almost a fivefold increase in the proportion of persons 65 and older during this period.

EFFECTS OF POPULATION AGING IN DEVELOPING COUNTRIES

The rate of population growth began to decline in Latin America and Oceania in the late 1960s and in Asia in the late 1970s. Table 4-1 shows that the rate in Latin America declined from 2.8 percent per year between 1960 and 1965 to 2.19 percent per year between 1980 and 1985. Smaller declines were experienced in Oceania and Asia. The numbers for Asia are dominated by the Chinese experience.

In contrast, the nations of Africa continue to experience very high

TABLE 4-5.   POPULATION SIZE AND RATE OF GROWTH IN
DEVELOPING REGIONS

	Population Size			Growth Rates	
	1990	1995	2000	1990–95	1995–2000
	(Millions)			(Percent per year)	
Africa	647.5	752.6	872.2	3.01	2.95
East	194.8	228.9	269.2	3.23	3.24
Middle	65.6	80.7	93.5	2.97	2.94
Northern	142.6	161.8	181.5	2.52	2.29
Southern	41.0	45.9	51.2	2.27	2.18
Western	199.5	235.2	276.9	3.30	3.26
Latin America	448.1	493.8	539.7	1.94	1.78
Caribbean	33.6	36.1	38.6	1.43	1.30
Central America	117.7	131.3	145.1	2.19	2.01
South America	296.8	326.4	356.0	1.90	1.74
Asia	3,108.5	3,404.1	3,697.8	1.82	1.66
South-East	440.8	482.6	523.8	1.81	1.64
Eastern	1,334.0	1,421.2	1,501.3	1.27	1.10
Southern	1,202.9	1,350.6	1,502.3	2.32	2.13
Western	130.8	149.7	170.4	2.70	2.60

Source: United Nations 1989:74–75.
Projections are based on medium variants.

rates of population growth. Between 1980 and 1985, twenty-five countries had population growth rates in excess of 3.5 percent per year. These nations were almost exclusively in the Mideast and Africa. The population size and rates of growth for various developing regions are shown in table 4-5. These data show that eastern, middle, and western Africa currently have growth rates of more than 3.0 percent per year, and these rates are expected to decline only slightly in the latter half of the 1990s. Thus, the countries of Africa are virtually alone in not experiencing any noticeable decline in their population growth rates.

Despite the relatively high rates of population growth in many developing countries, the decline in the rate of population increase is producing an aging of their populations. Table 4-2 shows that the median age of the population in developing regions declined from 21.2 years in 1950 to 19.0 years in 1970 but increased to 21.0 years by 1985. The median age is expected to increase to 23.8 by 2000 and to 29.7 in 2025. Throughout this period, the African population will remain much younger than the populations in other developing regions.

The population ratios shown in table 4-3 depict the recent aging of the populations in the developing regions. The proportion of the population aged 0 to 14 in these developing countries declined from 41.8 to 35.6 percent between 1970 and 1990, and further declines are projected for the next thirty-five years. The proportion of the population 60 and older increased slightly, from 6.0 percent in 1970 to 6.9 percent in 1990. The proportion of older persons is projected to increase sharply in the first quarter of the twenty-first century.

Most developing nations outside of Africa have entered the early stages of population aging. The pace of aging will quicken, however, during the next twenty-five years. This demographic transition will provide some opportunities for enhanced economic development as the proportion of children declines in the next two decades.

POPULATION AND LABOR FORCE AGING

Population aging obviously results in an aging of the potential labor force. Its age structure depends, however, on both the age structure of the population and the age-specific rates of labor force participation. Many of the same factors that influence population aging also have directly altered age-specific labor force participation rates. These factors include real economic growth and improvements in health care.

Three key trends in labor force participation rates typically have coincided with declines in the rate of population growth and the related aging of the population. These are a decline in the proportion of youths in the labor force; an increase in the proportion of women, primarily between the ages of 25 and 55, in the labor force; and a decline in the proportion of older persons, primarily older men, in the labor force. These changes in labor force participation rates are affected by government policies, including subsidized schooling and national retirement policies.

The potential impact of population aging on an economy depends, in part, on the accompanying changes in the age structure of the labor force. A series of economic relationships govern the net effect of population aging on labor force productivity, employment patterns, and economic growth.

First, a decline in the rate of population growth implies a slowdown in the growth rate of the cohort composed of potential new entrants into the labor force (see table 4-3). Thus, the economy must create fewer new jobs than if the cohort entering the labor force was larger. Considerable attention was given to this point in the United States in the 1970s when the large cohort entering the labor force was thought to have played a significant role in the rise in the unemployment rate.

Second, worker productivity is linked to the age structure of the labor force. In general, productivity increases with age as workers gain experience on the job. Beyond some point, however, a person's ability to perform various job tasks begins to decline. Thus, replacing youths with middle-aged workers tends to enhance total productivity, while a rapid increase in the percentage of very old workers might tend to lower productivity overall.

New entrants into the labor force introduce new skills based on the latest technology. Formal education enhances human capital, and new labor force entrants are able to learn the latest technology during their school years. Thus, a reduction in the percentage of new labor force entrants may retard the rate of introduction of new technology, which ultimately would lower the rate of economic growth.

Third, population aging tends to reduce the flexibility of the labor force. A more slowly growing labor force has greater difficulty responding to structural changes. A more rapidly growing labor force can channel young workers into growing industries, while attrition reduces the size of companies (and thus industries) where demand has declined. In economies where the labor force is growing less rapidly, expanding sectors of the economy attract workers away from declining industries.

Individual labor force mobility declines with age. Older workers are less likely to switch industries if their skills are firm-specific or if they face substantial loss in pension benefits with such a move (Allen, Clark, and McDermed 1991; Mitchell 1982). Thus, an older, more slowly growing labor force tends to be less responsive to economic fluctuations than a younger, more rapidly growing labor force. Population aging also retards the rate of promotion, thereby slowing the climb up the employment hierarchy (Keyfitz 1973; Cantrell and Clark 1982).

Fourth, in many countries, compensation increases with seniority. The increase in compensation associated with age and job tenure results in older workers being paid more than younger workers (Lazear 1979; Hutchens 1989). Long-term employment relationships and some form of seniority-based pay are the norm in may countries. The expected length of employment is linked to the rate of increase in compensation (Lazear 1979; Clark and Ogawa 1992a).

To the extent that increased compensation is not matched by increases in production, unit labor costs rise. Thus, an aging of the labor force will be associated with increasing production costs and firms will have incentives to reduce the number of older workers. If older workers are paid more than younger workers, it is not enough for older workers to be as productive as younger workers; they must be more productive to prevent labor costs from rising. These contracts will tend to reduce employment opportunities for older workers (Hutchens 1986).

Many firms, primarily in developed countries, have attempted to reduce the number of older workers on their payrolls by adopting a variety of early-retirement programs. Furthermore, many developed countries, especially in Europe, have attempted to lower national un-employment rates by reducing the number of older workers in the labor force. During the 1960s and 1970s, early-retirement incentives were incorporated into the national pension programs in several countries of Europe to entice older workers to retire (Clark 1992).

Fifth, population aging increases the ratio of retirees to active workers, which results in increases in the cost of providing social security benefits. Projections of very large increases in the costs of maintaining existing social security systems led many countries to amend their programs. Thus, during the 1980s, the United States, Japan, and some European countries approved legislation raising the age to receive normal retire-ment benefits or changing social security benefit formulas. These changes were made to reduce costs and encourage older workers to remain in the labor force.

The continued population aging in developed countries will increas-ingly set government policies at odds with firms' personnel policies. In most developed countries, firms continue to encourage older workers to retire in contrast with new government policies, which seek to delay retirement. Japan is an example. Firms have increased the age of man-datory retirement in response to government policies; however, early-retirement policies have been introduced, and firms are reducing the rate of increases in earnings with continued employment (Clark 1991; Clark and Ogawa 1992b).

DETERMINANTS OF THE LFPRS OF OLDER PERSONS

The proportion of older workers in the labor force is one of the key determinants of the impact of population aging on national economies. Retirement decisions are based on individual preferences, economic constraints limiting individual choices, personal characteristics, and health status.

Most studies of retirement have been limited to older men in developed countries. Research findings indicate that increases in household wealth increase the probability of retirement, as do pension and social security income (Quinn, Burkhauser, and Myers 1990). Greater demand for older workers as indicated by the availability of employment opportunities and the prevailing wage rate results in more older workers remaining in the labor force. Health limitations increase the likelihood that older workers will retire. Theoretically, retirement decisions in developing countries should be based on a similar choice process. There are substantial differences between these countries and developed countries, however, in their economic and social institutions and their family relationships. Key differences include the industrial structure of their economies, the lack of employer pensions, their much lower coverage and less generous benefits from social security, and the overall poorer health of their older persons.

Developing countries tend to have a lower degree of urbanization and a large proportion of the labor force employed in agriculture and self-employed. Generally speaking, workers' hours are more flexible and the LFPRs of their older workers are higher. Older men may remain as the head of an extended household, controlling the family's wealth and spending some limited amount of time working on family land or in a family business.

Coverage by employer pensions and social security often is limited to the government sector, the military, and the industrial sector in urban areas. While these plans may have early-retirement incentives and mandatory retirement provisions, only a relatively small proportion of the total workforce participates in formal retirement plans. Persons forced to retire from these career jobs often seek employment in other sectors of the economy.

Family support systems in developing countries often take the place of formal retirement plans. Family structure also influences retirement decisions. Single and widowed women are more likely to be in the labor force than married women. Further, the presence of children or grandchildren affects the value of time at home and the older person's possible sources of income.

Extreme differences in the absolute level of income between developed and developing countries are also very important in defining retirement possibilities. The very low incomes of some developing nations make it virtually impossible for workers to accumulate sufficient resources to retire independently. Even extended families may not have sufficient income to enable healthy older family members to cease working. John D. Durand (1975) found that the labor force participation rates of older persons declined with economic development and increases in real income (also see Clark and Anker 1990).

CROSS-NATIONAL DATA ON PARTICIPATION RATES

Labor force participation rates for 1980 have been collected for 151 countries by the International Labour Office. Average labor force participation rates for men and women 65 and older by region are shown in table 4-6. The average participation rates for men range from 71.8 percent in western and middle Africa to 6.6 percent in western Europe. Throughout the world, rates are much higher in the developing regions. Europe and North America have the lowest rates while Africa has the highest.

The labor force participation rates for older women are lower than for men in each of the regions. The pattern of participation across regions is similar for women as it is for men except in the Islamic nations of northern Africa. The extremely low rates reported for these countries may be attributable to significant undercounting of female workers in the official labor force surveys in part because of religious customs and attitudes (Anker 1983). Participation rates for older women in North America and Europe are 7.0 percent or less, while those for Africa are more than 27.0 percent except in the north.

The righthand side of the table shows similar information, but it is based on only the 114 nations with per-capita gross national products reported by the World Bank. For the most part, the truncation of the sample does not substantially alter the regional participation rates. Comparing participation rates with the level of income illustrates that higher real income is associated with a lower LFPR for older men. Thus, the highest participation rates occur in those areas of Africa with the lowest income per capita and the lowest in western and northern Europe and in North America, regions with the highest income. An exception is eastern Europe, which has low participation rates and a relatively low income per capita. With the exception of the Islamic countries, the pattern for females is much the same.

Robert L. Clark and Richard Anker (1989b, 1990) examined LFPRs for 1980 of older men and women in 151 countries. A detailed reporting is presented in Clark and Anker 1989b, while both their papers provide

TABLE 4-6. LABOR FORCE PARTICIPATION RATES OF PERSONS 65 AND OLDER, BY REGION, 1980

Region[a]	No. of Countries	LFPR[b]		Countries with GNPP Data	GNPP[c]	LFPR[d]	
		Men	Women			Men	Women
Africa							
Eastern	15	67.1	34.2	11	416	69.1	32.8
Middle	8	71.8	29.0	5	1,242	70.6	32.0
Northern	6	43.5	5.5	6	2,435	43.5	5.5
Southern	5	60.9	27.3	4	1,043	63.2	31.1
Western	16	71.8	28.1	14	456	71.0	28.8
Caribbean	9	35.8	13.6	5	2,054	52.8	21.6
Central America	7	58.6	9.4	7	1,287	58.6	9.4
South America	12	42.4	7.2	12	1,737	42.4	7.2
Asia							
East	6	41.1	17.0	4	4,248	39.3	12.3
South	18	53.2	15.0	11	847	52.7	14.3
Western	15	44.1	4.9	10	7,970	44.5	4.7
North America	2	16.9	7.0	2	11,305	16.9	7.0
Europe							
Eastern	7	15.3	6.9	1	1,930	4.0	3.0
Northern	7	18.3	6.9	7	10,987	18.3	5.9
Southern	7	23.7	5.2	6	4,318	20.4	4.8
Western	7	6.6	2.7	7	13,107	6.6	2.7
Oceania	4	31.7	11.6	4	4,905	31.7	11.6

Source: Clark and Anker 1989b.

[a]Countries are grouped by geographical regions as specified by the International Labour Office. The former USSR is included in eastern Europe. The South Asia region includes only eastern and middle South Asia, since Western South Asia is listed separately here.

[b]These columns indicate the average labor force participation rates of persons aged 65 and older for all countries in the region with information on labor force participation.

[c]GNPP represents the average per-capita gross national product in U.S. dollars for countries in the region that report GNPP data.

[d]These columns indicate the average labor force participation rates of persons aged 65 and older for countries in the region with GNPP data.

TABLE 4-7. LABOR FORCE PARTICIPATION RATE EQUATIONS, 1980

	Men		Women	
Variable	(1)	(2)	(1)	(2)
Intercept	143.43[a]	96.55[a]	61.25[a]	34.02[b]
	(7.56)	(26.95)	(5.77)	(16.84)
Log GNPP	−13.26[a]	−3.95[b]	−6.35[a]	−1.70
	(1.02)	(2.12)	(0.78)	(1.62)
PERPOP65		−0.86		0.08
		(0.58)		(0.36)
PERURB		−0.19[b]		−0.08
		(0.10)		(0.07)
SSLAW		−0.15[b]		−0.09
		(0.08)		(0.06)
WIDOWRATE		−0.18		0.04
		(0.12)		(0.10)
SSAGE		−0.04		−0.08
		(0.42)		(0.26)
AFRICA		15.70[b]		14.59[a]
		(7.24)		(5.40)
MIDEAST		−1.03		−4.35
		(6.85)		(5.13)
LATAM		9.02		0.97
		(6.07)		(4.63)
ASIA		−1.02		−0.23
		(7.10)		(5.22)
DEVPLAN		−19.97		−7.40
		(12.59)		(9.29)
ADJ R2	0.59	0.76	0.36	0.60
N	116	102	116	102

Source: Clark and Anker 1989a.
[a]Coefficient is significantly different from zero at .01 confidence level.
[b]Coefficient is significantly different from zero at .1 confidence level.

results of least-squares estimates of participation rate equations for older men and women.

Specifications in these studies were limited to information that was available from a single source for all countries in the sample. Participation rate data came from the International Labour Office, demographic data from the United Nations, income data from the World Bank, and social security data from the U.S. Social Security Administration.

Table 4-7 reports the results of these estimates for men and women. For each sex, participation rates are first estimated only as a function of the log of the gross national product per capita in U.S. dollars (Log

GNPP). The results indicate that increases in per-capita income across countries significantly reduce the proportion of older persons in the labor force. For men, a 10 percent increase in income is associated with a 1.3 percent decline in the labor force participation rate, while for women, a 10 percent increase in income is associated with a decrease of 0.64 percent. These simple specifications explain 59 percent of the variation in national participation rates for men and 36 percent for women.

Equation 2 in table 4-7 reports the results from an expanded specification incorporating the effects of demographic change, economic development, social security programs, and regional effects. National participation rates for older persons are assumed to be influenced by the proportion of the population 65 and over (PERPOP65), the percentage of the population living in urban areas (PERURB), and the proportion of the female population that is widowed (WIDOWRATE). WIDOWRATE is calculated by dividing the number of women aged 55 and over by the number of men of the same age minus one multiplied by one hundred.

SSLAW is an indication of the maturity of the national social security program and is calculated by subtracting the year the country's first social security law was enacted from 1980. SSAGE is the earliest age a person can receive social security benefits. The regional variables indicate the geographical location of the country. The omitted category represented the developed market economies of North America and Europe.

For men, the results provide a clear picture of declines in labor force participation with economic development. With economic development, real incomes rise and the proportion of the population living in urban areas tends to increase. In most cases, the development of comprehensive national social security programs has followed along with economic development. As noted above, the rate of population growth and hence an aging of the population also occurs in conjunction with economic growth. Each of these effects tends to reduce the LFPR of older men.

Table 4-7 indicates that changes in the variables accompanying economic growth will tend to reduce the LFPR of older men. The regional variables show substantially higher labor force participation in Africa and Latin America even after controlling for these economic and demographic effects. Similar effects are noted for women; however, the results are smaller and less significant.

TABLE 4-8. ESTIMATED COEFFICIENTS FOR LOG GNPP FROM LFPR
EQUATIONS FOR MEN AND WOMEN 55 AND OLDER

Age and Sex Group	Equation 1[a]	Equation 2[b]
Male		
55–59	− 3.03	− 1.46
60–64	− 7.42	− 3.25
≥ 65	− 13.26	− 3.95
Female		
55–59	− 5.10	0.29
60–64	− 6.40	− 0.70
≥ 65	− 6.35	− 1.70

Entries are the coefficients estimated from labor force participation rate equations similar to those in table 4-7. The values for persons 65 and older are directly from table 4-7.

[a]Equation includes only the constant term and log GNPP as explanatory variables; see table 4-7.

[b]Equation includes a constant term, log GNPP, other economic and demographic variables, and dichotomous variables indicating region; see table 4-7.

Clark and Anker (1989b) also examined the participation rates of persons 55 to 59 and 60 to 64. The estimated coefficients for Log GNPP from participation equations similar to those reported in table 4-7 are shown in table 4-8.

The analysis of men and women between 55 and 64 suggests that increases in real per-capita income produces declines in LFPRs for each of the age groups shown in table 4-8. Each of the income coefficients in the equations that include income as the only explanatory variable are significant at the .01 confidence level. For men, the size of the income effect increases substantially with advancing age; for women, this pattern is less clear. Including the additional explanatory variables described above in the equations reduces the size and significance of the income effect.

Clark and Anker (1989b, 1991) also explored the effect of these economic and demographic variables on the decline in participation rates with age. They examined the participation rate of men and women aged 65 and older relative to those 45 to 49. This ratio standardizes for the level of activity at earlier ages. For men, the results are very similar to those shown above since the effect of the standardization is to divide participation rates of those 65 and over by approximately one; the participation rate for men 45 to 49 is very close to 100 percent in all countries.

For women, this analysis shows the decline in participation rates with age and controls for the wide variation in the participation of women 45 to 49 across nations. These results show a large and more significant effect of income on the decline in the LFPRs of women. The estimated coefficient for Log GNPP for women using a specification similar to equation 2 is −4.56, implying that a 10 percent increase in real income will produce a 0.46 decline in the ratio of the participation rate of women 65 and older to that of women 45 to 49.

Finally, Clark and Anker (1991) explored the income effect on participation rates conditional on developmental status. Participation rate equations are estimated for countries above and below the world mean GNPP for persons 65 and over. The effect of per-capita income on the level of labor force participation is observed primarily among low-income countries. For men 65 and older, the estimated coefficient on Log GNPP for the low-income countries is −7.26. This coefficient is significantly different from zero at the 0.1 confidence level. For countries above the mean, the estimated coefficient is −0.39 and is insignificant. For women, the coefficients are −1.58 for countries below the mean and −0.20 for those above the mean.

The primary conclusions from the research studies by Clark and Anker are that increases in real income are associated with lower labor force participation rates across countries; changes in other variables associated with economic development also lower participation rates; the income effect on labor force participation increases with age; and the income effect occurs primarily among developing countries.

TRENDS IN LFPRs IN DEVELOPED COUNTRIES

Economic theory predicts that labor supply will decline with increases in real income. History indicates that much of this reduction occurs in the form of earlier retirement from the labor force. In addition to economic growth, other economic and social changes may produce a decline over time in the labor force participation rates of the elderly. Of specific importance are changes in government retirement policies.

Most developed countries have introduced national social security programs. Most of these countries have made retirement benefits available to persons younger than the normal retirement age, often without requiring actuarial reductions for these benefits. Some countries have set the normal retirement age below 65.

During the 1960s and 1970s, many European countries used their

74 *Robert L. Clark*

TABLE 4-9. LABOR FORCE PARTICIPATION RATES OF MEN 65 AND
OLDER IN SELECTED DEVELOPED COUNTRIES

Country	1950	1960	1970	1980	1985
			(percent)		
Australia	32.7	28.2	21.8	13.5	12.7
Belgium	19.4	9.4	6.2	4.6	4.4
Canada	40.9	30.4	21.7	14.6	13.8
Denmark	38.0	32.4	26.9	15.3	14.2
France	37.2	26.1	15.0	6.0	5.6
Germany	27.5	21.4	16.7	4.9	4.7
Italy	46.6	27.5	14.5	7.5	6.8
Japan	54.5	54.5	54.5	45.8	42.7
Netherlands	31.5	20.4	11.4	4.5	4.2
Sweden	36.4	27.7	19.0	10.3	9.7
United Kingdom	34.4	26.6	18.8	11.0	10.6
United States	45.0	33.9	25.5	19.1	18.2

Source: United Nations 1988.

social security programs to entice older workers out of the labor force, hoping that the reduction in the supply of workers would increase jobs for younger workers and reduce national unemployment rates. In some cases, social security benefits were made more generous and full benefits were made available at earlier ages. In other countries, access to early-retirement benefits for retirees was conditional on firms hiring new workers to replace the retirees (Mirkin 1987).

Table 4-9 shows LFPRs for men 65 and older for a sample of developed countries between 1950 and 1985. Sharp declines are reported for all the countries except Japan. The declines are especially large for the western European countries between 1950 and 1980.

Japan has by far the highest participation rate for older men. The Japanese participation rate of more than 40 percent can be compared with rates of 4 to 7 percent in western Europe and rates of 14 to 18 percent in North America. The high rates in Japan are somewhat puzzling given the widespread use of mandatory retirement in most firms at relatively young ages (Clark 1991).

These data and other information concerning the activity rates of older persons indicate that the normal retirement age in most developed countries is probably closer to 60 than to 65. Will this trend toward early retirement continue? Many of these countries have become very concerned with the rapidly increasing costs of their national retirement programs. An earlier age of retirement increases the ratio of retirees to active workers and raises the tax rate necessary to sustain any given level of retirement benefit.

Current projections indicate that all developed countries will face substantial increases in the cost of social security by 2000 and 2025. Raising the age of eligibility for benefits could reduce the expected total increase in the cost of these programs. Increases in the age of eligibility have been passed or are now being considered in many developed countries (Clark 1992). Other changes in national retirement policies are also being considered in an effort to keep older workers in the labor force.

Expected changes in national retirement policies will alter the incentives for retirement. These changes should slow and perhaps reverse the trend toward early retirement. The result of changes in government policy depend in part on the responses of employers. If firms continue to press for reductions in the number of older workers, employers could offset the incentives provided by government actions. In Japan, for example, employers are reducing the rate of wage growth with continued employment (Clark and Ogawa 1992b), and in the United States, firms continue to offer specific early-retirement incentives.

TRENDS IN LFPRS IN DEVELOPING COUNTRIES

Reliable data on labor force participation in developing nations are less prevalent. Clark and Anker (1992) examined such data in an effort to identify any trends in these countries. Their analysis reveals a general downward trend but with substantial fluctuations over time in the rates for both men and women.

During the 1980s, many developing countries experienced sharp economic downturns. If increases in real income reduce the participation rates of older persons, does economic stagnation and decline reverse these trends? Despite some hints of this relationship in the data, estimates by Clark and Anker do not reveal a systematic relationship between changes in real income and labor force participation rates during this period.

It is not surprising that short-term fluctuations in income do not produce noticeable trends in labor force participation rates. Long-term increases in the rate of economic growth produce cohorts of older persons with greater real income than previous generations. This higher wealth leads to early retirement. Short-term declines in economic growth reduce current income but may have only a small impact on the lifetime income of older persons. Thus, while these fluctuations have income effects that should increase the labor supply of older persons, they should be smaller in magnitude than the response to changes in long-term increases in economic growth. In addition, economic downturns reduce the availability of jobs and hence the wage offered to older workers. These effects tend to decrease the likelihood of older workers remaining in the labor force.

Additional research is needed to determine the impact of short-term economic downturns on the LFPRs of older persons in developing countries. If economic decline continues in these countries, we would expect the participation of older persons to begin to increase in the future.

CONCLUSION

Population aging in developed countries is well advanced; however, most of these nations will experience a further rapid increase in the proportion of their populations 65 and older during the next thirty-five years. In most developed countries, more than one-fifth of the population will be 65 and older by 2025. The changing age structure of the population has important effects on the cost of providing retirement income and health care to older persons. Age structure changes have direct effects on the labor force, average productivity, and labor costs.

A schism is developing between government retirement policies and those of employers. Increasingly, governments are encouraging delayed retirement, while firms still are seeking to reduce the size of their older labor force. The relative strength of these two conflicting forces will influence the proportion of older persons who remain in the labor force.

The participation rates of older men declined rapidly over the past forty years with increases in real income and the development of national retirement programs. The decline in participation rates has slowed in many developed countries in recent years as the proportion of men 65 and older who remain in the labor force has fallen below 10 percent. In the United States, the participation rates of older men have remained relatively stable over the past five years. There are a few signs, however, that the proportion of older men who will remain in the labor force will increase in the coming years.

Among developing countries, the participation rates of older persons have also declined with economic growth. During the last decade, many developing countries experienced a decline in real income; some countries had substantial declines. These declines reduced the availability of jobs to older workers but also reduced the economic ability to retire. The net effect on the labor force participation rates of older persons is unclear.

Declines in fertility rates have slowed the rate of population growth in most developing countries. These countries are experiencing the first stages of population aging. In the coming decades, developing countries must begin to consider issues associated with having an increased population of older persons. Employment and income issues must be addressed, and national retirement policies must be developed. Economic progress in the developing countries can be enhanced if they can avoid the mistakes made by the developed nations in establishing retirement policies that encourage early retirement.

PART II.
NEW JOBS FOR AN OLDER WORKFORCE

Chapter 5.
RESTRICTED JOB OPPORTUNITIES AND THE OLDER WORKER

Robert M. Hutchens

T HERE IS GOOD REASON to suspect that older workers confront more restricted job opportunities than otherwise identical young workers. When older males change jobs, they tend to reap smaller wage gains than young males. Indeed, older males who change jobs often experience a decline in wages as well as a decline in the socioeconomic status of their occupation (see Bartel and Borjas 1981; Carliner 1982; Parnes and Nestel 1981; Shapiro and Sandell 1985). In addition, several studies indicate that the offer arrival rates of older workers are lower than those of comparable younger workers. Finally, anecdotes indicate that older workers have difficulty finding jobs that make full use of their skills. When Packard Motor Company shut down, for example, the younger workers were more likely to find reemployment in the other Detroit auto companies (where their Packard skills could be used) than were the older workers with similar skills (Sheppard, Ferman, and Faber 1960).

Of course, such evidence does not provide a coherent answer to the question of whether and why older workers face different job opportunities than otherwise identical young workers. This chapter takes steps toward answering that question. It uses the neoclassical economic theory of job search to frame the idea of restricted job opportunities and presents preliminary tests of the resulting hypotheses. As such, it provides new information on the barriers confronting older workers.

A problem with explaining observed phenomena in terms of "restricted job opportunities" is that in most cases the same phenomena

I am indebted to Yoshio Okunishi and Annika Sunden for their excellent research assistance.

can be explained in terms of "tastes." For example, older workers may reap smaller wage gains when they change jobs because they *want* lower-wage jobs. They may be moving from stressful jobs to ones that are less demanding. They may be more willing than their younger counterparts to trade wages for positive job amenities. In the Packard Motor Company shutdown, older workers may not have wanted reemployment in another auto company.

This problem is not unique to the labor market for older workers. It is difficult to think of a labor market phenomenon that cannot be explained by variations in taste. Even the ubiquitous finding that people with more nonwage income supply less labor to the market can be viewed as a consequence of tastes (e.g., people with higher nonwage income have a greater taste for leisure, ceteris paribus). There is, however, a troubling "anything goes" aspect to explanations that rely on taste variation. Economists typically resort to such explanations only as a last resort. Theories of restricted job opportunities provide a plausible alternative.

There is no question that job opportunities can be and are often restricted. Classic examples are the racial segregation of professional baseball before 1947 and the existence of "marriage bars," whereby some employers simply excluded married women from the workplace (Goldin 1990). Similar evidence can be cited for older workers. In particular, a 1965 study of employer hiring behavior in five cities found that three out of five employers covered by the survey imposed upper age limitations (usually between 45 and 55) on new hires (U.S. Department of Labor 1965). Whether such restrictions still exist, why they exist, and whether they dramatically affect labor market outcomes remain interesting and open questions, however.

This chapter begins by sketching a theory of job search wherein older workers confront more restricted job opportunities than otherwise identical younger workers. The theory is consistent with the observation that older job changers reap smaller wage gains and are offered jobs less often than younger workers. The next section then states hypotheses. Preliminary results then appear, based on the January 1988 Survey of Displaced Workers. These data contain information on U.S. workers who were forced out of jobs because their plant or company closed down or moved. Since the plant-closing process is, arguably, exogenous to the individual, these data provide insights into the jobs available to different groups of workers. I conclude that the preliminary evidence provides mixed support for the theoretical model.

THEORETICAL FRAMEWORK

Restricted job opportunities may arise because younger workers have an unambiguous advantage over otherwise identical older workers: young workers have more years to devote to a job. For this reason, some employers will prefer to hire young workers rather than equally skilled and motivated older workers. These employers are not discriminating against older workers in that they are exercising an irrational prejudice. Rather, they are excluding older workers because they seek to maximize worker tenure with the firm.

It is reasonable to predict that some jobs are unlikely to fall within an older worker's job choice set.[1] One example is a job with a large "fixed cost" of hiring, such as firm-specific training. Each time the firm hires a new worker for a job with large fixed costs, it must bear these costs. As Walter Oi (1962) has argued, to minimize the burden of such costs, the firm will seek to form long-term relationships with workers and thereby minimize turnover. Since young workers have more years to offer than older workers, the firm is more likely to form a long-term relationship with a young worker, ceteris paribus. Thus, when jobs involve large fixed costs, the firm either will not hire older workers or will offer them lower wages than equally qualified younger workers. Although they employ older workers (who joined the firm when they were young), such firms tend not to hire *new* older workers.

To illustrate, consider a large firm that dominates the market for mainframe computers. When it hires new workers, it not only provides extensive training but also seeks to imbue these workers with its corporate culture. Since such training is expensive and time-consuming, the firm seeks to limit turnover by forming long-term implicit contracts with its workers. As such, when it hires new workers, it tends to focus on young workers. While older workers may be as qualified, their expected duration on the job is shorter; and consequently they are less desirable new hires.

Of course, there are other jobs in which, because of the nature of the technology used, employers are not particularly concerned about forming

1. This argument is drawn from Hutchens 1988.

long-term relationships and minimizing turnover. An example might be a job in a fast-food restaurant. In this case, employers may be indifferent about hiring equally qualified young or old workers. As a result, both the probability of a job offer as well as the offered wage will be the same for young and old.

Because the technology used in different jobs imposes different requirements for long-term attachments, young workers have a broader range of job opportunities than do older workers with the same skills and abilities. Since young workers are more likely to convincingly signal a willingness to spend several years in the same firm, they will be offered new jobs that involve long durations. Since older workers cannot signal this characteristic, they will tend to be shut out of such jobs and their new job opportunities will occur in jobs in which turnover is not particularly problematic.

This point can be made with a modification of the standard single-spell economic model of an unemployed worker's search from a known distribution of wage offers. As in a standard model, agents are assumed to be income maximizers. When they incur an instantaneous search cost c ($c > 0$), job offers arrive from a Poisson process with parameter λ independent of the level of c.

The model introduced here diverges from the standard model in its treatment of the offer distribution. Assume that successive offers are independent realizations from a known absolutely continuous distribution $f(w,k)$, $w \geq 0$, $k \geq 0$, where w is compensation and k is the minimum job duration that an employer requires when hiring a new worker. Although w encompasses monetary and nonmonetary components of the job (e.g., benefits), for simplicity w will henceforth be called "wages." In addition, we assume that once refused, a job offer is no longer available.

What makes this model different is the minimum job duration, k. For some firms (such as fast-food restaurants) k is small, while for others (such as manufacturers of mainframe computers), it is large. Although each firm knows its value of w and k, workers know only the distribution, $f(w,k)$. They obtain information on a specific firm's values of w and k when they search and receive an offer from that firm. (The standard economic search model assumes that each firm knows its value of w and workers do not, whereas this model assumes that each firm knows its value of both w and k and workers do not.)

For current purposes, assume a positive association between w and k. More rigorously stated, assume that $f(w, k)$ is of a form where employers with greater required job durations also tend to offer higher wages. Then $E(w|k)$—the expected value of w conditional on k—is monotonically increasing in k. This could plausibly arise in a world in which there is a shortage of workers who are able to commit to long job durations. In such a world workers who are able to commit to long job durations receive a wage premium.[2]

In this simplified format, the jobs offered by employers are assumed to last forever (there are no layoffs or forced retirements in this model[3]). Nevertheless, job searchers differ in the length of time they can be expected to remain in the job. Alternatively stated, searchers signal different expected job durations. Denote the ith searcher's expected job duration as $k^*(i)$, where $k^*(i)$ is public knowledge. (To simplify the notation, I shall refer to $k^*(i)$ as k^* henceforth.) Note that unlike the employer's value of k, there is no asymmetry of information regarding k^*; both searchers and prospective employers accurately observe k^*. Note also that since k^* does not depend upon current search behavior, it is an exogenous variable in the model.

An employer who looks over a room full of job applicants will see different values of k^*. Using observable demographic characteristics such as age, race, gender, and past job experience, the employer (implicitly) predicts how long an applicant will remain in the job. Some in the room might be viewed as likely to quit and return to school; still others may depart because of illness, home responsibilities, or retirement. In this regard the employer is acting like someone viewing a barrel with different kinds of light bulbs, some used, some new. Although it is not possible to say how long a specific bulb will last, one can form judgments about the expected duration of different kinds of bulbs based on observed characteristics.

To illustrate these ideas, suppose that for the ith searcher, k^* takes the form

$$k^*(i) = \{C - AGE(i)\}\,\{X(i)'B\},$$

---

2. In a more general model with endogenous quits, firms that require long durations would pay higher wages to discourage quits.

3. Among mature males who work full time, permanent job separations usually take the form of quits. Thus, a more general theory would bring in quits. See Burdett and Mortenson 1980 for research that brings in layoffs.

where $AGE(i)$ is the age of the ith searcher, C is a constant with the property $C > Max\{Age(i)\}$, $X(i)$ is a vector of demographic characteristics for searcher i, and B is a vector of parameters. Holding $X(i)$ constant, aging leads to lower values of k^*. Holding age constant, more "favorable" demographic characteristics (e.g., received diploma, no evidence of job hopping) lead to higher values of k^*.

An employer who requires a minimum job duration of k will make offers only to applicants with values of k^* greater than or equal to k. As such, younger workers have broader job opportunities than older workers with the same skills and abilities. Since younger workers have a larger value of k^*, other things equal, they receive offers from a broader range of employers. That in turn has implications for wages, offer arrival rates, unemployment, and the industrial sectors in which younger and older people find jobs.

Since this model is closely related to the standard search model, it can be formulated with considerable mathematical rigor. Indeed, as in the standard search model, one can derive expressions for the reservation wage, the distribution of accepted wage offers, and the distribution of completed spells of unemployment. This then leads to structural hypotheses linking the exogenous variables (k^*, c, r, and the parameters of $f(w,k)$) to endogenous variables, such as the offer arrival rate, the reservation wage, and the distribution of accepted wage offers.

I do not seek to test structural hypotheses here, so a mathematical development will not be undertaken. Rather, for purposes of the subsequent empirical work, it suffices to note three plausible theoretical hypotheses that arise from the model.

Theoretical hypothesis 1: $dE(k)/dk^* > 0$. This means that the expected value of k in new jobs increases with k^*. This is because workers receive offers only from firms with k less than k^*. As k^* increases, workers receive offers from firms with larger k. In consequence, the expected value of k in accepted jobs increases. Thus, the expected value of k for younger workers will be greater than the expected value of k for older workers, ceteris paribus.

Theoretical hypothesis 2: $dE(w)/dk^* > 0$. This states that the expected value of wages on new jobs increases with k^*. This is primarily because it is assumed that $E(w|k)$ increases monotonically with k. In consequence, as k^* increases, workers receive offers not only from firms with higher k but also from firms with higher w. The hypothesis implies that after controlling for skills and ability, young workers will enjoy higher wages than old workers.[4]

Theoretical hypothesis 3: $\lambda/dk^* > 0$. The third hypothesis states that the job offer arrival rate increases with k^*. Once again, this is because workers receive offers only from firms with k less than k^*. Even if workers with a small k^* search as intensely as those with a large k^* and even if they have the same skills and abilities, some firms make offers only to workers with large k^*. Thus, we would expect older workers to enjoy lower offer arrival rates, ceteris paribus.[5]

Finally, a fourth theoretical hypothesis is particularly useful in the subsequent empirical work:

Theoretical hypothesis 4: If k^* is of the form

$$k^*(i) = \{C - AGE(i)\}\ \{X(i)'B\},$$

then $dE(k)/d(Age)$, $dE(w)/d(Age)$, and $d\lambda/d(Age)$ become more negative as $X(i)'B$ increases.

This implies that the effects of age on expected job duration (k), wages (w), and offer arrival rates (λ) should be especially pronounced for people with characteristics other than age that are associated with high k^*.[6]

Are these hypotheses unique to this theory? Of course not. One can surely develop alternative theories, including those built on taste variation, that generate similar hypotheses. These hypotheses are, however, useful first approximations for looking at the data.

DATA AND TESTS

I shall assess whether the above model is roughly consistent with actual behavior using the January Survey of Displaced Workers (SDW) supplements to the Current Population Survey (CPS). The CPS collects labor market information on a nationally representative sample of the U.S. civilian population. People who worked during the survey week

---

4. The derivation of this result is complicated by the fact that reservation wages change when k^* increases. It can, however, be shown that, since the reservation wage increases with k^*, the prediction also holds in this case.

5. Previous empirical work by Wiji Narendranathan and Stephen Nickell (1985), Hyun-Joon Chang (1985), and Theresa J. Devine (1988) provides empirical support for this hypothesis.

6. The hypothesis is simply a consequence of the chain rule. For example, the change in the expected value of k with respect to a change in Age is

$$dE(k)/d(Age) = (dE(k)/dk^*)(dk^*/d(Age)) = -(dE(k)/dk^*)(X'B).$$

Thus, as $X'B$ increases, $dE(k)/d(Age)$ becomes more negative.

are asked questions about their current job, including wages, hours, industry, and occupation. For the January 1988 supplement, respondents were also asked whether they lost or left a job in the past five years and, if so, whether it was because the "plant or company closed down or moved." The group thus identified as displaced workers was then asked additional questions about predisplacement jobs. Thus, the SDW contains information on both the predisplacement and the postdisplacement jobs of about 2,700 persons displaced over the period 1983–88.

These data have two major advantages over other data on job changers. First, as noted by Robert Gibbons and Lawrence Katz (1992), everyone in the sample actually lost a job, so the ratio of false industry (or occupation) transitions to reported transitions should be at a minimum. Second, the job changers in the displaced worker survey did not select themselves into the sample through quits or layoffs, so there is good reason to claim that the process generating the data is exogenous to the individual. That greatly simplifies the task of controlling for sample selection.

The claim that the process generating the data, that is, displacement, is exogenous to the individual is supported by several recent empirical papers[7] and plausible theoretical arguments. With regard to the latter, consider plant shutdowns. When a plant shuts down, a wide spectrum of workers—senior and junior, good and bad, underpaid and overpaid— are released to find their best alternative jobs. In this case, if otherwise identical younger and older workers find very different jobs, then we can be reasonably confident that this difference is not attributable to the characteristics of the workers who were released but rather reveals information on the alternative job opportunities that they confront. Thus, although the displacement process is nonrandom, it is exogenous to the individual. Using an approach similar to one used by James J. Heckman (1979), one can show that when multivariate models of alternative wages (and other job characteristics) are estimated with such data, the coefficients are both unbiased and applicable to all workers.[8]

---

7. Ronald G. Ehrenberg and George H. Jakubson (1988) find no evidence that advanced notice of a plant closing leads the firm's most productive workers to quit before being displaced. Daniel S. Hamermesh (1984) tests the hypothesis that plant closings affect wages and investment in human capital in periods before a closing and found no empirical support for it. Gibbons and Katz (1992) find evidence consistent with the claim that plant closings are exogenous while layoffs are endogenous.

8. Consider the problem of estimating a worker's alternative wage (W_A). In the population,

To assess the plausibility of the theory developed above, we need to identify jobs in industries and occupations characterized by long job durations. One way to proceed is to use the job duration index $I(m,n)$ developed in Hutchens 1986. This index takes the form

$$I(m,n) = \frac{\text{\% of all newly hired workers in industry } m \text{ and occupation } n \text{ that are over age 55}}{\text{\% of all workers in industry } m \text{ and occupation } n \text{ that are over age 55}}$$

Low values of this index should reveal jobs with long durations. When the index takes low values, the denominator is large (since the industry-occupation pair employs older workers) but the numerator is small (since the industry-occupation pair does not hire older workers). Consistent with this, I found (1986) that older workers in industry-occupation cells with low values of $I(m,n)$ have longer job tenures, other things held constant. Workers are usually hired into these jobs when they are young and remain in them through much of their working lives. As documented in Hutchens 1986, these also tend to be high-wage jobs with pensions.

This paper uses the above index as a proxy for the theoretical concept k. Recall that k is the employer's minimum required duration of a job. Note that the index $I(m,n)$ is effectively the inverse of k. Large values of the index should correspond to small values of k, and small values of the index should correspond to large values of k.

$W_A = Z_1'C_1 + Z_2'C_2 + U_A$, and Z_1 is a $(1 \times L)$ vector of demographic variables (e.g., age, education, region of residence, race, and so on); Z_2 is a $(1 \times N)$ vector of dummy variables indicating the industry and occupation of the person's current job; C_1 and C_2 are vectors of parameters, and U_A is an error term that is uncorrelated with Z_1 and Z_2, that has zero expected value, and that has finite variance. Let a sample be selected from this population through the following selection rule: an observation is included in the sample if $S > 0$, where $S = Z_1'D_1 + Z_2'D_2 + U_S$, D_1 and D_2 are parameter vectors, and U_S is an error term. Note that this sample selection rule yields a nonrandom sample. As argued in Heckman 1979, if U_A and U_S are correlated $(Cov(U_A, U_S) \neq 0)$ then application of least squares to this sample will yield biased estimates of C_1 and C_2. For example, estimation of the alternative wage equation in a sample of quitters is likely to yield biased estimates of C_1 and C_2. This is because people who quit are likely to be people with comparatively high alternative wages, implying $Cov(U_A, U_S) \neq 0$. In the case of plant shutdowns, sample selection depends primarily on the industry and occupation of the worker's current job. Neither the individual's alternative wage nor his unobserved productivity characteristics are considered when the plant shutdown sample is "selected." As such, since the models control for industry and occupation (Z_2) as well as observed demographic variables (Z_1), there is good reason to argue that $Cov(U_A, U_S) = 0$, implying unbiased estimates of C_1 and C_2. Moreover, since these are population parameters, they are applicable to *all* workers.

To get as close to a concept of "job" as possible, I compute this index for narrowly defined industry-occupation pairs. The index is computed for 2,205 jobs, defined by thirteen occupation categories and approximately two hundred industry categories (e.g., salesperson in the railroad industry).[9] Since meaningful numbers at that level require a large data set, I pooled the January 1983 and January 1987 Current Population Surveys, both of which contain information on job tenure. The denominator is the proportion of all employed (but not self-employed) individuals in an industry-occupation pair who are older than 55. The numerator is the proportion of all workers with a tenure of less than five years who are over 55. An example of a low value (.18) is a fabricator in machinery manufacturing. An example of a high value (1.16) is a fabricator in miscellaneous repair service.

The index was assigned to records in the CPS Survey of Displaced Workers on the basis of each worker's predisplacement and postdisplacement industry and occupation. If, for example, the predisplacement industry and occupation code on a displaced worker's record indicated she was a machine operator in the auto industry, then the value of the index for machine operators in the auto industry was assigned to that record. Similarly, if the worker's postdisplacement code indicated he was a handler in the restaurant industry, then the value of the index for handlers in the restaurant industry was assigned to the record.

These data can be used to examine whether the above theory yields plausible predictions. Four operational versions of the theoretical hypotheses described earlier are as follows:

> *Operational hypothesis 1:* In a sample of mature displaced workers, the index value of the postdisplacement job will increase with age. Alternatively stated, older workers will tend to find new jobs in industries and occupations characterized by short job durations.

> *Operational hypothesis 2:* In a sample of mature displaced workers, older workers will tend to find postdisplacement jobs that are less desirable (i.e., lower monetary compensation, fewer benefits such as health insurance, and fewer job amenities) than those found by younger workers.

> *Operational hypothesis 3:* Evidence for the first two hypotheses will be particularly strong for workers whose predisplacement jobs

---

9. There were fewer than 200 × 13 pairs because some industry-occupation combinations had no observations.

were characterized by long job durations. That is, compared with the full sample, the absolute value of $d(Index)/d(Age)$ and $d(Compensation)/d(Age)$ will be larger for workers with predisplacement jobs in industries and occupations characterized by long job durations.

Operational hypothesis 4: In a sample of mature displaced workers with predisplacement jobs in industries and occupations characterized by long job durations, older workers will be less likely than younger workers to obtain a postdisplacement job in the same industry and occupation.

The first two operational hypotheses flow directly from the first two theoretical hypotheses. As workers age, they tend to have lower values of k^*. In consequence, they are not offered jobs with long expected job durations. Since these are also the most desirable jobs, younger workers end up with better compensation than older workers. The third operational hypothesis posits that younger workers with low $I(m,n)$ predisplacement jobs will have previously succeeded in signaling a large k^*. They are likely to succeed again. In contrast, their older colleagues will find it impossible to signal a large k^*. Thus, these younger and older workers should find very different postdisplacement jobs. Workers with predisplacement jobs in industries and occupations characterized by long job durations have, on average, higher values of $X'B$. Thus, $dE(k)/d(Age)$ and $dE(w)/d(Age)$ should be more negative in this sample than for the full sample.

The fourth operational hypothesis is related to previous points. Consider a firm in which jobs tend to last a long time. If that firm shuts down, it releases both younger and older workers into the labor market. (The older were hired when they were young and have grown older in the job.) Because the younger workers can still signal a long expected job duration, they should be able to find new jobs in the same industry and occupation. Since the older workers can no longer signal such intent, they must move to industries and occupations that hire workers with shorter expected job durations. Thus, when the predisplacement job is in an industry and occupation characterized by long job durations, displaced older workers should be less likely than displaced younger workers to find a new job in the same industry and occupation.

To examine these hypotheses, I estimated multivariate models of the form $Y = X_1B_1 + X_2B_2 + u$, where Y is the dependent variable, X_1 is

TABLE 5-1.   SUMMARY OF THE SURVEY SAMPLE

Age	
30–34	27.7%
35–39	22.3
40–44	17.4
45–49	13.2
50–54	10.4
55–59	9.0
Education	
Less than 12 years	17.4%
12 years	38.7
13–15 years	23.2
16 or more years	20.7
Region	
Northeast	18.9%
North central	24.6
South	31.3
West	25.4
Married	73.6%
Nonwhite	10.7%
Urban	70.3%
Year displaced	1985.29[a]
Proportion of postdisplacement employed who changed industry or occupation[b]	
Changed:	
3-digit industry	68%
3-digit occupation	67
either 3-digit industry or occupation	79
2-digit industry	57
2-digit occupation	50
either 2-digit industry or occupation	69
Number of observations	2,710

[a]N = 2,689.
[b]N = 2,000.

a vector of dichotomous age indicators, X_2 is a vector of control variables, and u is an error term. Included as dependent variables were both continuous variables (e.g., the postdisplacement wage) and discrete variables (e.g., whether or not the postdisplacement job provides health insurance). Linear regressions were estimated for continuous dependent variables, and logit models were estimated for discrete dependent variables. The X_1 vector indicates age effects. To capture nonlinearities, dichotomous age variables were used. The X_2 vector contains several control variables. Included as controls were variables indicating region, years of education, race, tenure in the predisplacement job, residence in a Standard Metropolitan Statistical Area (SMSA), year of displacement, the index value for the predisplacement job, whether the predisplacement job was part time or full time, and dummy variables indicating predisplacement industry and occupation.

The analysis was restricted to a sample of male displaced workers between the ages of 30 and 59. In each case, displacement was caused by a plant or company closure or move that occurred in the previous five years. The age and gender restrictions were imposed to assure that those in the sample had a strong attachment to the labor market. It was hoped that this would minimize sample selection bias arising from postdisplacement joblessness.

EMPIRICAL EVIDENCE

Tables 5-1 and 5-2 present summary statistics for the data. Note from table 5-2 that at the time of the Current Population Survey (January 1988) almost 20 percent of the displaced workers were unemployed and another 6 percent were out of the labor force. Thus, despite efforts at minimizing sample selection bias due to postdisplacement joblessness, that may be a problem here. Note also the magnitude of industry and occupation change. Of those with jobs in January 1988, fully 69 percent had changed either their two-digit industry or occupation. The industry and occupation data in table 5-2 provide information on the direction of these movements. As might be expected, there is clear evidence of a movement out of manufacturing and into the service sector. The fraction in durable and nondurable manufacturing dropped from a predisplacement 32 percent to a postdisplacement 17 percent; the fraction in services increased from 13 percent to 15 percent. Consistent with this, weekly wages dropped from a predisplacement average of $463 to a postdisplacement $405, and the index increased from a predisplacement value of .4273 to a postdisplacement .4619. Thus, on average, people moved away from long-duration toward short-duration jobs.

Table 5-3 presents descriptive cross-tabulations by age. The major surprise here is the extent to which unemployment and out-of-labor-force status increased with age. As indicated in columns 2 and 3, 22 percent of the men aged 40 to 44 were without a job at the time of the survey, whereas the percentage rose to 36 percent for men aged 55 to

TABLE 5-2. PRE- AND POSTDISPLACEMENT STATISTICS

	Predisplacement	Postdisplacement
Unemployed	0	19.85%
Out of labor force	0	6.35%
Industry		
Agriculture, forestry, and fishing	0.0214	0.0151
Mining	0.0587	0.0162
Construction	0.1808	0.1100
Manufacturing—durable	0.2351	0.1262
Manufacturing—nondurable	0.0837	0.0483
Transportation, communications, and public utilities	0.0804	0.0775
Wholesale and retail trade	0.1653	0.1343
Finance, insurance, and real estate	0.0358	0.0358
Services	0.1257	0.1506
Public administration	0.0137	0.0232
	1.000	.738
Occupation		
Executive and managerial	0.1192	0.0911
Professional specialty	0.0723	0.0679
Technical and related	0.0343	0.0196
Sales	0.0978	0.0937
Administrative support	0.0432	0.0376
Service	0.0469	0.0539
Precision production, craft, and repair	0.2690	0.1760
Operator, fabricator, and laborer	0.2945	0.1830
Farming, forestry, and fishing	0.0229	0.0151
Armed forces	—	—
	1.000	.738
Percent part time	7.7%	7.7%
Weekly wage	$462.76[a]	$404.83[b]
Health insurance	69.1%	61.3%
Tenure	6.12[c]	N.A.
Index	0.4273[d]	0.4619[e]
Index LT[f]	0.301	0.233

[a] N = 2,452.
[b] N = 1,660.
[c] N = 2,669.
[d] N = 2,334.
[e] N = 1,873.
N.A. = not available.

59. Fully 28 percent of the men aged 55 to 59 had not worked since displacement. This is surprising and disturbing. These men had been attached to the labor force and were not yet eligible for social security. Why were so few working?

Such findings raise interesting research questions; however, they also pose significant difficulties for the current analysis. Disentangling the relationship between age and the characteristics of postdisplacement jobs is nearly impossible when so many older workers have no postdis-placement job. To make further headway while minimizing this sample selection problem, I have focused in the subsequent tables on a group of workers with predisplacement characteristics associated with a rela-tively high probability of postdisplacement employment. In particular, the sample is henceforth restricted to married males with high school diplomas who at the time they were surveyed had had at least one year to find a postdisplacement job. Columns 5, 6, and 7 of table 5-3 present data on this subsample.[10]

The multivariate results in table 5-4 provide information on the op-erational hypotheses. Here I report the age coefficients in several logit and linear regression models.[11] These models are estimated based on the sample of married males who completed high school and who were displaced at least one year before the January 1988 survey. The column 1 results come from a logit model of joblessness in which the dependent variable takes the value 1 when an individual is not working at the time of the January 1988 survey and is 0 otherwise. The coefficient on age 35 to 39 is normalized to zero. Thus, a negative (positive) coefficient for some age group indicates that people in that age group have a lower (higher) probability of joblessness than otherwise identical people in the 35 to 39 age group.

Note that the magnitude of the column 1 age coefficients increases with age. Older workers are more likely than younger workers to report no postdisplacement job. Thus, although these workers were displaced at least one year before January 1988, and although the model includes controls for education, race, region, and predisplacement industry and

10. Another way to handle this problem would be through statistical adjustments for sample selection, such as those detailed in Heckman 1979. Such methods require as-sumptions about identification and functional form, and conclusions can be very sensitive to those assumptions. My methods have the advantage of not requiring these identification and functional form assumptions.

11. Estimates of the full models are available from the author.

TABLE 5-3. CROSS-TABULATIONS BY AGE

Age (1)	Full Sample			Subsample		
	Out of Labor Force (2)	Unemployed (3)	No Postdisplacement Job (4)	Out of Labor Force (5)	Unemployed (6)	No Postdisplacement Job (7)
30–34	4.27%	19.73%	16.14%	2.24%	7.35%	3.90%
35–39	4.31	18.08	16.33	2.14	6.41	4.73
40–44	4.67	17.20	15.05	3.52	8.81	4.48
45–49	6.13	21.73	17.85	3.09	8.64	6.33
50–54	11.66	24.73	24.91	11.81	8.66	10.40
55–59	15.16	21.31	28.03	14.66	7.76	17.39
Number of observations =		2,710			1,226	

TABLE 5-4. AGE COEFFICIENTS FROM LINEAR REGRESSIONS AND LOGITS ESTIMATED ON SEVERAL DEPENDENT VARIABLES FOR THE FULL SAMPLE
(t-statistics in parentheses)

Age	(1) JOBLESS (Logit)	(2) INDEX (Regression)	(3) INDEX < .3 (Logit)	(4) LOG(PREDISP WEEKLY WAGE) (Regression)
30–34	.2234 (0.7)	.0519 (1.9)	.3378 (1.5)	−.0903 (2.1)
35–39	0.0	0.0	0.0	0.0
40–44	.5232 (1.6)	−.0144 (0.5)	−.2011 (0.8)	.0481 (1.0)
45–49	.4061 (1.1)	−.0262 (0.3)	−.0271 (0.1)	.0858 (1.6)
50–54	1.3007 (3.7)	−.0811 (2.0)	−.4966 (1.7)	.0035 (0.1)
55–59	1.521 (4.3)	−.0190 (0.5)	−.1400 (0.4)	−.0001 (0.0)
Observations	1,098	886	909	983

Age	(5) LOG(POSTDISP WEEKLY WAGE) (Regression)	(6) PREDISP HEALTH INS (Logit)	(7) POSTDISP HEALTH INS (Logit)	(8) CHANGED EITHER IND OR OCC (Logit)
30–34	−.0122 (0.3)	.0105 (0.0)	−.5133 (2.3)	.4962 (2.1)
35–39	0.0	0.0	0.0	0.0
40–44	.0333 (0.6)	−.0362 (0.1)	−.2323 (0.9)	.1953 (0.8)
45–49	.1749 (2.8)	.6803 (2.1)	.0388 (0.1)	.1445 (0.5)
50–54	−.0329 (0.5)	−.4417 (1.4)	−.1554 (0.5)	.3240 (1.0)
55–59	−.3112 (4.4)	.0984 (0.3)	−.3037 (0.9)	.0511 (0.2)
Observations	821	1,098	959	909

occupation, there is still a strong tendency for joblessness to increase with age. Interestingly, this tendency develops well before the fiftieth birthday.

The second column in table 5-4 presents results from a linear regression model on the postdisplacement index. The sample is restricted to people who were employed at the time of the January 1988 survey. If the first operational hypothesis were correct, the coefficients would become more positive with age. There is no evidence of that.

Column 3 in table 5-4 provides an additional check on the latter result. Here the dependent variable takes the value 1 when a worker has a postdisplacement job in an industry or occupation with an index value less than or equal to .3 and is otherwise 0. Once again, there is no strong evidence indicating that older people have a lower probability of getting jobs with index values less than .3. Thus, the data do not support the first operational hypothesis.

The fourth and fifth columns of table 5-4 pertain to the relationship between age and the logarithm of the predisplacement and postdisplacement weekly wage. Here we find that the predisplacement wage peaks at age 40 to 45 and then gradually declines with age. The postdisplacement wage is similar in that it peaks at age 40 to 45, but after that the drop is much more dramatic. Indeed, according to these results, the postdisplacement weekly wage of 55- to 59-year-old workers is 49 percent below the postdisplacement weekly wage of workers aged 40 to 45. For the predisplacement weekly wage, this difference was only 9 percent. These findings are doubly remarkable because they come from multivariate models that control for education and predisplacement industry and occupation. This strong negative relationship between age and postdisplacement wages implies solid evidence in favor of the second operational hypothesis.[12]

The sixth and seventh columns of table 5-4 present results on health insurance coverage. Interestingly, neither the predisplacement nor the postdisplacement probability of health insurance coverage varies with age. Thus, these columns do not support the second operational hypothesis.

Column 8 in table 5-4 shows the relationship between age and the probability of moving to a new industry-occupation cell. For this pur-

---

12. It would be better to test this hypothesis using hourly wages. Unfortunately, the requisite data are not available.

pose, jobs were classified into approximately two hundred industries and thirteen occupations and the dependent variable was set equal to 1 if the individual moved to a postdisplacement job in either a different industry or a different occupation than the predisplacement job and to 0 otherwise. The coefficients reveal no relationship between this variable and age.

Table 5-5 presents models that are identical to those in table 5-4 except that they are estimated for a sample of workers in jobs whose predisplacement job index was less than .4. This restricts the sample to workers who, before displacement, were in jobs with long expected durations. Results from this sample yield information on the third and fourth operational hypotheses. As indicated in the table, the sample was cut in half when it was restricted in this way.

The results are quite similar to those in table 5-4. Once again, column 1 suggests that joblessness increases with age. Columns 2 and 3 provide no meaningful evidence that within this subsample older people are more likely to end up in short-duration jobs. The results on the wage rate in column 5 are exactly what was expected: as workers age, they tend to move toward low-wage jobs. Columns 4 and 7 indicate that younger and older workers have about the same level of pre- and post-displacement health insurance coverage.

The result in column 8 of table 5-5 is a surprise. According to the fourth operational hypothesis, older displaced workers should have a *higher* probability of changing their industry or occupation, but the evidence points in the opposite direction. As workers age, their probability of changing industry or occupation falls. This suggests that older workers do not face restricted opportunities in their original industry and occupation.

Finally, table 5-6 presents evidence on the hypothesis that the table 5-5 subsample exhibits larger absolute values of $d(Index)/d(Age)$ and $d(Compensation)/d(Age)$ than the table 5-4 full sample. Table 5-6 facilitates comparisons by presenting coefficients from tables 5-4 and 5-5 for the two age groups. The table yields little support for the hypothesis.

In summary, tables 5-4, 5-5, and 5-6 provide limited support for the four hypotheses. There is no support for the hypothesis that older workers tend to obtain jobs in industries and occupations characterized by short job tenures. Either the hypothesis is incorrect or the index used here does not adequately reveal short-term jobs. The tables indicate that older workers tend to find postdisplacement jobs with lower compen-

TABLE 5-5. AGE COEFFICIENTS FROM LINEAR REGRESSIONS AND LOGITS ESTIMATED ON SEVERAL DEPENDENT VARIABLES FOR SUBSAMPLE WITH PREDISPLACEMENT INDEX OF .4 (t-statistics in parentheses)

Age	(1) JOBLESS (Logit)	(2) INDEX (Regression)	(3) INDEX < .3 (Logit)	(4) LOG(PREDISP WEEKLY WAGE) (Regression)
30–34	.7492 (1.4)	−.0714 (1.6)	.5370 (1.5)	−.1018 (1.7)
35–39	0.0	0.0	0.0	0.0
40–44	.4428 (0.7)	−.0085 (0.2)	−.1256 (0.3)	.0213 (0.3)
45–49	.7630 (1.3)	.0191 (0.4)	−.1886 (0.5)	.1828 (2.6)
50–54	.9825 (1.5)	−.0446 (0.7)	.7307 (1.6)	−.0055 (0.1)
55–59	1.829 (3.1)	.0217 (0.4)	.0925 (0.2)	−.0301 (0.4)
Observations	466	377	384	411

Age	(5) LOG(POSTDISP WEEKLY WAGE) (Regression)	(6) PREDISP HEALTH INS (Logit)	(7) POSTDISP HEALTH INS (Logit)	(8) CHANGED EITHER IND OR OCC (Logit)
30–34	.0199 (0.3)	.1528 (0.6)	.1990 (0.5)	.5489 (1.1)
35–39	0.0	0.0	0.0	0.0
40–44	.0916 (1.2)	−.5365 (1.2)	.0778 (0.4)	−.4850 (1.1)
45–49	.1985 (2.2)	.5757 (0.9)	−.0609 (0.1)	−.3901 (0.8)
50–54	−.0138 (0.1)	−.4819 (0.8)	−.2402 (0.5)	−.3196 (0.6)
55–59	−.3664 (3.6)	.6752 (0.9)	−.2667 (0.5)	−.6802 (1.2)
Observations	358	439	407	366

TABLE 5-6. COMPARISON OF SELECTED COEFFICIENTS FROM TABLES
5-4 AND 5-5
(t-statistics in parentheses)

	(1) INDEX (Regression)		(2) INDEX $< .3$ (Logit)	
Age	Full Sample (Table 5-4)	Subsample (Table 5-5)	Full Sample (Table 5-4)	Subsample (Table 5-5)
50–54	−.0811 (2.0)	−.0446 (0.7)	.4966 (1.7)	.7307 (1.6)
55–59	−.0190 (0.5)	.0217 (0.4)	−.1400 (0.4)	.0925 (0.2)

	(3) LOG(POSTDISP WEEKLY WAGE) (Regression)		(4) POSTDISP HEALTH INS (Logit)	
Age	Full Sample (Table 5-4)	Subsample (Table 5-5)	Full Sample (Table 5-4)	Subsample (Table 5-5)
50–54	−.0329 (0.5)	−.0138 (0.1)	−.1554 (0.5)	−.2402 (0.5)
55–59	−.3112 (4.4)	−.3664 (3.6)	−.3037 (0.9)	−.2667 (0.5)

sation. This evidence is, however, restricted to wages; the results on health insurance coverage are inconclusive. Also, compared with the full sample, there is no evidence that $d(Index)/d(Age)$ and $d(Compensation)/d(Age)$ are larger in absolute value for workers with predisplacement jobs in industries and occupations characterized by long job durations. Again, this result could be an artifact of the index. Finally, there is no support for the fourth hypothesis, and in fact the evidence points in the opposite direction. In the sample of mature displaced workers with predisplacement jobs in industries and occupations characterized by long job durations, the older workers were *more* likely than the younger workers to obtain a postdisplacement job in the same industry and occupation.

CONCLUSION

This paper examined whether and why older workers face different job opportunities than otherwise identical younger workers. The data indicate that, compared with otherwise identical younger workers, older workers receive lower wages and experience greater joblessness.

Some of the most intriguing results were obtained for workers who, before displacement, had jobs in industries and occupations characterized by long expected durations. In this case, the older workers were somewhat more likely than their younger counterparts to find postdisplacement jobs in their previous industry and occupation.

It is interesting to speculate about these results. Perhaps older workers do not, in fact, confront more restricted job opportunities in their predisplacement industry and occupation. They have valued skills. They have contacts and information about job opportunities. Perhaps it is only when they move outside this familiar territory that their age affects their opportunities and that only then, other things being equal, younger workers have an advantage. Perhaps the comparatively high joblessness of older workers follows from this. While the younger workers move on to greener pastures, the older workers remain unemployed, waiting for a job in their predisplacement industry and occupation.

Unfortunately, the data do not permit strong conclusions about job opportunities. Although the fact that older workers suffer greater wage declines and joblessness than younger workers is thoroughly consistent with the idea of restricted job opportunities, other evidence is less supportive. Before final conclusions can be drawn, better measures of expected job duration must be developed. The index used here may have substantially more noise than signal. Moreover, it is necessary to provide a more complete treatment of sample selection bias. At this point, I must simply conclude that, while there is good reason to suspect that older workers confront restricted job opportunities, solid evidence is hard to come by.

Chapter 6.
THE JAPANESE APPROACH
TO FINDING JOBS
FOR OLDER WORKERS

Marcus Rebick

J APAN IS CURRENTLY the most rapidly aging country in the Organization for Economic Cooperation and Development. In 1970, less than 5 percent of the population was over age 65. By 1989, that figure had reached 11.6 percent, and Japanese Welfare Ministry projections estimate the proportion will be 23 percent in 2015.[1] If we consider the proportion of the population aged 15 to 64, then in 1970, 11.5 percent were over the age of 55, the traditional age of mandatory retirement. By 1989, the proportion had grown to 16.5 percent, and the forecast is for 19.2 percent of 15- to 64-year-olds to be over 55 by 2015. Ensuring that older workers can find jobs if they need them is becoming an important social issue in Japan. Despite the widespread use of the term "lifetime employment" in the popular press, Japanese firms have traditionally set mandatory retirement ages that are low by American standards. In 1974, the median retirement age among workers in firms was 55. Over the last seventeen years, it has risen to age 60, but 97 percent of all Japanese firms still institute mandatory retirement at age 60 or younger. Despite the young age of mandatory retirement,

I wish to thank Olivia Mitchell, Robert Hutchens, Akira Kage, Minoru Ito, Naoki Mitani, Scott Davis, Richard Hinz, and Yoshio Okunishi for useful discussions and comments. The Japan Institute of Labour provided access to data through their Older Workers' Research Project. Yoshio Okunishi was very helpful in providing the data in readily accessible form for analysis. Financial support from the Cornell East Asia Program and the Japan Institute of Labour is also gratefully acknowledged.

1. The demographic figures come from Association of Employment Development for Senior Citizens 1991:20.

the labor force participation rates (LFPR) of Japanese men and women over the age of 60 are the highest in the OECD.[2]

Several reasons are given for the high participation rates of older Japanese. Among these are the moderately low social security earnings replacement rates (40 percent in 1990), the lag in the response of older Japanese to the recent increase in social security replacement rates (Seike 1985, 1989), stronger bequest motives (Dekle 1990; Otake 1991), greater satisfaction with work (Kawakita 1989), fewer opportunities and greater costs for the enjoyment of leisure (Japan Ministry of Labor 1990), and the importance of the self-employed sector in the Japanese economy (Rebick 1990). Here I am concerned with one other factor that may contribute to the higher participation rates—the availability of better job matches for postcareer workers. Put simply, my thesis is that Japanese workers are able to use more of their human capital after mandatory retirement, either through reemployment with their career job employer or through reemployment elsewhere in the same subcontracting group of firms. Reemployment with the same firm is possible because age discrimination has so far not been challenged by Japanese labor legislation. Employment in other firms within the same subcontracting group is possible because of the prevalence of subcontracting in Japan and because the movement of personnel between firms within the same group is an accepted personnel practice. Although I do not attempt to quantify how much these practices contribute to the higher participation rates for older people in Japan, I do seek to show that these practices overcome one of the worst disadvantages of the institutions of mandatory and/or pension-induced retirement—the loss of human capital for displaced workers who wish to continue working as employees beyond the end of their career jobs.

The high participation rates for workers over age 60 combined with the prevalence of mandatory retirement by age 60 indicates that post-career jobs or bridge jobs must be a significant feature of the Japanese labor market. Postcareer jobs and partial retirement became topics of interest over the last decade in the United States as the Retirement History Survey and other longitudinal studies became available for in-

---

2. In 1989, the rates for men and women older than 65 were 35.8 percent and 15.8 percent, respectively. Robert L. Clark and Richard Anker (1988a) show that when the LFPR of men over the age of 65 is regressed on real gross national product for some 150 countries, Japan is a significant outlier above the downward-sloping regression line, especially in the case of men.

tensive research on the process of retirement. Although it is debatable whether increasing the participation rates of older Americans is desirable from the viewpoint of economic efficiency, it is likely that any such increase will have to come through the development of postcareer job opportunities, rather than through longer tenure in career jobs.[3] The reason is that the prohibition on mandatory retirement in the United States has had little impact on the age of retirement from the labor force. Several research studies have indicated that private pension plan provisions are responsible for much of the timing of retirement behavior and that even when the age of first social security recipiency is raised, the effects on the LFPRs of older workers are likely to be minimal.[4] Therefore, if we are to see an increase in the employment rate of older workers, it will likely be as a result of the increased availability of attractive postcareer job opportunities.

Since Japan seems to have been quite successful so far in providing these opportunities, it may be valuable to see how this has been accomplished. Even if there is no desire to raise American participation rates for older workers, the Japanese experience can help us more fully understand the retirement process in that the labor market for its older workers operates under different economic and institutional constraints.

The next section of this chapter provides details on Japanese labor force participation rates and the timing of retirement in Japan. The role of Japanese public pensions in lowering the labor market retirement age will be briefly discussed. The choice between part-time and full-time work in postcareer jobs will also be discussed with reference to the incentives provided by the Japanese public pension system. Subsequently, I describe the employment and occupational patterns for those Japanese who engage in postcareer jobs, focusing on the relation between career and postcareer occupations. I then look at the ways in which postcareer employees find new jobs, in particular the important role of the career employer in providing new opportunities. I turn then to an examination of the wages of employees after mandatory retirement, with

3. Not all Japanese share the opinion that job creation for older Japanese is a major priority. The position of the main labor union federation, Rengo, is that earlier labor force retirement with better pension coverage ought to be a priority. In its view, the negative view of retirement held by older Japanese reflects the high cost of enjoyment of leisure in Japan, both because of the low investment in the physical capital used for leisure service industries and the low investment by individuals in the skills needed to enjoy leisure activities.
4. For a survey of this literature, see Quinn, Burkhauser, and Myers 1990:108–11.

TABLE 6-1. LABOR FORCE PARTICIPATION RATES OF OLDER WORKERS
IN JAPAN AND THE UNITED STATES, 1989

Age Group	Men		Women	
	Japan	U.S.	Japan	U.S.
55–59	91.6%	78.8%	52.2%	54.5%
60–64	71.4	54.2	39.2	35.3
65 +	35.8	16.0	15.8	7.8

Source: OECD labor force statistics.

emphasis on the consequences of changing employers and changing
occupations. Finally, I attempt to interpret why direct participation of
the career job employer in finding postcareer job employment is such
an important phenomenon in Japan.

THE "NET RETIREMENT" PROFILE IN CROSS-SECTION

Table 6-1 compares the labor force participation rates for men and
women over the age of 55 in both Japan and the United States. The
rates for men are clearly much higher in Japan, and the gap between
the countries widens with age. The differences are less notable for
women, except for the oldest subgroup, those over the age of 65. Since
fewer than one-third of these women are actually employees (see table
6-2), it is likely that the high overall rate of self-employment and family
enterprise in Japan is responsible for much of the U.S.-Japan difference.[5]
For men, however, the difference is less likely to be explained by the
importance of the self-employed and family sector. Table 6-2 indicates
that 22 percent of the men over the age of 65 are either employees or
directors of companies. Even without the self-employed, Japanese men
would have a higher labor force participation rate in this age group.

To gain a better understanding of the major influences on retirement
in Japan, it is useful to look at the net rate of retirement from the labor
force for individual age groups in Japan. In the U.S. case, the well-
known declines in labor force participation rates at ages 62 and 65
immediately suggest that the eligibility for reduced social security benefits
at age 62 and for full benefits at age 65 plays an important role in the
decision to retire. Figure 6-1 plots the slope of the age-participation

5. In the United States, 9 percent of the labor force were self-employed and family
workers in 1985. In Japan, the proportion was 26 percent. (Japan Ministry of Labor
1988b:213)

TABLE 6-2.   EMPLOYMENT STATUS OF OLDER JAPANESE BY AGE GROUP
AND SEX, 1988

	Men			Women		
	55–59	60–64	65–69	55–59	60–64	65–69
Employees and directors	62	37	22	25	13	8
Directors	11	9	7	2	2	2
Employees	51	28	15	23	11	6
% part-time employees	5	9	9	13	12	12
% managerial employees	16	17	14	2	0.5	0.4
% white-collar employees[a]	48	42	43	59	50	52
% blue-collar employees[b]	52	58	58	41	50	48
Self-employed and family workers	25	27	28	21	20	16
Family workers	1	3	4	12	11	8
Other	2	4	4	6	6	4
Not working	12	32	46	48	60	71
Want to work	7	17	18	20	19	16
Do not want to work	5	15	28	28	41	55
Employees Who Left Career Jobs at Age 55[c]						
Employees and directors	58	35	20	21	15	10
Directors	6	5	4	1	1	1
Employees	51	30	17	21	15	9
% part-time employees	13	26	34	38	49	52
% managerial employees	5	5	8	2	1	1
% white-collar employees[a]	48	51	46	54	62	58
% blue-collar employees[b]	52	49	54	46	38	42
Self-employed and family workers	8	11	15	7	8	5
Family workers	1	2	3	5	5	3
Other	3	5	5	8	7	4
Not working	31	48	59	64	70	81
Want to work	22	28	25	36	32	27
Do not want to work	9	20	34	28	38	54

Source: Older Persons Survey 1988.

[a] White-collar occupations include specialists, managers, office work, trade, real estate, and the service sector.

[b] Blue-collar occupations include security, agricultural work, transport, communications, production work, including skilled trades, construction, and manual work.

[c] Career job is defined as the job from which one exits as a result of mandatory retirement or a job with mandatory retirement that one leaves for a job without mandatory retirement.

profile for Japanese men in 1970 and 1985, both census years for which age-specific data are available. Defining retirement as the move to non-participation status, this profile could be called the "net retirement profile" since it shows the net drop in labor force participation as age increases. As the figure indicates, there is at most a 5 percent net

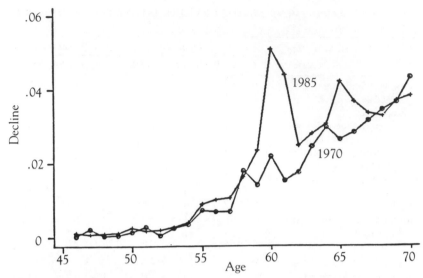

Source: Japanese census.

FIGURE 6-1. LABOR FORCE PARTICIPATION RATE OF JAPANESE MEN, 1970 VERSUS 1985

retirement of the male labor force at any given age. This is a small number by U.S. standards, where drops of eighteen and ten points in men's LFPRs occur at ages 62 and 65, respectively (see chap. 9).

The most striking features of figure 6-1 are the large spikes in the profile at age 60-61 and age 65-66 that emerged by 1985. Both spikes coincide with the earliest ages when public pension benefits are made available to men under Japanese pension law.[6] Private sector male employees are eligible for benefits under the employee pension system at age 60.[7] The self-employed and others not covered by the employee pension system or the various public employee pension plans are eligible for benefits under the national pension system at age 65.[8] In addition,

6. The following discussion relates to the public pension systems as they existed until 1985, when major reforms were undertaken. Although the reforms substantially reorganized the pension system, the actual benefits received by different groups of beneficiaries under the new system are still similar to those under the old system.

7. For women, the eligibility age was set at 55 until 1987, but since then the age is gradually being raised to 60, a process that will be complete in the year 2000.

8. Employees of firms with fewer than five employees are not under mandatory coverage by the employee pension system. Spouses of employees are eligible for survivors' benefits

public sector employees have their own pension plans with eligibility set at 56, but since the public sector sets mandatory retirement at age 60, we would not expect a major spike at age 56. The absence of the spikes in the net retirement profile for 1970 is explained by the relatively low level of benefits provided at that time. Average annual benefits under the employee pension system replaced only 19 percent of average annual compensation for private sector employees in that year.[9] By 1985, however, the replacement rate had increased to 38 percent, mainly through reforms made in the early 1970s.

The spike at age 60 also corresponds with the modal age of mandatory retirement in 1985. Although the timing of mandatory retirement undoubtedly exerts some influence, especially for public sector employees, the absence of any major spike at age 55 in 1970, when the majority of private sector employees faced mandatory retirement at age 55, indicates that mandatory retirement in itself is unlikely to be responsible for withdrawal from the labor force. Rather, it appears that the doubling in the public pension earnings replacement rate over the 1970s is most likely responsible for the emergence of the spikes (Rebick 1990; Seike

Alan L. Gustman and Thomas L. Steinmeier (1985a) and Christopher J. Ruhm (1990) have emphasized the importance of partial retirement in the overall transition to fully retired status in the United States. Table 6-2 includes figures for part-time employment for different age groups of older workers. It is evident that the percentage of employees engaged in part-time work increases from ages 55-59 to ages 60-64. Although preferences for leisure, declining wages after mandatory retirement, and declining health play a role in encouraging part-time work, there are also features of the Japanese pension system that affect the decision to work part time. I briefly look at these in the remainder of this section.

Japanese employee pensions have an earnings test for employees between the ages of 60 and 64 that reduces the maximum pension payment by fixed percentages as monthly *wage* income rises above certain levels (see table 6-3). This schedule generates discontinuities in total income

---

under the employee pension system but may also be covered separately under the national pension system.

9. Average compensation is taken from the Monthly Labor Survey (Japan Ministry of Labor, various years) and average pension benefits from the *Yearbook of Social Insurance* (Japan Ministry of Welfare, various years).

TABLE 6-3.   REDUCTIONS OF MAXIMUM PENSION PAYMENTS IN
JAPAN, 1988

Monthly Wage (Yen)	60–64	65 +
Less than 95,000	20%	0%
95,000–155,000	50	0
155,000–210,000	80	0
Over 210,000	100	20

Source: Japan Ministry of Welfare, annual operations report, 1988.

as wage income increases. This, in turn, encourages employees to choose jobs that hold wage earnings below the lowest earnings test point (95,000 yen in 1988). Since bonus payments are not considered income from the point of view of the social security system, employers can devise compensation packages whereby semi-annual bonuses make up abnormally large proportions of annual compensation. A survey by Nikkeiren (1990) reports the case of Tokyo Gas, where bonuses amount to as much as 50 percent of total compensation for workers over the age of 60, well above the 25 to 30 percent levels found on average in large firms for workers below the age of mandatory retirement. The same survey reports cases of other companies where monthly earnings are deliberately set below the first or second earnings test point and bonuses are used to raise total compensation to competitive levels. Even if monthly wage compensation is held below the minimum earnings test point, however, social security payments are still reduced by 20 percent. This is where part-time status can become significant.

According to Japanese pension law, only full-time workers are considered part of the mandatory coverage sector. For this purpose, full time is defined as working more than three-fifths of the average number of hours worked by regular employees of the firm. Consequently, any employees who work less than three-fifths of the regular hours are not required to pay social security premiums and are also eligible to receive their entire pension if they are over 60. As a result, some employees may choose to work part time if full-time earnings do not adequately compensate for the loss in leisure time *and* the 20 percent reduction in pension benefits. Of course, the worker also loses any increase in future pension levels that may result from contributions after age 60. The formula for the employee pension payments multiplies average earnings over the contribution period by the length of the contribution period.[10] The formula sets a ceiling of thirty-five years on the contribution period, however, and it is likely that many employees will not be concerned with future pension losses should they choose the part-time option. According to figures in the 1987 annual operations report of the Social Insurance Bureau, 29 percent of the men aged 60 or younger, who began receiving pensions after March 1986, had already accumulated thirty-five or more years of contributions to the pension system (Japan Ministry of Welfare 1987).[11] These workers in particular are likely to prefer part-time work, other things being equal.

Private pensions are an important feature of employee contracts, especially in large companies. Typically, the employee receives a present value of forty months of his final monthly basic wage, not including overtime or bonus payments (Association of Employment Development for Senior Citizens 1991:122-23). Depending on the company, this may be taken either as an annuity or as a lump sum, but favorable tax treatment and outstanding debts have continued to make the lump-sum option popular. Since the private pension reflects a one-time anticipated addition to wealth, private pensions are unlikely to have much of an effect on the age of retirement from the labor force. Recently, many Japanese companies have introduced early-retirement pension provisions similar to those of American pension plans. Since workers are generally eligible for public pensions after the early retirement age, most of these plans have had a negligible effect on retirement from the labor force.

In conclusion, despite the increased rate of net retirement brought on by improved pension benefits and the prevalence of mandatory retirement at age 60, labor force participation remains high for Japanese

10. For example, in 1986, the formula for the annual basic pension of a male age 60 was (in yen):(contribution period) × (2,492 + average monthly wage × .01) × inflation adjustment. The contribution period was measured in months up to a maximum of 420. The average monthly wage was adjusted to bring past earnings levels in line with inflation and economic growth. In addition, there was a supplementary pension for spouses and dependent children that would amount to 186,000 yen/year per dependent (Japan Ministry of Welfare 1987:44).

11. My computation is based on the following figures: a total of 354,000 men were receiving the employee pension under the new pension law introduced in 1986 (Japan Ministry of Welfare 1986). To be considered under the new law, one had to have been born after April 1, 1926, and to have started receiving benefits after March 1986. Of the 354,000 men that fell into this category, 102,000, or 29 percent, had thirty-five or more years of coverage in the system.

in their 60s. In the next section, I look at the employment status and job characteristics of older Japanese workers.

EMPLOYMENT AND OCCUPATIONS OF OLDER JAPANESE

Table 6-2 gives the current employment status of older Japanese by age group and sex. This information comes from the 1988 Survey of Employment Conditions for Older Persons (hereafter Older Persons Survey), a survey of 26,000 individuals aged 55 through 69.[12] This survey does not use the strict definition of labor force participation used by the Japanese Census, a definition comparable to the one used in the U.S. Current Population Survey. Instead, the nonemployed (those who did not work for pay in May 1988) are divided into those who self-report a desire to work and those who do not. If we include those who want to work in the labor force, then both the participation rate and the unemployment rate are higher than that reported by the Census. Here, however, I am mainly interested in those who are working.

Looking at the top panel of table 6-3, both men and women have a high proportion of self-employed and family workers (hereafter SEF workers) in these older age groups. The true labor force status of some of these workers is questionable, given that some people may report themselves as self-employed for reasons of pride or because their businesses are used as tax shelters. The second panel provides the same breakdowns for the subsample of those individuals who report that they were employees at age 55 and that they no longer work at their "career jobs."

For the remainder of this chapter, I define *career job* as it is defined implicitly in the Older Persons Survey as either a job from which an individual exits via mandatory retirement after age 54 or as a job with mandatory retirement that an individual left before mandatory retirement. Mandatory retirement does not necessarily entail separation from the firm in which the individual held the career job. In other words, recontracting with the employer is possible after mandatory retirement. In the subsample of postcareer job individuals summarized in table 6-3, the proportion of SEF workers is also high, reaching 15 percent of the population for 65- to 69-year-old men and almost 10 percent for 55- to

12. The survey was previously conducted in 1980 and 1983, but each sample is independent.

59-year-old women. Self-employment is clearly an important form of postcareer employment.

The same survey tells us that in 1988, 61 percent of those 65- to 69-year-old men who had been employees at age 55 had experienced mandatory retirement from their career jobs (although not necessarily from their firm). The corresponding figure for women is 34 percent. Even before mandatory retirement became illegal in the United States in the 1980s, the proportion of American employees who left their career employment via mandatory retirement was never that high (Quinn, Burkhauser, and Myers 1990; Fields and Mitchell 1984). Since this group of workers has experienced an involuntary end to their career jobs, they are particularly interesting to policy makers concerned about promoting employment opportunities for older workers in Japan.

Table 6-3 also provides information on the occupations of the subgroup of employees. The proportion of blue-collar workers increases with age. Studies such as that by Akira Motokawa and Ryuji Mori (1981) indicate that blue-collar workers retire earlier from the labor force, after controlling for health status and pension benefits, so that this increase in the proportion of blue-collar workers is most likely due to their having lower pension benefits.

Table 6-4 gives transition matrices for different occupational categories within the employee-director subsample both before and after mandatory retirement.[13] Since the sample of women who remain employees or directors after mandatory retirement is small (only 236 observations), much of the remainder of this essay will focus on men. I look at transition matrices for the two most common ages of mandatory retirement, 55 and 60, separately, since the proportion of employees in blue-collar occupations falls with age.

Based on table 6-4, older Japanese workers overwhelmingly remain in their occupational group after experiencing mandatory retirement from a career job. In fact, if we look at the thirty-one detailed occupational groups defined by the survey, only 38 percent of postcareer workers who remain employees experience occupational changes, if we

13. The Older Persons Survey provides information only on occupational status at age 55 and at the time of the survey. Consequently, to avoid the possibility of occupational transitions that occur long after mandatory retirement, I consider only those individuals who experienced mandatory retirement in the two-year period immediately preceding the survey.

TABLE 6-4. TRANSITION MATRICES FOR EMPLOYEE-DIRECTOR SUBSAMPLE

Mandatory Retirement at Age 55

	Status in May 1988	
	White Collar	Blue Collar
Status at Age 55 — White Collar	.95	.05
Status at Age 55 — Blue Collar	.02	.98

Mandatory Retirement at Age 55

	Status in May 1988	
	Manager	Nonmanager
Status at Age 55 — Manager	.90	.10
Status at Age 55 — Nonmanager	.03	.97

Mandatory Retirement at Age 60

	Status in May 1988	
	White Collar	Blue Collar
Status at Age 60 — White Collar	.88	.12
Status at Age 60 — Blue Collar	.09	.91

Mandatory Retirement at Age 60

	Status in May 1988	
	Manager	Nonmanager
Status at Age 60 — Manager	.71	.29
Status at Age 60 — Nonmanager	.05	.95

Source: Older Persons Survey (author's tabulations).

Age 55 refers to the occupational group at age 55. May 1988 refers to the occupational group at the time of the survey. Only employees or company directors who left their career jobs between 1987 and 1988 are included in the sample. It is assumed that the occupation at the end of the career job was the same as at age 55, so that these transition matrices reflect the career job to postcareer job transition.

exclude from the sample those who were managers at 55 and those who were managers after mandatory retirement.[14] Although most workers tend to remain in their macro-occupational group, some 12 percent of employees who were white-collar workers at age 55 had become blue-collar workers after mandatory retirement at age 60. The corresponding percentage for blue-collar workers moving to white-collar status is 9 percent.

If we include managers in our consideration of occupational change, some 10 percent of Japanese managers at age 55 became nonmanagers after mandatory retirement at age 55. After mandatory retirement at age 60, 30 percent lost their managerial status. Less than 5 percent of those who were not managers by age 55 found managerial jobs after exiting from their career jobs. It is not clear that movement from managerial to nonmanagerial status entails a real change in occupation, but from the employee's viewpoint, the loss of a managerial role may involve some loss in the quality of the job match.

HOW DO POSTCAREER EMPLOYEES FIND JOBS?

I now turn to the question of how postcareer employees in Japan find their jobs. The role of the career job employer in assisting workers with job placement is an important feature of the labor market for older workers in Japan.

The Older Persons Survey indicates that in 1987-88, 56 percent of men and 71 percent of women who remained employees after mandatory retirement at age 55 were reemployed by their career job employers. For men and women who reached mandatory retirement at age 60, the percentages were 37 percent and 60 percent, respectively. Mandatory retirement represents a point at which the long-term labor contract of the career job is terminated and the worker now recontracts for shorter periods of time, often with the old employer. In the Japanese case, legal concerns about age discrimination do not prevent employers from deliberately lowering the wages of older workers, as they would in the United States. This ability to recontract with older employees at lower compensation is likely to lead to more efficient use of older labor, since workers need not switch employers to find work at a lower wage, some-

---

14. Managers are excluded since their occupational skills, except for management, are not reported.

thing that they seem constrained to do under current interpretation of American labor law.

In addition to reemploying workers at mandatory retirement, some employers arrange to have employees transferred directly to other firms before their mandatory retirement (*shukko*). At first, the employees may retain membership (*seki*) at the sending firm where they had their career jobs, but at the age of mandatory retirement, or just before it, the majority of these employees are formally transferred to the receiving firm. A 1987 survey of 2,700 men who had reached the age of mandatory retirement in their career firms between 1982 and 1986 indicates that 8.0 percent had been directly transferred to other firms before mandatory retirement (Association of Employment Development for Senior Citizens 1988:86).[15]

Besides the direct-transfer system, there are more informal ways in which employees are introduced to postcareer job employment in other firms. According to the same survey of workers who reached mandatory retirement age in 1982, roughly one-half of the men who found work at new companies after leaving their career jobs, did so with companies in the same corporate group or with suppliers or customers of their old firm. This corresponds fairly well with the 50 percent of men who claim to have found postcareer work in different companies either with the help of their old employers or by invitation from a new firm. (This includes the 8 percent who were directly transferred.) Consequently, through a variety of formal transfers, reemployment by their old employer, and informal introductions to new employers, up to three-quarters of those employees who continue as employees after termination of their bridge jobs are assisted in finding employment by their old employer or by their old employer's business associates.

Since these jobs are either in the same corporate groups or supplier networks as their old jobs, much of the specific and general human capital invested in the employee may be matched well with the new job. A 1984 survey of 11,500 male workers who had reached mandatory retirement reports that two-thirds of reemployed workers reported that

---

15. I considered only employees with ten or more years of tenure at their original firms to be in career jobs. That left a sample of 2,447 employees in career jobs, of which 196 were permanently transferred out of their firms before mandatory retirement. Unlike the Older Persons Survey, this survey was a mail-response survey with a response rate of 44 percent. The sample characteristics and responses to questions similar to those on the Older Persons Survey give no indication that the sample was biased.

their job content remained unchanged after mandatory retirement (Older Persons Employment Development Association 1985). For the group who moved to subsidiaries or related firms, about one in three reported that their job content was unchanged, while the proportion dropped to about one in ten for all others who changed companies. Similarly, the 1988 Older Persons Survey shows that the probability of remaining in the same occupation is 90 percent if one is reemployed in the same company but only 63 percent if one switches companies.[16] Reemployment either within the company or within the same corporate group leads to better job matches. If this is the case, the Japanese system may offer some efficient methods of managing the postcareer job employment transition.

COMPENSATION AFTER MANDATORY RETIREMENT

Longitudinal data for older workers do not exist in Japan, and the best data source reporting the effect of mandatory retirement on wages are the reports of the Older Persons Employment Development Association (1980, 1985). These surveys ask individuals who remained in employee status after mandatory retirement what their wage changes were in percentage terms (monthly base wage only). Both of these reports indicate that employees who remain with their former employers after mandatory retirement experience a median wage drop of 20 to 25 percent. Those who are directly transferred to new jobs with the help of their old employers experience median wage declines in the range of 36 to 38 percent, while those who find jobs themselves experience median drops of 40 to 45 percent. Figure 6-2 presents a stylized view of this wage profile, illustrating the wage changes as determined by employment patterns. In table 6-5, I use the Older Persons Survey to investigate the effects of switching employers, after controlling for the age of mandatory retirement, occupation, and whether or not there has been a change in occupation.

Table 6-5 reports the results of several regressions of the log of monthly income on current occupation, age, and a dummy variable for whether or not the occupation is the same as at age 55 for full-time male workers

16. Removing those who had managerial occupations at age 55 or at the time of the survey does not substantially alter these figures. The percentages of men remaining in the same occupation are presumably higher than the percentages who report identical job content since job content may vary within occupational groups.

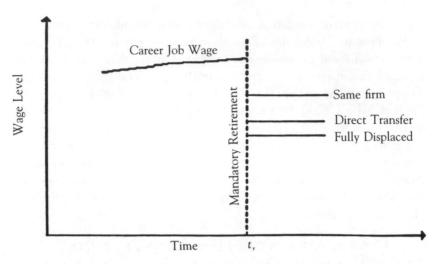

FIGURE 6-2.   WAGE PROFILES AROUND CAREER JOB SEPARATION

who exited from their career jobs by 1988. The results from model 1 indicate that changing occupations has a downward impact on wage levels of 16 percent (0.15 log points). Thus, any factors that help older Japanese workers to remain in the same occupational group are likely to raise earnings and to encourage participation after exit from the career job.

Models 2 through 5 include a dummy variable for whether or not the employee is currently working for an employer other than his career job employer. In all models this variable is significant and sizable, indicating that, other things being equal, changing employers is correlated with 15 percent lower wages. The interpretation of this variable is problematic, since employers may retain their best employees. If this is the case, a selection process is chiefly responsible for the lower wages of those who change employers, rather than the quality of the job match. More support for the notion that this coefficient reflects better use of specific human capital comes from model 3, in which a variable reflecting the number of years since separation from the career firm is included. The positive and significant coefficient on this variable seems to indicate that some of the 21 percent (.19 log point) loss in earnings from changing employers may be recovered over time, at a rate of more than 1 percent per year. If the coefficient on employer change reflected only ability

TABLE 6-5.   LOG EARNINGS OF JAPANESE MEN IN POSTCAREER JOBS, 1988

Variable	(1)	(2)	(3)	(4)	(5)
Occupation change dummy	−.15	−.12	−.11	−.11	−.11
	(0.03)	(.03)	(.03)	(.03)	(.03)
Employer change dummy	—	−.14	−.19	−.15	−.19
		(.03)	(.04)	(.03)	(.04)
Years since employer change	—	—	.013	—	.016
			(.006)		(.009)
Years since career job exit	—	—	—	.0095	−.003
				(.0061)	(.0096)
Age	−.024	−.023	−.030	−.029	−.029
	(.004)	(.004)	(.005)	(.006)	(.006)
Health-status dummy	.100	.097	.098	.097	.098
	(.04)	(.04)	(.04)	(.04)	(.04)
Number of observations	1303	1303	1303	1303	1303
R^2	.30	.31	.31	.31	.31

Source: Older Persons Survey 1988.

The dependent variable is log earnings for May 1988. The sample includes all full-time male employees or directors of companies who have either experienced mandatory retirement or who left their career company before the mandatory retirement age. Sample size is restricted to observations without missing data for all variables in the data, whether or not the variable is used in particular models. All regressions include occupation dummies for thirty different occupational groups as controls. Observations are weighted according to the sample weights provided for each observation by the survey. Occupational dummy results are available from the author.

(1) The occupation change dummy is equal to 1 if the occupation at the survey date is different from the occupation when the individual was 55 years old.

(2) The employer change dummy is equal to 1 if the employer today is different from the employer in the career job.

(3) Years since employer change is the number of years since the individual left their career-job employer. This is set equal to zero if the individual is still with their career-job employer.

(4) Years since career job exit is the number of years since the individual left his career job, either through mandatory retirement or by leaving the firm if there was no mandatory retirement from the career job.

(5) The health status dummy is set equal to 1 if the individual reports himself to be healthy and to 0 if self-reported health status is "not very healthy" or "sick."

differences, we would not expect any significance for this variable, since age is already controlled for in the regression. Consequently, I conclude that at least some of the wage loss that is correlated with changing employers reflects a loss in the quality of the job match and/or in specific human capital. Model 5 provides an even stricter test of this conclusion

TABLE 6-6. RELATIVE SIZE OF CAREER AND POSTRETIREMENT FIRMS
EMPLOYING MALES IN JAPAN, 1988

	Size of Postretirement Firm		
Size of Career Firm	Smaller	Same	Larger
≥ 1,000	82%	18%	—
300–999	81	17	2%
100–299	68	27	5
30–99	54	36	10
5–29	10	73	17

Source: Older Persons Survey 1988.

by including a variable for the number of years since exit from the career job. The effect of adding this variable is to lower the size and significance of the coefficient for years since changing employers. The result is that model 5 provides weaker confirmation of the hypothesis but is still basically supportive of it.[17]

A second result of models 2 through 5 is that the addition of the employer change variable reduces by 3 or 4 percent the size of the effect of changing occupations from the 16 percent drop of model 1. The correlation of employer changes and occupational changes indicates that the occupational change variable was picking up some of the effect of switching employers in model 1.[18]

One final point should be made about changing employers after exiting from the career job—the move is almost always to a smaller firm. As indicated in table 6-6, for those men who leave firms with one-thousand

17. An examination of the residuals from the regressions does not indicate any decline in the variance of the residuals since the end of one's career job. This suggests that the increase in wages among those who change employers is not due to a selector process whereby those who earn less are more likely to retire earlier.

18. One potential problem with the results is that the compensation measure in the Older Persons Survey includes only monthly cash compensation in May 1988 and not bonuses and fringe benefits. The absence of a measure for bonuses is problematic given that many firms pay substantial bonuses to postcareer job employees in order to keep monthly wages below the employee pension earnings test points. I see no theoretical reason, however, to suspect that employees who change employers are more likely to have larger bonuses. Similarly, since health insurance coverage is provided for all employees in Japan and for everyone over the age of 65, the differences in pay should not be compensation for any difference in health coverage. Finally, company pensions are generally dispensed at mandatory retirement, and postretirement employment will generally not include pension benefits. I therefore conclude that the monthly wage compensation differences that I am measuring are representative of differences in total compensation.

or more employees, fewer than one in five find jobs in other large firms. For the groups that leave middle-sized firms (100 to 299 and 300 to 999 employees), 20 to 25 percent find work in similar-sized firms, but less than 5 percent find work in larger firms. For those who leave smaller firms (30 to 99 employees), 36 percent find work in similar-sized firms, but only 10 percent move to larger firms, leaving more than half that to move to smaller firms. This move down the firm-size scale is an important aspect of the postcareer job employment pattern that is closely connected to the vertical organization of Japanese industry. The next section examines why the phenomenon of employer-assisted job moves is so important for older workers in Japan, considering this organizational pattern.

Industrial Organization and Retirement Patterns

An important feature of Japanese industrial organization is the extensive use of subcontracting through networks of firms known as vertical *keiretsu* (Caves and Uekusa 1976).[19] An interesting feature of the vertical *keiretsu* is the loan or transfer of labor between firms within the subcontracting group. According to the Survey of Employment Management in 1986, 500,000 employees were on temporary transfer or *shukko* from one firm to another. This represented about 1 percent of all the employees in all the firms surveyed. An additional 26,000 were permanently transferred to other firms. In both cases roughly two-thirds of those transferred went to firms within the same *keiretsu*. Although some of these were older workers who were pushed out from their career firms, others were used to disseminate technology, to improve communications between cooperating firms, and to exercise control over other firms.

A question that naturally arises is whether it is useful to view these vertical corporate groupings as equivalent to one large American firm rather than as many independent firms. In that case, many of the postmandatory retirement workers who were employed by other firms in the same vertical *keiretsu* would be considered essentially reemployed by the same industrial enterprise. There are several problems with this view. The first is that many subcontractors have more than one downstream

19. The term *keiretsu* is also used to refer to "horizontal" groups of large firms with historical links, or with common financial or banking relationships. I will use the term *vertical keiretsu* to refer to the vertically disintegrated networks of subcontracting firms and their customers.

customer. A second problem is that enterprise unionism divides the workforce of the Japanese vertical *keiretsu* in a way that would not occur in the integrated American firm. Some theories of Japanese subcontracting go so far as to suggest that labor market segmentation under enterprise unionism is the primary reason for the prevalence of subcontracting groups in Japan.

Michael Smitka (1991), for example, suggests that cultural preferences may make egalitarian pay structures more desirable in Japan than in the United States. The continuing demands for pay by seniority from Japanese unions throughout the twentieth century can be seen as one manifestation of this tendency.[20] If firms face constraints on the variance in compensation (controlling for worker attributes such as sex, age, seniority, and education), then economic pressures may necessitate the division of workers into separate firms according to the differing marginal products of their labor. In this case, the division of the company into several different units with different compensation schemes becomes attractive. Enterprise unionism naturally supports such a segmentation of the workforce through subcontracting. Consequently, the segmentation of the labor force in the vertical *keiretsu*, as well as the fact that many of the subcontractors have more than one downstream customer, indicates that the giant firm analogy for the *keiretsu* is not entirely accurate.

In this setting, the transfer of workers to subcontracting firms after mandatory retirement becomes desirable for several reasons. First, the employee can be used as an instrument of managerial control in the new firm. Second, if workers are divided among firms according to their productivity, and less productive workers are in smaller firms, it may be optimal to move the less productive, older employees to smaller firms within the same corporate group. The smaller firms pay less, while at the same time some of the specific human capital accumulated in the larger firm will still be useful within the corporate group. Third, the range of positions in different firms may serve as rewards to employees for their diligence during the tenure of their career job.[21]

---

20. Andrew Gordon (1985) devotes large sections of his historical account of Japanese labor relations to demands from the labor movement for pay according to seniority and to the degree to which management has met these demands.

21. The last explanation invites the objection that it might be just as easy to pay rewards directly in cash rather than so indirectly. Egalitarianism, however, is just as likely to prevent this as it is to block the extensive use of merit pay in regular compen-

Job transfers for the purposes of managerial control or as a reward mechanism are less likely to be important when employees move to trading partners that are not subcontractors. In this case, the move may be desirable simply because it improves communications and trust between the firms concerned. In some cases, the postcareer firm may be rewarding the employee for favors received in the past. An example of this kind of behavior in a related context is the placement of ex-government bureaucrats in high-paying managerial or advisory positions in private firms following retirement from their ministries. This movement, known as *amakudari*, literally the descent from heaven, is important both for maintaining government-business communication and for rewarding government ministries that have been helpful in the past to the firms in question.

CONCLUSIONS

This chapter has surveyed some of the main features of the employment patterns of older workers in Japan, focusing on the role of the career job employer in finding postcareer jobs for workers at the age of mandatory retirement. The advantages of retaining post-mandatory retirement workers in terms of preserving job matches have been documented, as well as the positive effect on postcareer job wages of maintaining the same occupation. After mandatory retirement, older employees' wages decline by 20 to 25 percent if they remain with the same employer. Those who transfer to new jobs with the help of their former employers experience median wage decreases of 36 to 38 percent, while those who find jobs themselves experience declines of 40 to 45 percent. Much of the decline is attributable to changes in occupation: remaining within the same occupational group is associated with a 10

---

sation. Enterprise unions do bargain with employers over the terms of company pensions and/or lump-sum retirement payments. In almost all cases, the agreements set these payments according to fixed schedules that allow little discretion on the part of management. Postcareer jobs, however, have one characteristic that makes it more difficult for the union (or other forms of worker representation) to push for stricter equality: they are indivisible. As indivisibles, it becomes virtually impossible to bargain over the sharing of these opportunities. Furthermore, different postcareer jobs have specific attributes that may make them differ in value according to individual tastes. For these reasons, firms that are constrained from paying either immediate or delayed compensation for productivity may choose this form of indivisible reward to reward effort on the part of employees. We should not overlook the possibility that introductions to these jobs are useful as an important motivating device, especially during the final years of the career job.

percent smaller reduction in wages, other things being equal. Remaining with the same employer can account for an additional 15 percent moderation in the decline, although this may be because the employer selects more able workers.

The Japanese experience suggests that the difficulty American employers have in lowering the compensation of older workers may have adverse effects on U.S. productivity. It is possible that if American labor law and institutional norms could be altered to make it easier for firms to recontract with older employees at lower wage rates, then better job matches for older employees might be found and a more efficient outcome could be attained.

Chapter 7.
HEALTH INSURANCE CHOICE
AND THE OLDER WORKER

Melissa W. Barringer and Olivia S. Mitchell

ONE WAY IN WHICH firms have adjusted to having more diverse workforces and to increasing health-care costs is by providing workers with a measure of choice over key features of their health insurance plans. In this chapter we examine differences in health plan selection behavior between older and younger workers in flexible benefits plans and the implications of these findings for health-care costs and utilization patterns.

Employers who offer flexible benefits plans generally contribute a defined amount of funds toward the purchase of employees' benefits. Workers are then allowed to select, from among options with various cost and coverage characteristics, the benefit package that best meets their needs. Typically, many health-care options are available (see Meisenheimer and Wiatrowski 1989 and Hewitt Associates 1989). For example, many firms permit employees to choose between a fee-for-service plan (FFS), such as Blue Cross/Blue Shield, and a prepaid health plan, such as a health maintenance organization (HMO). Some firms offer more than one FFS and HMO plan, ranging from high-premium plans that provide a great deal of coverage to less expensive plans with higher deductibles and higher co-insurance rates. Employers also often permit workers to contribute additional funds, beyond the basic employer allocation, to "buy" more expensive plans with lower deductibles, lower co-insurance rates, and perhaps higher plan maximums and more inclusive coverage rules.

The authors gratefully acknowledge generous research support from the ILR Center for Advanced Human Resources at Cornell University. Useful comments were provided by Silvana Pozzebon. The authors remain solely responsible for opinions contained herein.

Previous studies of flexible benefits plans clearly demonstrate that employee demand for health insurance is sensitive to the relative price of the options (see Holmer 1984 and Feldman et al. 1989). In addition, previous studies have found that population subgroups have divergent health-care needs and that peoples' preferences differ regarding the ways in which their health care is delivered. Thus personal characteristics such as sex and marital status appear to affect plan choice in systematic ways. For example, women are more likely to prefer and use preventive services and hence are more likely to choose HMO plans (which typically cover such services) over more traditional fee-for-service alternatives (which do not) (see Feldman et al. 1989 and Dowd and Feldman 1985). Income also affects plan choice. Higher-income workers are more likely to resist the long waits associated with some HMOs and to value the choice of physicians permitted by FFS plans (see Juba, Lave, and Shaddy 1980; McGuire 1981; and Welch and Frank 1986). Clearly, the demand for health care varies tremendously across workers, and recognition of this fact has been one reason for the growth of flexible benefit plans over the last decade.

One characteristic that has been relatively underexamined in the literature on health insurance choice is the effect of age. This chapter asks whether older workers' selections of health insurance plans in a flexible benefits context differ greatly from those of younger employees. The goal is to determine whether demands for health insurance would be predicted to change as the workforce ages and if so how much and in what directions.

First, we sketch the qualitative choice model used to assess the effect of age on workers' choice of a health insurance plan. Next, we describe the data set employed to test for age patterns, along with summary statistics on choice patterns by worker characteristics. Finally, we present estimation results and use them to simulate changes in plan demand under alternative workforce scenarios.

How Employees Choose Health Plans in a Flexible Benefits Setting

We examine health insurance plan selection behavior in a large firm where employees are permitted to choose from among six health insurance options. As in previous studies of employee choice in a flexible benefits scenario, we follow the expected utility model formulation of choice under uncertainty.[1] This approach predicts that employees will select the health insurance plan that makes them as well off as possible, or, in economic terms, the one with the highest expected utility. In this case, utility is assumed to depend on the employee's expected costs under the plan and his or her perceptions of the plan's quality (Holmer 1984).

In particular, the model assumes that employees' choice of plan will depend on the characteristics of each plan. Each plan is defined by its own premium level, co-insurance rate, deductible, and out-of-pocket maximum. Since these characteristics influence expectations about the costs of choosing a plan, they are hypothesized to affect the probability that employees will select that plan. Additionally, it has been suggested in the literature that the nonfinancial attributes of each plan should be considered, including the degree of choice participants can exert regarding which medical care provider is elected.[2] Traditionally, prepaid (HMO) plans have offered less choice over providers than fee-for-service plans, though recently developed independent practice association plans (IPAs) have the features of prepaid plans yet offer some (albeit limited) choice over physicians.

In addition to these plan-specific variables, our model posits that employee-specific factors may affect choice. Some of these have theoretically ambiguous effects, such as worker pay levels. On the one hand, higher pay enables workers to buy more expensive plans, but on the other hand, on average, higher-income workers are likely to be healthier than poorer workers (see Feldstein 1988).[3] Higher-paid workers may be more willing (and able) to accept the risk of incurring uncovered medical expenses, which would suggest they would opt for a plan with a lower premium and thus a less generous plan. Alternatively, as income increases, workers can afford to purchase more of all valued goods and services, including coverage for medical expenses and the choice of a health-care provider. In general, the effect of

1. Many of these are reviewed in Feldman et al. 1989.
2. Other nonfinancial choice-specific variables would include the waiting time until appointments can be made, the plan's emphasis on prevention versus cure, and the quality of the physicians and other medical care providers available through the plan (Feldman 1989). Unfortunately, no data on these other characteristics are available in our data set (or in most studies of flexible benefits plans to date).
3. There is also some evidence that higher-income workers are less risk-averse (see Friedman 1974).

higher pay on plan choice is theoretically ambiguous and must be settled by examining the data.

Previous studies have suggested that other worker-specific factors also influence the choice of a health insurance plan. Thus, higher-paid workers seem to prefer the more traditional FFS plans to prepaid plans (see Juba, Lava, and Shaddy 1980; Merrill, Jackson, and Reuter 1985; Welch and Frank 1986). Women tend to consume more medical care and may desire more preventive care than men (see Sindelar 1982; Dowd and Feldman 1985).[4] Marital status also influences the decision since married workers tend to need more preventive and more out-patient coverage (particularly for their children) than single workers (see Taubman and Rosen 1982).[5] Further, as will be shown, employers often subsidize workers choosing family coverage by offering them a plan at less than its true market price. Hence employees claiming a dependent are relatively subsidized compared with single workers, which, in effect, raises the number of credits available to allocate across plans. Conversely, a married worker may have coverage through a working spouse and thus opt for the minimum-cost plan when presented with a choice of plans in a flexible benefits setting.

We have also hypothesized that age will powerfully affect health plan choice. Older workers are expected to behave differently from younger workers, both because they face objectively different health risks and because their subjective tastes in health plans may be different from those of younger workers. To the extent that choice over health plans differs systematically by age, the data are said to reveal "biased selection."[6] Some analysts have suggested that older workers prefer health insurance coverage that permits them to continue long-standing relationships with medical care providers (see Feldman et al. 1989). Older workers also face different health risks than younger workers, particularly if they have chronic diseases or lifestyle-induced ailments, which can be more serious than they are in younger workers.[7] This would certainly

4. Feldman et al. (1989) report that women tend to select health-care plans that provide more preventive care.
5. Married persons also appear to consume less health care than single people, in part because spouses tend to provide substantial amounts of in-home care not readily available to many single people.
6. Patterns of biased selection are reviewed by Gail Wilensky and Louis Rossiter (1986) and more recently by Bryan Dowd et al. (1991). Age differences have not been the focus of previous studies, unlike the current study.
7. For a discussion of differential health risks between older and younger workers, see Mitchell 1988.

suggest that employee age should be taken into account in a multivariate model of employee choice of health plans in a flexible benefits setting. Furthermore, older workers may be more likely to select a fee-for-service plan over just about any prepaid alternative if choice is valued strongly enough, or they may judge an FFS plan to be superior to some prepaid plans but not others. It is also possible that a well-specified model should allow for age interaction effects. Thus, older workers may be less sensitive to changes in premiums and other financial characteristics of the plan than their younger counterparts. A natural test of this hypothesis is to interact age with plan variables to see whether the responses of older workers differ systematically (are smaller) than for younger employees.

DATA AND PROCEDURES

Data on employees' health plan selections were derived from corporate payroll and benefits records provided by a large private sector manufacturing firm for the 1989 plan year.[8] Because the data are from corporate payroll and benefits records, response rates were 100 percent, in contrast with some studies that relied on voluntary participation in the data collection effort and therefore had much lower response rates and possibly significant selection bias.[9]

The records examined here cover both salaried and hourly workers in a broad range of job titles and pay levels. For the current analysis, we focus on one site because complete data are not yet available for all regions; later research will extend the analysis to employees of the same firm at six distinct geographical sites. The firm in question provided large sample sizes for analysis; in particular, the group under study is 5,194 employees. Previous studies have been limited by data sets on a few hundred covered employees; this larger group should offer more statistical precision for key coefficient estimates.

There are other advantages of our data set worth mentioning. Employees in this firm have six plans from which to chose, with substantially different cost-sharing and premium characteristics. Many previous studies focused on participants who had to choose from among only two or three plans, which greatly limited the degrees of freedom over which choice parameters were estimated. Our study rectifies this shortcoming. Related to this is the fact that cost responses within and across plan

8. For confidentiality reasons, the firm cannot be identified.

9. For instance, Feldman et al. (1989) report a 48 percent response rate, and Juba et al. (1980) reported a 46 percent rate.

TABLE 7-1.   CHARACTERISTICS OF EMPLOYEES AT FIRM STUDIED

	Mean	s.d.	Correlation Matrix		
			1	2	3
Age	39.71	10.90			
Salary (1,000$)	39.05	21.34	0.27		
Married	0.70	0.46	0.28	0.23	
Female	0.36	0.48	−0.19	−0.40	−.026
N = 5,194					

types can be estimated because we have data on choices across three FFS and three prepaid plans; this is not possible when employees have only one FFS and one prepaid option (Feldman et al. 1989).

Table 7-1 describes the characteristics of the 5,194 employees in the data set. The average age of this population was about 40, and the average annual salary was about $39,000 ($1989). Approximately 70 percent of these employees were married and 36 percent were women.

Employees of this firm are offered three prepaid plans with varying premiums and associated cost-sharing rules, and three fee-for-service plans, also with different premiums and cost-sharing rules.[10] The three FFS plans are fairly different in their coverage and premiums, as indicated in table 7-2 (more detail appears in appendix A). The "traditional" (preflex) FFS plan costs a single employee $933 per year and provides a low deductible ($120/year for a single employee), a low in-patient hospital co-insurance rate (10 percent), and a cap on health expenditures (the "out-of-pocket" maximum) of $1,250 per year. (All figures are in 1989 dollars.) The premium for the "transitional" FFS plan is 21 percent less, in exchange for which the employee is at risk of bearing higher health-care costs: the deductible amount is twice as high ($300 for a single employee), as is the co-insurance rate—20 percent. (In the transitional FFS plan, the out-of-pocket maximum is unchanged.) The third FFS plan has a 38 percent lower premium than the traditional plan but also a very different character: it provides only what might be termed catastrophic coverage, since the substantially higher deductible ($2,000 for a single employee) equals the out-of-pocket maximum, after which the plan pays the full cost of care (the co-insurance rate is 0 percent). The premium rates for all of these plans are supposed to reflect true

10. Employees are required to select one option and are not permitted to opt out of coverage completely.

TABLE 7-2.   CHARACTERISTICS OF SIX HEALTH INSURANCE PLANS

	Premium	Deductible	In-Patient Co-Insurance	Out-of-Pocket Maximum
Fee-for-service plans[a]				
Traditional	High	Low	Low	Low
Transitional	Medium	Medium	Medium	Low
Catastrophic	Low	High	Zero	Low
Prepaid Plans[b]				
IPA Plan 1	High	Zero	Medium	Zero
IPA Plan 2	High	Zero	Medium	Low
HMO	High	Zero	Zero	Zero

See appendix A for further detail.

[a]Fee-for-service plans, such as Blue Cross/Blue Shield, are those in which health-care providers are reimbursed on a per-service basis.

[b]Prepaid plans, such as health maintenance organizations or independent practice associations, are those in which health-care providers are paid a lump sum and agree to provide all covered services at no, or minimal, additional cost to the insured.

expected costs since the firm offers these plans on a self-insured basis and intentionally sets premiums equal to the full cost of employees' health-care expenditures.[11]

Table 7-2 also summarizes the key features of the three prepaid plans offered by this firm, one being a health maintenance organization and the remaining two being independent practice associations. The HMO option costs a single employee $1,225 per year in premiums, more than any of the FFS plans, in exchange for a zero percent co-insurance rate and no deductible. While this plan is the most generous, employees are restricted to choosing medical practitioners who are employed by the HMO and medical centers affiliated with it. IPA plans are similar in that services are provided in exchange for a preset fee rather than on a reimbursement basis. The IPAs offer substantially more flexibility to participants, however, in that they permit employees to select medical service providers from a list of independent practitioners working under contract for the IPAs. Neither IPA has a deductible, and both have only a 20 percent co-insurance rate for in-patient care; where they differ is in the out-of-pocket limit and the premium. IPA plan 1 has a premium of $983 per year with no out-out-of- pocket maximum, while IPA plan

11. It could be that the full administrative costs of operating the plans are not fully valued in the FFS premiums. This arises when administrators of self-insured plans (who are often company employees with many responsibilities) do not actually allocate every last penny to flexible benefits plan costs versus other personnel functions (Mitchell and Andrews 1981). If such a subsidy had existed, it should have been constant across FFS plans and thus should not have altered the relative value of the FFS options.

2 charges 6 percent more in exchange for a $500 out-of-pocket maximum. All three prepaid plans are operated by third parties, and premiums are presumably set at market rates.[12]

As in many flexible benefits plans, the employer provides employees with "credits" or benefit dollars that may be used to pay for their plans. In addition, employees may buy benefit dollars by trading in vacation days and/or via a salary reduction plan; in any event, premiums are paid on a pretax basis regardless of which plan is chosen. The firm allocates benefit dollars based on employees' self-declared family status. Thus, someone claiming single status is granted fewer benefit dollars than an employee with one or more dependents. Since this flexible benefits plan was introduced only recently (data are derived from the plan's second year of operation), employees are granted sufficient benefits dollars to guarantee them the traditional FFS plan they had the previous year.[13]

RESULTS

Because the dependent variable, employee health plan choice, is a categorical variable, we used logistic regression techniques to estimate the effects of the explanatory variables.[14] In this section, we present two sets of results: coefficients obtained from estimation of the logit model and the simulated effects of changes in the explanatory variables on participation rates across health insurance plans.

---

12. Since prepaid plans are purchased from insurance companies, their premiums are probably not subsidized, as discussed in the previous footnote. Employee premiums for the FFS plans may therefore appear to employees to be slightly less expensive if this administrative cost practice is in effect.

13. Employees could also use benefit dollars to purchase dental, disability, and life insurance options or additional vacation days. They could also elect to participate in health-care and dependent-care flexible spending accounts. Unused benefits credits were forfeited at the end of each year (Barringer et al. 1991).

14. Choice-specific factors collected in a vector X_{ij} are defined for each individual i over health insurance coverage choice j, while worker-specific factors expressed as a vector Y_i are invariant to the health-care plan chosen. In a conditional logit framework, employee i gains utility U_{ij} from having selected option j, where the deterministic portion of utility depends on X_{ij}, Y_i, and a residual factor μ_{ij}, assumed to be distributed according to the extreme value distribution. In such a setup, the probability that individual i will select a particular option j^* is given as P_i $(j = j^*) = [exp\ (U_{ij}^*)/\Sigma J\ exp\ (U_{ij})]$. The denominator is defined over all j ($= 1$ to J), and utility is generally assumed to be linear ($U_{ij} = \beta X_{ij} + \pi_j Y_i + \mu_{ij}$). Maximizing the likelihood function produces estimates of β and π_j, with one coefficient β estimated per element of X_{ij}, and for elements of Y_i, normalization requires that only $J - 1$ coefficient estimates of the π_j terms are estimated. In the special case where age differences in behavior are evaluated, choice-specific and age terms are also estimated (Maddala 1983).

PREFERRED MODEL

Several variants on a basic logit model were explored. We limit our discussion here to the results of the model that did the best job of predicting actual participation rates while avoiding estimation problems such as multicollinearity.[15] The preferred model relates each employee's health insurance choice to a linear function of the premiums and deductibles of all the plans and to the employee's salary, sex, and marital status. In addition, the employee's age is interacted with the plan-level premiums and deductibles. The plan co-insurance rate is not included in this model because it proved to be too closely related to other cost-sharing provisions and thus generated unrealistic results.

Turning to table 7-3, we report first the plan-specific effects, either alone or interacted with age. Several results stand out. On the one hand, higher premiums reduce employees' willingness to choose some plans, as predicted by economic theory, and the effect is a statistically significant one. On the other hand, the positive coefficient on the age interaction term suggests that as workers age, plans with higher premiums become more attractive. The latter effect is quite small, however, and is not particularly robust, since in a different variant of the choice model the coefficient takes on a negative sign (see appendix B). Thus, there is scant evidence that older workers respond differentially to changes in health-care plan premium costs. Higher deductibles do reduce the appeal of a plan, as would be expected. Again, the age interaction effect is quite small and not statistically significant, indicating that sensitivity to deductibles does not vary with age.

The effects of other employee characteristics on choice probabilities are reported next. Because these variables remain constant for a given individual across plans, the logit model estimates their effects on the probability of selecting each plan, compared with a reference option, which here is the traditional FFS plan.

Higher-paid workers prove to have a substantially lower probability of selecting all but the traditional FFS option, and these results are significant at conventional levels. Patterns for women versus men are less clear-cut: women seem to prefer the traditional FFS plan over both

15. Results of two other models that also performed relatively well are presented in appendixes B and C. One includes as explanatory variables each plan's premium, deductible, and in-patient co-insurance rate and the employee's age, salary, sex, and marital status. The other omits the linear age term, replacing it with three age interactions (age*premium, age*deductible, and age*co-insurance).

TABLE 7-3. DETERMINANTS OF HEALTH PLAN CHOICE: ESTIMATED LOGIT COEFFICIENTS
(t-statistics in parentheses; traditional FFS plan is reference category)

Explanatory Variable	Coefficient Estimate	Fee-for-Service Plans		IPA Plan 1	Prepaid Plans	
		Transitional	Catastrophic		IPA Plan 2	HMO
Premium	-0.23*** (-5.68)					
Deductible	-0.09*** (-7.42)					
Age * Premium	0.002** (2.42)					
Age * Deductible	-0.0002 (-0.72)					
Salary		-0.02*** (-9.45)	-0.03*** (-9.46)	-0.03*** (-16.78)	-0.02*** (-13.88)	-0.05*** (-13.54)
Female		-0.33*** (-3.71)	0.78*** (7.54)	-0.01 (-0.11)	0.19*** (2.86)	-0.33** (-2.41)
Married		-0.89*** (-7.69)	2.00*** (11.89)	-0.19* (-1.83)	0.34*** (4.31)	-0.29* (-1.87)
Log likelihood	-7580.64					
Chi-square (DF)	3451.52 (14)					
N = 5,194						

*Significant at p = .10 in two-tailed test.
**Significant at p = .05 in two-tailed test.
***Significant at p = .01 in two-tailed test.

the transitional FFS plan and the HMO, but they also seem to find the traditional FFS plan less attractive than either the catastrophic plan or IPA plan 2. These results are hard to explain but may indicate that health risks are more diverse among women than among men.

Finally, the effects of marital status are statistically significant across all plans. We find that married workers concentrate in the catastrophic FFS plan and IPA plan 2 while avoiding the transitional FFS plan and the other two prepaid plans. This pattern is difficult to explain, since low FFS and IPA plan 2 offer such different risk and cost characteristics; further analysis on this pattern is required.

In a logit model, estimated coefficients are somewhat difficult to interpret because the effect of one variable also depends on the values of all other variables. For this reason, it is sometimes difficult to assess the magnitudes of estimated effects directly. The model's nonlinear structure makes it difficult to assess visually the effects of changes in explanatory variables. For this reason, table 7-4 offers several simulations, computed as the fraction of employees selecting each option under a range of alternative scenarios. Line 1 reproduces the observed distribution, wherein 40 percent of all employees elected the traditional FFS plan, 27 percent opted for the IPA plan 2, and the remaining one-third spread themselves over the four remaining options. The least popular option was the HMO, whereas more similar numbers elected the transitional and catastrophic FFS plans and IPA plan 1. In line 2, predicted probabilities are presented using plan and employee data and coefficient estimates for the preferred model (see appendix C for results from other models). Average predicted probabilities for each plan are calculated by computing the probability for each individual employee of selecting the plan and then taking the mean. The "base-line" projections do a very good job of replicating actual selection patterns, in that predicted and actual probabilities are very close.

We next simulate how participation rates, or "market share," would be predicted to change in response to changes in *plan characteristics*. If the traditional FFS premium were to rise by 10 percent, from $933 per year for a single employee to about $1,026, it would be roughly comparable in cost to the IPA plan 2 premium. As one might expect from previous results suggesting that these two plans are comparable in workers' eyes, the fraction choosing the traditional plan would be expected to drop by about 15 percent; many (but not all) of those moving away from the traditional health-care option would move to IPA plan 2. If

TABLE 7-4. EFFECTS OF PLAN AND EMPLOYEE VARIABLES: ILLUSTRATIVE PROBABILITIES

| | Probability of Selecting Health Plan[a] | | | | | |
| | Fee-for-Service Plans | | | Prepaid Plans | | |
Plan/Employee Change	Traditional	Transitional	Catastrophic	IPA Plan 1	IPA Plan 2	HMO
Actual fraction selecting	0.40	0.13	0.07	0.09	0.27	0.04
Base-line probabilities	0.39	0.13	0.08	0.10	0.26	0.04
Premium for traditional FFS plan up 10%[b]	0.33	0.15	0.08	0.11	0.29	0.04
Deductible for traditional FFS plan up 10%[b]	0.39	0.13	0.08	0.10	0.26	0.04
Age up 10 years[b]	0.50	0.11	0.07	0.08	0.21	0.03
All female employees[b]	0.38	0.10	0.11	0.09	0.29	0.03
All male employees[b]	0.40	0.15	0.05	0.10	0.25	0.05

[a]Predicted probabilities are computed by averaging responses across all employees using coefficient estimates from table 7–3.
[b]All else held constant.

the traditional FFS plan deductible were to rise by 10 percent, which is a relatively modest dollar change, we would expect to see relatively little movement.

Turning next to *employee characteristics*, we present the predicted effects on plan choice of simulated changes in the age and sex composition of the workforce. First, we examine the effects of a ten-year increase in the average age of the workforce, from age 40 to age 50. This change is in line with demographic projections for the labor force as a whole as the baby boom ages. We find that the most substantial differences in plan selection are anticipated for the traditional FFS plan, which will experience about a 28 percent increase in participation. This increase is offset by declines in the prepaid plans, especially in IPA plan 2, where coverage falls by about 19 percent. It may be that the choice restrictions imposed by prepaid plans take on more importance as workers age.

If the firm's workforce were to become completely female, the model predicts declines in coverage by the traditional and transitional FFS options, with the catastrophic FFS plan and IPA plan 2 growing more popular. This could be because women have health coverage through their spouses and the catastrophic FFS plan is by far the least expensive. In contrast, an all-male workforce would probably select the traditional FFS plan more often, even controlling for other factors.

OTHER FORMULATIONS

Other models, not described in detail here, were also examined. For instance, one model adds a linear and an age-interacted co-insurance term; another omits the interaction terms and replaces them with linear age and in-patient co-insurance terms (results are reported in appendixes B and C). Estimated effects of most of the explanatory variables are stable across models. When age interaction terms are excluded from the estimation model, the effect for the employees' sex is altered: the results suggest that women are more likely to select the transitional FFS and HMO plans over the traditional FFS plan, whereas just the opposite effect is observed using models that include interaction terms. Linear age effects for all of the choices are negative and statistically significant, indicating that older workers are much more likely to select the traditional FFS plan than any other options. Surprisingly, coefficients on the co-insurance terms are positive, suggesting that plans with high employee co-payment provisions are more attractive. This unexpected pattern may be a function of the unusual cost-sharing provisions in the catastrophic FFS plan, which offers a high deductible and zero co-insurance. Thus, if workers tend to select a plan offering low overall cost sharing but a higher co-insurance rate than the catastrophic FFS plan, it implies a preference for higher co-insurance, while, in fact, the preference is for lower cost sharing overall.

One model included both the in-patient and the out-patient co-insurance rates specific to each health insurance plan. Multicollinearity between these two variables, however, required us to select one for inclusion in the model; here we selected the in-patient rate, since it exhibited more cross-plan variance. We also sought to examine a model that included both age and age interaction terms, but multicollinearity again prevented this model from being estimated. Finally, we estimated a model that included a categorical variable indicating whether it was a prepaid plan or not, as suggested by Roger Feldman et al. (1989). If prepaid plans severely limit the choice of medical care providers and if workers value choice, this would be picked up by a negative sign on this "prepaid" coefficient. This model also could not be estimated, however, because of the low variability in the data. It is anticipated that including more establishments in the sample will loosen this constraint.[16]

CONCLUSIONS AND DISCUSSION

To assess the relative importance of demographics and plan charac-teristics on health-care plan choice, we estimated models of employee choice and simulated changes in demand for health plans under different circumstances. Most important for this paper, we found that if the workforce aged by ten years, from age 40 to age 50, the most substantial changes anticipated in plan choice or "market share" would be a marked increase in demand for a traditional fee-for-service plan. Specific findings from our data may be summarized as follows (these conclusions hold all else constant):

1. A higher health insurance plan premium reduces employees' will-ingness to choose that more expensive option. Older workers respond to changes in health plan premium costs much as younger workers do.

2. A higher deductible reduces the chance that a given plan will be

---

16. In ongoing research, we are seeking to refine the measure of choice employees can exert over medical care providers. Early results suggests that participants view IPA plans as much more similar to FFS plans along the choice dimension, even though they are prepaid plans.

selected. Older workers do not significantly differ from younger workers in their response to changes in the deductibles for their plans.

3. Older workers and more highly paid workers are more likely to select a traditional fee-for-service plan over other options.

Some of our findings can be compared with those found in previous studies of health-care choice in flexible benefits plans. Only one analysis has addressed age differences and in far less detail than here. That study, by Feldman et al. (1989), concluded that older persons strongly prefer choice over physicians, a finding with which we concur based on our findings. Our work goes further by testing for age-specific responses to changes in other plan features. We did not find older workers to be any less willing than younger workers to move to a prepaid plan if premiums and other cost-sharing features make it cost-effective to do so.

Previous studies have yielded conflicting results regarding the effect of employee premiums on the demand for health insurance. Some analysts have concluded that the demand for health insurance is not responsive to price (see, for example, Feldman 1989; Juba, Lave, and Shaddy 1980; Holmer 1984; Marquis and Holmer 1986; and Barringer et al. 1991), while others report a negative and significant effect for employee premiums, similar to that indicated here (see Piontkowski and Butler 1980; McGuire 1981; Welch 1986; and Feldman et al. 1989). Part of the explanation for different behavioral outcomes across studies may be that participants confronted radically different choice sets from one study to another. Inevitably, the effects of explanatory variables will vary across settings (see Merrill et al. 1985). It is also possible that studies that find no significant effect of premiums can be explained by their inadequate controls for other costs such as the deductible amount and the co-insurance rates (see Feldman et al. 1989). Our results show that the demand for health insurance plans is sensitive to price once other plan-specific cost-sharing provisions are controlled.[17]

Future work will take several tacks. In testing whether older workers' health insurance choices differ significantly from their younger counterparts, it will be useful to join to this data set a separate survey conducted at the individual worker level on each employee's health status and, if married, on the spouse's health-care coverage. This will enable us to determine with more care whether the effects differ according to

17. When these cost-sharing provisions are not included, the estimated coefficient on employee premium is positive and nonsignificant (Barringer et al. 1991).

health status and to assess the accuracy of the model when additional health status terms are included. We are also investigating more complex nested logit models to determine whether or not older workers' groupings of similar plans differ from the similarity index implicit in younger workers' behavior. Last, adding data from other plant sites will provide more variation in premiums and other plan variables, which will presumably increase the precision with which these coefficients can be estimated.

TABLE 7A. PLAN VARIABLES

	Fee-for-Service Plans			Prepaid Plans		
	Traditional	Transitional	Catastrophic	IPA PLAN 1	IPA Plan 2	HMO
Annual deductible						
Employee only	$120	$300	$2,000	$0	$0	$0
Employee +1	$240	$600	$4,000	$0	$0	$0
Employee +2 or more	$300	$750	$5,000	$0	$0	$0
In-patient co-insurance rate						
Plan pays	90%	80%	100%	80%	80%	100%
Employee pays	10%	20%	0%	20%	20%	0%
Out-of-pocket maximum						
Employee only	$1,250	$1,250	$2,000	None	$500	None
Employee +1	$2,500	$2,500	$4,000	None	$500	None
Employee +2 or more	$2,750	$2,750	$5,000	None	$500	None
Employee premium						
Employee only	$933	$731	$580	$983	$1,045	$1,225
Employee +1	$2,031	$1,613	$1,261	$2,031	$2,125	$2,563
Employee +2 or more	$2,926	$2,213	$1,825	$2,926	$2,926	$3,025
Fraction selecting	40%	13%	7%	9%	27%	4%

TABLE 7B. DETERMINANTS OF HEALTH PLAN CHOICE: ESTIMATED LOGIT COEFFICIENTS
(t-statistics in parentheses; traditional FFS plan is reference category)

Employee Variable	Fee-for-Service Plans		Prepaid Plans		
	Transitional	Catastrophic	IPA Plan 1	IPA Plan 2	HMO
Age					
Model 1	-0.05*** (-13.54)	-0.04*** (-8.25)	-0.02*** (-5.69)	-0.02*** (-7.83)	-0.03*** (-4.40)
Model 2	N/A	N/A	N/A	N/A	N/A
Model 3	N/A	N/A	N/A	N/A	N/A
Salary					
Model 1	0.0 (0.46)	-0.01*** (-3.08)	-0.03*** (-9.74)	-0.02*** (-7.28)	-0.02*** (-4.08)
Model 2	-0.02*** (-9.45)	-0.03*** (-9.46)	-0.03*** (-16.78)	-0.02*** (-13.88)	-0.05*** (-13.54)
Model 3	-0.02*** (-8.20)	-0.03*** (-8.90)	-0.04*** (-14.50)	-0.02*** (-10.85)	-0.05*** (-12.58)
Female					
Model 1	0.18* (1.76)	1.46*** (12.33)	0.07 (0.70)	0.29*** (3.61)	0.33** (2.04)
Model 2	-0.33*** (-3.71)	0.78*** (7.54)	-0.01 (-0.11)	0.19*** (2.86)	-0.33* (-2.41)
Model 3	-0.34*** (-3.58)	0.73*** (6.97)	-0.06 (-0.65)	0.12 (1.55)	-0.35** (-2.45)
Married					
Model 1	-0.48*** (-3.88)	2.17*** (11.72)	0.03 (0.29)	0.57*** (6.45)	0.25 (1.41)

	Coefficient Estimate				
Model 2	−0.89*** (−7.69)	2.00*** (11.89)	−0.19* (−1.83)	0.34*** (4.31)	−0.29* (−1.87)
Model 3	−0.82*** (−6.99)	2.00*** (11.89)	−0.11 (−1.00)	0.43*** (5.18)	−0.32** (−2.00)

Plan Variable	Coefficient Estimate	Plan Variable	Coefficient Estimate
Premium		Age * premium	
Model 1	−0.16*** (−6.39)	Model 2	0.002** (2.42)
Model 2	−0.23*** (−5.68)	Model 3	−0.002** (−2.12)
Model 3	−0.05 (−1.01)		
Deductible		Age * deductible	
Model 1	−0.07*** (−9.01)	Model 2	−0.0002 (−0.72)
Model 2	−0.09*** (−7.42)	Model 3	−0.002*** (−5.83)
Model 3	−0.01 (−0.74)		
IP co-insurance		Age * co-insurance	
Model 1	0.06*** (5.41)	Model 3	−0.002*** (−7.54)
Model 2	N/A		
Model 3	0.08*** (6.43)		

(continues)

TABLE 7B. *(continued)*

		Chi-square (DF)	
Log likelihood			
Model 1	−7459.14	Model 1	1694.52 (18)
Model 2	−7580.64	Model 2	3451.52 (14)
Model 3	−7551.42	Model 3	3509.96 (16)
N = 5,194			

*Significant at p = .10 in two-tailed test.
**Significant at p = .05 in two-tailed test.
***Significant at p = .01 in two-tailed test.

Model 1: Choice = f(premium, deductible, IP co-insurance, age, salary, female, married).
Model 2: Choice = f(premium, deductible, salary, female, married, age· premium, age· deductible).
Model 3: Choice = f(premium, deductible, IP co-insurance, salary, female, married, age· premium, age· deductible, age· IP co-insurance).

TABLE 7C. EFFECTS OF PLAN AND EMPLOYEE VARIABLES: ILLUSTRATIVE PROBABILITIES

| Plan/Employee Change | Probability of Selecting Health Plan[a] | | | | | |
| | Fee-for-Service Plans | | | IPA Plan 1 | Prepaid Plans | |
	Traditional	Transitional	Catastrophic		IPA Plan 2	HMO
Actual fraction selecting	0.40	0.13	0.07	0.09	0.27	0.04
Base-line probabilities						
Model 1	0.41	0.11	0.07	0.10	0.27	0.04
Model 2	0.39	0.13	0.08	0.10	0.26	0.04
Model 3	0.39	0.13	0.08	0.10	0.26	0.04
Age up 10 years[b]						
Model 1	0.48	0.08	0.06	0.10	0.25	0.03
Model 2	0.50	0.11	0.07	0.08	0.21	0.03
Model 3	0.24	0.16	0.09	0.12	0.33	0.05
Salary up 10%[b]						
Model 1	0.42	0.12	0.07	0.09	0.26	0.03
Model 2	0.42	0.13	0.07	0.09	0.26	0.03
Model 3	0.41	0.13	0.07	0.09	0.26	0.03
All-female employees[b]						
Model 1	0.35	0.11	0.13	0.09	0.28	0.04
Model 2	0.38	0.10	0.11	0.09	0.29	0.03
Model 3	0.39	0.11	0.10	0.09	0.28	0.03
All-male employees[b]						
Model 1	0.44	0.12	0.04	0.11	0.26	0.03
Model 2	0.40	0.15	0.05	0.10	0.25	0.05
Model 3	0.39	0.15	0.05	0.10	0.26	0.04

(continues)

TABLE 7C. *(continued)*

| Plan/Employee Change | Probability of Selecting Health Plan[a] | | | | | |
| | Fee-for-Service Plans | | | Prepaid Plans | | |
	Traditional	Transitional	Catastrophic	IPA Plan 1	IPA Plan 2	HMO
All-married employees[b]						
Model 1	0.38	0.09	0.13	0.09	0.28	0.03
Model 2	0.37	0.09	0.15	0.09	0.27	0.03
Model 3	0.37	0.09	0.15	0.09	0.28	0.03
All-single employees[b]						
Model 1	0.46	0.17	0.02	0.11	0.20	0.03
Model 2	0.39	0.23	0.03	0.11	0.20	0.05
Model 3	0.40	0.22	0.03	0.11	0.20	0.05
Premium for traditional FFS plan up 10%[b]						
Model 1	0.34	0.13	0.08	0.11	0.30	0.04
Model 2	0.33	0.15	0.08	0.11	0.29	0.04
Model 3	0.33	0.15	0.08	0.11	0.30	0.04
Deductible for traditional FFS plan up 10%[b]						
Model 1	0.41	0.12	0.07	0.10	0.27	0.04
Model 2	0.39	0.13	0.08	0.10	0.26	0.04
Model 3	0.39	0.13	0.08	0.10	0.27	0.04
IP co-insurance for traditional FFS plan up 10%						
Model 1	0.42	0.11	0.07	0.10	0.26	0.04
Model 2	N/A	N/A	N/A	N/A	N/A	N/A
Model 3	0.39	0.13	0.08	0.10	0.26	0.04

[a]Predicted probabilities are computed by averaging responses across all employees using coefficient estimates from table 7–3.
[b]All else held constant.

Chapter 8.
COST-OF-LIVING ADJUSTMENTS IN PENSIONS

Alan L. Gustman and Thomas L. Steinmeier

T HIS CHAPTER EXAMINES cost-of-living adjustments in pensions. Its aim is to describe pension COLAs and their effects on the level of compensation and pension wealth, on the rate of accrual of pension wealth and compensation with continued work, and on variation in compensation among generations of retirees. It also attempts to derive implications for the role of pension COLAs in the labor market and discusses whether there is a strong case from the labor market perspective for or against policies that would mandate pension COLAs or regulate their availability and funding.

Defined benefit pension plans, the type of primary plan that covers the greatest number of workers, typically pay the same dollar benefit in each year of retirement.[1] Accordingly, the real value of the yearly pension declines with years in retirement, at a more rapid rate the higher

This paper is based on our report "The Adequacy of Pension Benefit Levels," submitted to the U.S. Department of Labor, Pension Welfare Benefit Administration, contract number J-9-P-8-0099, August 1991, as part of the National Bureau of Economic Research Programs in Labor Studies and Aging. Opinions expressed are those of the authors and not those of the Department of Labor or the NBER. We thank Kim Katzenberger, Euysung Kim, Leo Kropywiansky, and Scott Miller for their help in constructing the data set from the Wyatt Company, Sylvester Schieber of the Wyatt Company for making those data available, Allen Pulsifer for programming the simulation model, and Jun Jong, Charles McCain, Ashley O'Neill and David Spurr for help with running the simulations. We are also grateful for comments from Al Rees and other participants at the Cornell University "New Jobs for an Aging Economy" conference at which this paper was presented and to Steven Allen and Linda Moncrief.

1. Defined benefit pensions promise to pay a yearly pension benefit to workers who qualify on the basis of age and service. The benefit is based on a formula. In the simplest formula, the benefit is determined by multiplying a generosity factor, say 1 percent, by

the rate of inflation. The effect of inflation on the real value of a pension benefit stream is sometimes mitigated by a cost-of-living adjustment, but there is wide diversity among firms in their policies: they are ad hoc rather than automatic; the fraction of benefits that is protected by a COLA, and the incidence and timing of COLA increases, vary widely among firms; and there is wide variation in the relationship of the size of the COLA increase to years of retirement. In addition, there is some question whether inflation and pension COLAs have significant effects on the incentives created by pensions.

Although some pension plans have provisions whereby benefits are adjusted automatically in response to cost-of-living changes, almost no pension COLAs are declared prospectively.[2] There are no promises to adjust pension benefit amounts after retirement; rather, adjustments are made on an ad hoc basis. Typically, COLAs do not adjust pensions to cover the full amount of the cost-of-living change. Both the frequency with which pension benefits are adjusted for cost-of-living changes, and the size of the adjustments in benefits, vary widely, both among firms and over time.[3]

Fewer than half of pension-covered workers receive a COLA increase at any time within a five-year period. Consider, for example, results from the Employee Benefit Survey (EBS), a survey of medium- and large-sized firms conducted by the U.S. Department of Labor. In each of the years from 1983 through 1989, about a quarter to just over half of the full-time pension participants were in plans that made at least one adjustment in the five-year period preceding the survey date (Mitchell 1992).

The basic benefits in a defined benefit pension plan accrue nonlinearly with continued employment. The benefit accrual rate increases with tenure and is characterized by sharp discontinuities upon qualification

---

average salary in the last or highest paid years of employment and then multiplying by years of covered service. In the case of the other leading type of plan, the defined contribution plan, funds are accumulated in an account and retirement benefits are determined by the returns to the accumulated funds. For details on the frequency of plan types, other pension characteristics, and the values of the benefits promised by a representative sample of U.S. plans, see Gustman and Steinmeier 1989a and 1992.

2. Using the Employee Benefit Survey, the Bureau of Labor Statistics reports that "only 4 percent of all participants were in plans that provided for automatic increases in pension benefits to compensate for increases in the cost of living" (U.S. Department of Labor 1989:80).

3. See Allen, Clark, and Sumner 1986; Allen, Clark, and McDermed 1992; and U.S. Department of Labor, *Employee Benefits*, various issues.

for early and normal retirement benefits (Bulow 1982). In addition to affecting the real value of any nominal pension, the level of inflation may affect the shape of the pension accrual profile (Kotlikoff and Wise 1985, 1987).

Labor economists have argued that the shape of the accrual profile creates incentives that affect worker mobility, productivity, and retirement and that the creation of these incentives is a major reason firms adopt pensions with certain provisions. (For a review of this literature, see Gustman and Mitchell 1992.) Because inflation may affect the key incentives that have been the focus of labor market analysis, pension COLAs may also affect these incentives. Our central concern is with the implications of alternative levels of inflation, and COLA provisions, on the valuation of pensions and the incentives they create.

The first part of this chapter describes briefly the stylized facts about pension COLAs and some of the features of the formulas specifying COLA adjustments. We then use available data to describe changes in the pension benefits of retirees over time and the effects of pension COLAs on pension benefits. Estimated changes in pensions received by retirees are calculated from available longitudinal surveys of individuals. The data indicate that pension COLAs were less important in the 1980s than in the 1970s but that through 1987 they continued to cover about half the increases in the cost of living. COLA provisions are evaluated along with the basic pension benefit by constructing a twenty-year file from reports published by the Wyatt Company for the fifty largest industrial companies. These data suggest that if the inflation experience in the 1968–78 decade persisted, cost-of-living increases would have raised the current value of pension benefits by about one half, whereas if the inflation experience were that of the 1978–88 period, cost-of-living adjustments would have raised the current value of pension benefits by about 14 percent. Moreover, our results confirm findings from earlier studies that COLA increases are larger for those who have been retired longer.

The second part of the chapter focuses on increasing our understanding of the role of pension COLAs in the labor market. What progress we make is in some sense negative, in that we rule out what we considered on a priori grounds to be promising explanations for pension COLAs. Because the data do not allow us to isolate the effects of changing inflation on the costs of retirement, quitting, and being fired, we construct a simulation model of the firm and its pension plan. The model is used to examine the consequences of the leading theories that have been used to explain pensions when these theories are used to explain pension COLAs. We find that pension COLAs have a very small effect on the key incentives emphasized by labor market theories of pensions. Accordingly, it seems unlikely that firms provide pension COLAs to preserve these key incentives in the face of inflation.

Pension COLAs smooth the course of retirees' retirement incomes. We also find that once pension contributions and adjustments in wages are taken into account, pension COLAs may not necessarily act to reduce the variance among cohorts in real lifetime incomes. In the face of inflation shocks, the distribution of real incomes across cohorts may be reduced, unchanged, or increased as a result of the presence of COLAs.

PROVISIONS OF PENSION COLAS

It is useful to begin with some examples of provisions for pension COLAs, taken from surveys devised by the Wyatt Company over time. These are drawn from a longitudinal sample of pension benefit formulas and COLA provisions collected from the fifty largest industrial companies in the United States.

Provisions prescribing ad hoc COLAs may take a number of forms. One apparent distinction is between plans that express COLAs in marginal terms and those that express them as cumulative adjustments. As we shall see, most changes occur only sporadically. Accordingly, pension benefit changes often have to provide higher increases for those who have been retired for a longer time, even if their aim cumulatively is to provide a proportionate adjustment for all retirees to offset the effects of inflation.

As a first example, consider three postretirement increases reported for Eastman Kodak. Each is a marginal increase to be paid according to the year of retirement. These increases were granted in 1979, 1980, and 1985. The 1980 increase, for example, called for an increase of 12 percent for those retired before 1973, 8 percent for those retired between 1973 and 1978, and 4 percent for those who retired in 1979. Even though an increase was granted in 1979, in the case of the 1980 increase, the percentage increase also varied with year of retirement.

A second example is that of AT&T, which granted five increases from 1979 through 1988, all in the form of marginal increases. Most retirees received a specified maximum rate, such as 7.5 percent in 1982.

TABLE 8-1. FREQUENCY OF VARIOUS COLA INCREASES IN MEDIUM AND LARGE FIRMS

Type of Increase	Percentage of Covered Workers Experiencing Increase
Monthly dollar amount does not vary by date of retirement	3%
Monthly dollar amount varies with date of retirement	4
Percentage of current benefit does not vary with date of retirement	27
Percentage of current benefit does vary with date of retirement	20
Proportionate increase per year of retirement	20
Increase of a dollar amount per year of service	21
Other	5
Total	100

Source: Employee Benefit Survey 1988, table 84.

For any increase, the proportionate change was somewhat lower for those retired for only one year (5 percent for those retired for one year in 1982).

Other examples include Coca-Cola, which reported cumulative increases through 1988 by single year of retirement, ranging from 3.3 percent for those who retired in 1984 to 297.3 percent for those who retired in 1948. BP America used a similar scheme in which the cumulative increase over the pension at retirement varied with year of retirement.

Although there are some exceptions, the large firms Wyatt surveyed granted pension cost-of-living increases to both early and normal retirees. Excluding early retirees from COLA adjustments would have more strongly encouraged delayed retirements. Still other plans specified service requirements for the COLAs even though they provided adjustments in proportion to years of retirement. Maximum and minimum levels of adjustments are also noteworthy. Sometimes these were specified in proportionate terms and sometimes in dollar amounts. Some plans specifically excluded deferred vested employees from the COLAs.

The diversity in the formulation of pension cost-of-living increases is illustrated in table 8-1. Again, the effect of these increases on the difference in compensation associated with a decision to remain with the firm would depend on the extent to which the reported changes occur on a fairly regular basis. For example, if each yearly increase is meant to be higher for those who have been retired for a longer period, then pension COLAs would encourage earlier retirement. Because the timing for granting cost-of-living increases is irregular, however, the fact that for 44 percent of participants increases vary with years of retirement may reflect the need to make adjustments for long-term retirees whose benefits had not been adjusted for a number of years. In that case, higher COLA increases for those who have been retired longer would not be a sign that the firm is using the pension COLA to encourage earlier retirement. Accordingly, statistics such as those in table 8-1 are not sufficient to determine how COLA adjustments affect the reward for continued work with the firm.

If adjustments that vary with years of retirement encourage earlier retirement, the opposite effect is achieved by the adjustments made by the plans covering 20 percent of the covered workers. In these plans, the adjustment is larger the longer the years of service.

Empirical Analyses of Pension COLAs

PENSION COLAS IN SURVEYS OF RETIREES

We next investigate the size of the pension cost-of-living adjustments in a number of data sets.

A number of longitudinal surveys include older individuals and report some measure of pension incomes for the retired. If family structure and labor market status remain unchanged, variation in pension incomes should reflect either the effect of cost-of-living adjustments or the impact of other scheduled adjustments of the pension once reporting error is eliminated. An example of other such changes is a reduction in pension benefits at the time the individual becomes eligible for social security benefits. Another example is a yearly adjustment in an annuity that has a cost-of-living component attached.

Longitudinal information on pension benefits received may be analyzed using a number of leading surveys of households and individuals, but here we will emphasize results from the longest of these panel data sets, the Panel Study of Income Dynamics (PSID). Other data sets used are the Retirement History Survey (RHS), the National Longitudinal Surveys of Older Men and of Mature Women (NLS), and the Survey of Consumer Finances (SCF). Because these surveys do not cover the

TABLE 8-2. SIMPLE AVERAGE OF ANNUAL CHANGES IN PENSION
INCOME, 1974–79

Survey	Percentage Change in Benefit
NLS men	.013
PSID	.035
RHS	.021
ACS	.036
CPI	.085

Source: Authors' calculations and Allen, Clark, and Sumner 1986.
NLS = National Longitudinal Survey; PSID = Panel Study of Income Dynamics;
RHS = Retirement History Survey; ACS = Allen, Clark, and Sumner 1986; CPI =
Consumer Price Index.

same years, comparisons of the changes in pension benefits across surveys
require some adjustment. Moreover, some collect information annually,
while others survey only every two or three years. Even the same survey
may not maintain a constant time period between waves. Table 8A (in
the chapter appendixes) summarizes the sample period and the periods
over which changes in benefits are calculated for the various surveys of
retirees considered in this section.

There is a six-year period, 1973–74 through 1978–79, for which the
results are available for the PSID, the NLS men's survey, and the RHS.
This period is the same one studied by Steven G. Allen, Robert L.
Clark and Daniel Sumner (1986) using a nationally representative sample of persons in defined benefit plans. Table 8-2 shows the simple
average of the annual increases and the corresponding increase in the
consumer price index (CPI). We find that in the PSID, pension changes
calculated match those reported by Allen, Clark, and Sumner. Increases
computed using the NLS men's survey are only about one-third the size
of those from the PSID, and the results from the RHS fall between these
increases. According to our results, a simple average of the pension and
annuity increases accounted for between 15 and 42 percent of the increases in the cost of living over a six-year period in the mid–1970s.

The differences among the micro surveys may be explained in a number of ways. Different questions were asked, and the sampled populations
were different. Also, the surveys included different cohorts. The timing
of the increases suggest that older cohorts receive larger increases. For
example, participants in the RHS were born between 1906 and 1911
and thus were 65 to 70 years old in 1976. Those in the NLS men's
survey were born between 1913 and 1922 and were only 54 to 63 in

TABLE 8-3. INCREASES IN PENSION AND ANNUITY INCOMES AND
INFLATION RATE

	1971–79	1979–87	1971–87
CPI	.076	.058	.068
PSID	.035	.028	.031
Ratio of row 2 to row 1	.46	.48	.45
Average of pension change over CPI change in each year	.54	.56	.55

Source: Authors' calculations.

1976. We found that the NLS participants reported lower benefit increases, and Allen, Clark, and Sumner (1986) also reported that increases were larger the greater the number of years since retirement.
Both findings are consistent with the COLA provisions summarized
previously.

There was a decline in the pension benefit levels reported between
1975 and 1976 for the NLS men's survey. It is possible that some pensions
did decline, perhaps because early-retirement adjustments were provided
only until the retiree qualified for social security benefits. To allow for
this possibility, we recalculated our results for both the NLS and the
PSID data for those who were age 67 or older. The results indicate that
retirees age 67 or older received lower percentage increases than did all
individuals in the PSID sample but higher increases when the NLS
men's survey was used. From these results, we cannot determine that
systematic effects of temporary early-retirement incentives account for
observed declining pension payments over time. A less comforting alternative is that there are substantial errors in reported pensions and
annuity incomes.

What do these figures suggest about the extent to which postretirement benefit increases tracked inflation in recent years? We focus first
on the PSID, the one survey that covers most of the period of interest,
and compare pension and annuity changes with CPI changes. Here it
appears that there are no major differences in the ratio of the COLA
to the CPI change between the period of the 1970s and the years for
which we have data in the 1980s. According to the results in table 8-
3, the ratio of the average cost-of-living change to the average CPI
change is about 46 percent for the 1970s and only slightly higher for
the 1980s. The average of the ratios is also similar between the periods.

TABLE 8-4.   PENSION CHANGES IN THE PSID VERSUS COST-OF-LIVING (CPI) CHANGES

	PSID Change	CPI Change	COLA/CPI
1971–72	.038	.033	1.15
1972–73	.030	.062	.48
1973–74	.018	.110	.16
1974–75	.061	.091	.67
1975–76	.048	.058	.83
1976–77	.035	.065	.54
1977–78	.016	.077	.21
1978–79	.031	.113	.28
1979–80	.044	.135	.33
1980–81	.042	.104	.40
1981–82	.038	.061	.62
1982–83	.025	.032	.78
1983–84	.013	.043	.31
1984–85	.025	.036	.70
1985–86	.015	.019	.77
1986–87	.023	.037	.63

Source: Authors' calculations.

As noted previously, there is some evidence that some older cohorts received increases that disproportionately benefited long-term retirees, perhaps so that they could catch up for the period of high inflation in the late 1970s and early 1980s. The data in table 8-4 suggest that there is some tendency toward a catch-up of the pension changes to cost-of-living changes after 1982, when the inflation rate fell from double-digit levels. This is evident from the numbers for 1982 onward in the last column of the table; for five out of six years, the ratio of pension change to CPI change exceeded 0.6.[4] Nevertheless, the data in table 8-4 clearly reflect the effects of declining inflation. From 1982 through 1987, the yearly increase in pension and annuity income fell to about two percentage points.[5]

4. There is additional evidence that cost-of-living changes are made with a lag, creating a catch-up phenomenon. Using data from the Employee Benefit Survey from 1982 through 1987, for those retired five years, total ad hoc COLA increases were roughly 7 percent. The increases were roughly 21 percent over that same period for those retired fifteen years. The cost-of-living increase (CPI-1) was 18 percent over that period (U.S. Department of Labor 1989:80).

5. Using the Employee Benefit Survey, a participant-weighted survey, Allen, Clark, and McDermed found that "by the end of the decade, the average increase in benefits across all plans had fallen relative to inflation" (1992:324). This decline is not evident in PSID data for the period that overlaps with that in the Allen, Clark, and McDermed

PENSION COLAS IN LARGE FIRMS: THE WYATT SAMPLE

We have constructed a longitudinal data file using published data from the Wyatt Company on the pension plans of the fifty largest industrial firms. This survey covers a twenty-year period. It is unbalanced in that the set of firms is not the same in all years.[6] Fortunately, the survey inquires about COLA increases granted over a number of years in the past. In particular, the surveys until 1978 asked about COLA increases back to 1969. After that, they inquired about COLA increases over the past decade. As a result, COLA increases are available in some cases for years in which particular firms were not included in the sample.

Postretirement increases sometimes have a minimum service requirement. For all calculations of eligibility for postretirement increases, the following tables assume that the individual had thirty years of service and retired at age 60. Our conclusions are not changed when calculations are made for three other combinations of retirement age and service: age 60 and twenty years of service, age 65 and thirty years of service, and age 65 and twenty years of service.[7]

Table 8-5 reports on the relative frequency of pension COLAs by year of retirement. Those who retired between 1968 and 1977 received pension increases in 25 percent of the years from 1968 through 1978. From 1978 through 1988, these same cohorts received pension increases in 26 percent of the years, even though average CPI changes were lower in these years. It is clear from the results, however, that those retiring in 1980 and later received increases in fewer years than those with the same years of retirement in the earlier decade.

Data in appendix 8B indicate the size of the yearly COLA increases relative to the base pension. The base pension, in turn, is calculated

---

(1992) study. The latter attribute much of the decline to a fall in the incidence of COLA adjustments. In the next section, we consider incidence and the value of COLA adjustments in the context of a sample of very large firms.

6. When weighting by employment is required, the number of employees is taken from COMPUSTAT, a service that provides financial and other relevant data on these same firms. Compensation numbers for use in calculating the value of the pension from the pension formula are also taken from this source. Earnings growth assumptions are based on the *Economic Report of the President* 1988.

7. Over the 1968–88 period, ninety-six firms appear in the top fifty Wyatt sample. Of these, firms that appeared for less than six years were eliminated from the sample. In addition, we did not attempt to code plans at Ford, General Motors, Goodyear, Procter and Gamble, and Xerox, which included profit-sharing elements. Further details on the composition of the sample are available on request.

TABLE 8-5.   YEARS IN WHICH POSTRETIREMENT BENEFIT INCREASES
WERE GRANTED

Year of Retirement	Mean Percentage Change		
	1968–78	1978–88	1968–88
1968	25.5%	28.3%	26.3%
1970	25.2	26.3	24.8
1971	24.6	26.3	24.6
1972	26.6	26.0	25.2
1973	26.8	25.7	25.0
1974	24.8	25.5	24.2
1975	23.6	25.7	24.9
1976	22.8	25.6	24.7
1977	24.2	23.2	23.4
1978		23.6	23.6
1980		17.9	17.9
1982		12.6	12.6
1983		9.3	9.3
1984		7.1	7.1
1985		7.2	7.2
1986		0.0	0.0
1987		0.0	0.0

Source: Authors' calculations, based on Wyatt Company data.

from the reported pension formula, using assumed levels of retirement
age, service, and calculated earnings. These results suggest that COLA
increases are proportionately larger for those who have been retired
longer. For example, those retired sixteen to twenty years received
increases that averaged 2.2 percent per year between 1984 and 1988,
while those retired one to five years received increases averaging only
1.1 percent over the same period.

Table 8-6 reports on the cumulative values of the postretirement
benefit increases by year of retirement and compares those increases with
cumulative cost-of-living changes. Again we find that COLA increases
are larger for those retired longer. For example, between 1978 and 1988,
those retired in 1968 received payments in the form of increases that
had a value averaging 40.1 percent of the payments under the base
pension, while those retiring in 1976 received COLA increases averaging
23.3 percent of the payments under the base pension. The results are
comparable for those retiring in intervening years.

COLA increases are concentrated in the later years of retirement.
Thus, they have a proportionately smaller impact on the present value
of the pension than does the basic pension.

TABLE 8-6. CUMULATIVE POSTRETIREMENT INCREASES IN PENSION BENEFITS AND CORRESPONDING INFLATION RATES BY YEAR OF RETIREMENT, 1968–78 AND 1978–88

Year of Retirement	Pension Benefit Increases			CPI Increases			Pension Benefit Increases as a Percentage of CPI Increases		
	1968–78	1978–88	1968–88	1968–78	1978–88	1968–88	1968–78	1978–88	1968–88
1968	54.9%	40.1%	115.4%	97.8%	70.8%	237.9%	56.1%	56.6%	48.5%
1970	38.6	32.8	84.6	79.3	70.8	206.2	48.8	46.4	41.0
1971	33.4	31.0	75.0	73.7	70.8	196.7	45.4	43.8	38.2
1972	17.2	29.5	52.4	63.5	70.8	179.3	27.0	41.7	29.2
1973	14.4	27.5	46.5	47.3	70.8	151.5	30.6	38.8	30.7
1974	11.2	26.2	41.0	34.9	70.8	130.5	32.2	37.0	31.5
1975	6.8	25.4	34.3	27.6	70.8	117.9	24.7	35.8	29.1
1976	4.7	23.3	29.3	19.8	70.8	104.6	23.8	32.8	28.0
1977	2.7	19.5	23.0	11.3	70.8	90.2	24.0	27.5	25.5
1978	0.6	17.7	18.4		70.8	70.8		25.0	26.0
1980		10.4	10.4		36.4	36.4		28.7	28.7
1982		4.3	4.3		24.5	24.5		17.7	17.7
1983		2.8	2.8		19.3	19.3		14.4	14.4
1984		1.4	1.4		15.2	15.2		9.3	9.3
1985		1.0	1.0		13.1	13.1		8.0	8.0
1986		0.0	0.0		9.2	9.2		0.4	0.4
1987		0.0	0.0		4.8	4.8		0.8	0.8

Source: Authors' calculations, based on Wyatt Company data.

TABLE 8-7.   DISCOUNTED VALUES OF INITIAL PENSIONS AND
POSTRETIREMENT BENEFIT INCREASES GRANTED, BY YEAR OF
RETIREMENT, 1968–78 AND 1978–88

Year of Retirement	Initial Value of Pension	Value of Postretirement Increases			Percentage Increase in Pension Value Due to Postretirement Increases		
		1968–78	1978–88	1968–88	1968–78	1978–88	1968–88
1968	$20,437	$5,801	$2,279	$8,079	28.5%	8.6%	39.7%
1970	21,099	4,974	2,190	7,165	22.4	7.9	32.2
1971	26,099	5,711	3,116	8,828	21.8	9.2	33.1
1972	27,985	3,098	3,255	6,353	10.4	9.7	21.2
1973	29,069	2,756	3,386	6,142	9.0	9.7	19.8
1974	32,664	2,520	3,804	6,324	7.2	10.0	18.2
1975	36,600	1,643	4,367	6,010	4.7	10.6	15.9
1976	42,559	1,495	5,302	6,797	3.7	11.2	15.4
1977	49,430	1,048	5,586	6,635	2.4	10.2	12.9
1978	52,235	319	5,658	5,977	0.6	10.1	10.8
1980	55,181		3,354	3,354		5.9	5.9
1982	62,459		1,442	1,442		2.3	2.3
1983	76,701		1,188	1,188		1.7	1.7
1984	75,700		672	672		0.9	0.9
1985	86,952		638	638		0.7	0.7
1986	110,568		37	37		0.0	0.0
1987	110,338		38	38		0.0	0.0

Source: Authors' calculations, based on Wyatt Company data.

We next explore the relative importance of pension COLAs to the current value of pension incomes. To do so, we compute annual benefit amounts and discount them to the date of retirement (and express them in dollars as of the date of retirement). The discount rate used to value wages received before retirement was the prevailing long-term interest rate, while the discount rate used in years after retirement was the long-term interest rate as of the date of retirement.

The value of the basic pension, the COLA increase, and the fraction of the pension accounted for by COLA increases are reported in table 8-7. For someone who retired at the beginning of the period, pension COLAs accounted for $8,079, or 40 percent of the $20,437 in basic pension received between 1968 and 1988. Partly because the inflation rate was higher in the first decade than in the second, 72 percent of the present value of COLA adjustments was received between 1968 through 1978. Analogous results for the later cohorts cannot be computed over the entire time period because they received benefits for only a fraction of the 1968–78 period.

TABLE 8-8.   WAGE AND PENSION VALUES FOR SELECTED
RETIREMENT YEARS

Year of retirement	1968	1968	1978
Period for projection	1968–78	1968–88	1978–88
Present value of wages	$195,055	$195,055	$522,850
Present value of initial pension	$20,437	$20,437	$52,235
Present value of pension with postretirement increases	$30,882	$29,096	$59,879
Percentage increase in pension value due to postretirement increases	51.6%	42.6%	13.8%
Ratio of pension values to the Present Value of wages			
Without postretirement increases	10.4%	10.4%	9.8%
With postretirement increases	15.6%	14.7%	11.2%

Source: Authors' calculations, based on Wyatt Company data.
These figures assume the worker retires at age 60 with thirty years of service and were
calculated assuming that future percentage increases will be the same as during the
indicated periods.

On the assumption that future increases will be the same as those
observed in the indicated period, table 8-8 projects pension and COLA
increases into the future. The covered individual is one who retired at
age 60, in 1968 or 1978, with thirty years' service. As would be expected,
the importance of pension COLAs varies very widely with the inflation
rate. On the one hand, given the inflation experience of the 1968–78
period, the COLA may equal half the value of the basic pension, raising
the fraction of benefits accounted for by the pension from 10.4 percent
to 15.6 percent of the present value of the wage. On the other hand,
given the inflation experience of the 1978–88 period, a 1978 retiree
would receive a pension COLA with only 14 percent of the present
value of the basic pension. In the case of the more modest inflation
rate, and perhaps because of adjustments in the basic pension formula,
the pension COLA raised the present value of benefits from 9.8 percent
of the present value of the wage to 11.2 percent.

Similar calculations were made using combinations of retirement ages
of 60 and 65 and of twenty and thirty years of service. Because of the
economic environment of the 1968–78 period, the fraction of benefits
accounted for by COLAs ranged from 40 to 50 percent, whereas the
range was from 12 to 15 percent in the 1980s.

Of course, these findings do not provide a definitive link between
pension COLAs and the rate of inflation. Given the intermittent nature

of the COLA changes, it is difficult to isolate the pattern of any lags in the system. Nevertheless, from the information presented above, it is apparent that such lags do exist. Accordingly, the COLA increases in later years overstate the likely level of adjustment that would be observed were the rate of steady-state inflation to remain at the level observed for the 1978–88 period.

Explanations for Pension COLAs

Much of the pension literature has focused on explaining the consequences of a worker's long-term attachment to a firm for the financing of pensions, for defining property rights in the pension, for defining the obligation of the firm to the worker, for determining the implications of pensions for wage profiles, and for evaluating the consequences of pensions for turnover. (For a recent review, see Gustman and Mitchell 1992.) Some theories (e.g., Bodie 1990) seek to explain why pension indexing may be incomplete and made available on an ad hoc basis. From the perspective of finance theory, for instance, the pension is seen only as a device to provide retirement insurance. Zvi Bodie (1990:43) describes the pension promise, together with an ad hoc pension COLA, as "participating annuities that offer a guaranteed minimum nominal benefit determined by the plan's benefit formula which is enriched from time to time at the discretion of management based on the financial condition of the plan sponsor, the increase in the living costs of retirees, and the performance of the fund's assets."

Available theories of pensions leave us skeptical of the power of two of the explanations—that, except for effects through the regulation of retirement age, pensions are used to enhance productivity by discouraging shirking, and that they are used to regulate mobility so as to economize on costs of hiring and training (see Gustman and Steinmeier 1987, 1989a, and forthcoming for extensive evidence). At the very least, many unanswered questions prevent us from using these theories to explain fully the provisions of pension COLAs. Nor is there substantial direct evidence that explains plan characteristics or accrual profiles so as to enable us to choose from among these competing explanations for defined benefit plans or to weight the competing explanations according to their relative importance. Nevertheless, we will examine the sensitivity of the relevant incentives to cost-of-living pension adjustments.

In our view, the most promising line of research for our purposes suggests that inflation and pension COLAs may affect retirement incentives significantly. If so, firms may design COLAs with an eye toward influencing retirement outcomes. Our strategy is to investigate the likely importance of these alternative explanations for pension COLAs by examining the effects of inflation and pension COLAs on the key incentives emphasized by these theories. Particular incentives will be important, including the increment in pension wealth that influences the decision to remain until normal retirement age after qualifying for early-retirement benefits and the increment that influences the mobility decision and the cost of dismissal for shirking. On the one hand, if we find that pension COLAs have important effects on these incentives, then we would consider the explanation to be plausible, while recognizing that doubts remain about some of the explanations for pensions. On the other hand, if we find that inflation and pension COLAs do not have important effects on the incentives to retire, to move, and/or not to shirk, incentives that are emphasized by pension theories, then it is unlikely that firms' policies regarding pension COLAs are being shaped by these motivations.

SIMULATING THE EFFECTS OF PENSION COLAS ON LABOR MARKET INCENTIVES

A further aim of this study is to investigate how inflation alters labor market incentives, including the rewards of long job tenure and the penalties for quitting. A number of formidable problems prevent us from isolating these effects in most empirical data, including the surveys used to this point. The Wyatt data would seem to be most suited for such an analysis, but the Wyatt survey does not report benefits for vested terminated workers. Hence, we cannot calculate the accrual profile as workers approach early retirement age, which is central to the calculation of the incentive to move and the incentive to shirk. The Wyatt panel is also so short that it is extremely difficult to distinguish the effects of inflation on the pension formula from those of other influences and thereby to isolate the full effects of inflation on the accrual rate from early to normal retirement age.

We therefore turn to simulation analysis to analyze further the relation of pension COLAs to retirement, mobility, and shirking incentives. This analysis demonstrates that pension COLAs are not likely to have important effects on these key incentives. We therefore conclude that the changes in incentives are not large enough to have motivated the adoption of pension COLAs.

Our simulation model of the firm and its pension plan includes four key elements of compensation: the wage, the basic pension, cost-of-living adjustments to the pension, and contributions to the pension fund.

Following Gustman and Steinmeier 1989b, we begin with a firm in steady state. The first set of calculations pertains to the structure of the labor force, to each worker's productivity, and to the group of retirees. A distribution is specified for age of hire and desired age and/or service at retirement. Every year, one of each type of worker is hired. Total employment at the firm is then set equal to the steady-state workforce that is consistent with the hiring and retirement (turnover) scheme. For example, if two 25-year-old workers were hired each year, one who would retire at 55 and one at 62, the steady-state labor force for the firm would number sixty-seven. All workers are assumed to die at age 80. The plan is instituted for a firm in such a steady state in an initial year, arbitrarily set to 1970, and the pattern of steady-state hiring and retirement continues after the plan is adopted. Assumptions are made about base productivity, economywide and individual productivity growth rates, the interest rate for discounting the benefits, and the return-on-plan investments if different from the interest rates the covered individuals use.

The next set of calculations pertains to pension benefits for each worker, computed conditional on this wage. Each pension plan, once instituted in 1970, runs through to termination in 2080. All pension plans investigated are built around final average salary-defined benefit formulas, and parameters represent alternative treatments of the eligibility requirements for early and normal retirement, vesting requirements, crediting of work before formulation of the plan, postretirement increases, the period over which earnings are averaged, actuarial bonuses for early retirement, and other characteristics that play a central role in determining pension values and key pension incentives (Bulow 1982; Kotlikoff and Wise 1985, 1987; Gustman and Steinmeier 1989a).

The liabilities of the pension plan, and thus the contribution rate required to balance the pension fund, are conditional on the wage. Each individual's wage is a fraction of current year productivity, where the fraction is one minus the contribution rate. Accordingly, the wage depends on the contribution rate. The model solves simultaneously for the wage and contribution rate that balance the pension fund and leave total compensation, the sum of all contributions and wages paid in any year, equal to total worker productivity. The value varies with the rate of inflation and is affected by COLA provisions. It is likely that in steady state, the value of the compensation package would adjust to different rates of inflation and to the presence of COLA protection. Our analysis of the effects of steady inflation and alternative COLA provisions assumes that there are full compensating adjustments that arise through the wage. In some cases, we find that it is important to take the compensating differences into account. For a number of important results, however, the findings do not depend on the size of any compensating differences in the wage. Note also that the model does not take account of any feedback effects from the pension to productivity or hiring.

A $10,000 productivity base is assumed in 1970. Economywide wage growth is assumed to be either 5 or 10 percent per year. Productivity growth due to tenure is 1 percent. The interest rate is alternatively set at either 6 percent or 11 percent. (For the period of the 1970s and 1980s examined in our data, the interest rate exceeded average compensation growth by about three percentage points. Results from a sensitivity analysis to the differences between the rate of wage growth and the interest rate are discussed below.) The benefit formula pays 1 percent of the average salary in the last three years of attachment times years of service. A proportionate contribution rate to finance the pension is imposed, with the plan being funded on a projected liability basis. It is assumed that there is a payout at plan termination, in 2080, which is made to cover either the legal liability or the projected liability, as specified for the particular version under consideration.

HOW INFLATION AND PENSION COLAS AFFECT PENSION RETIREMENT AND MOBILITY INCENTIVES

The effects of alternative inflation rates, COLA provisions, and COLA funding schemes are examined insofar as they alter the incentives for early retirement versus normal retirement, as well as the penalty created by backloaded pensions for turnover at an early age. These latter pensions are important since they determine workers' incentive to stay until retirement age and the incentive not to shirk on the job and risk being fired (Lazear 1979, 1983). For this simulation, the worker is assumed to join the firm at age 25 and to retire at either 55 or 62. Thus, by working to normal retirement age, an individual who stays to age 62 works an additional seven out of thirty years, or 23.3 percent more, or 3.3 percent of the basic thirty-year period of attachment for each additional year of work. The effects of inflation and pension COLAs for a worker hired in 1980, ten years after the pension plan was adopted at the firm, appear in table 8-9. Dollar figures reported in the table are deflated to the initial year of plan adoption, 1970. The first row of each panel reports the pension benefit. The next row reports total compensation, which is the sum of the pension plus the wage, where the wage is calculated as the difference between the individual's productivity and the pension contribution. Next is the pension-wage ratio, followed by the ratio of compensation to productivity, and finally the difference between compensation for working until age 62 versus compensation for working until age 55. In each of the table's four panels, different inflation and COLA patterns are assumed. Two panels use a 6 percent interest rate, one without a COLA and the other with a fully anticipated automatic COLA at 3 percent, which is funded on a projected liability basis. The other two panels report results for an 11 percent interest rate, with and without a 5.5 percent automatic COLA. Economywide wage growth is 1 percent less than the interest rate, and wages increase by 1 percent with each year of tenure.[8]

Pension benefit backloading proves to be an important phenomenon. In panel A, for example, row 1 shows that the ratio of the pension at 62 to the pension at 55, which involves an actuarially fair reduction for early retirement, is 1.86 to 1. The ratio of pension benefits to the wage is reported in row 3. For those who leave after age 55, the ratio is .068, while it is .103 for those who leave at age 62, in row 3. Although working seven additional years after a career from age 25 to 55 increases work effort by 23.3 percent, lifetime compensation is increased by 27.5 percent for the additional work, a compensation rate that is 18 percent higher than in the first thirty years. (If there are special early-retirement incentives, the backloading will, of course, be less. But other simula-

---

8. Note that the use of the same 1 percent personal productivity growth factor at both a 6 percent and 11 percent discount rate and the changing ratio between economywide growth and the interest rate, 5 and 6 percent versus 10 and 11 percent, produces some slight discrepancy between the levels of productivity in the examples, which use the different interest rates. An analogous phenomenon may be observed between the overall compensation levels resulting when the two different interest rates are used.

TABLE 8-9.   IMPLICATIONS OF INFLATION AND COLAS FOR PENSION
INCENTIVES TO RETIRE AT EARLY VERSUS NORMAL RETIREMENT AGE

	Leave at 55	Leave at 62
A. 6 Percent Interest, 5 Percent General Wage Growth, 1 Percent Experience Growth, No COLA		
Pension benefits	$17,286	$32,162
Total compensation	$269,848	$344,168
Pension/wage ratio	0.068	0.103
Compensation/productivity ratio	0.982	1.014
Compensation 62/compensation 55		1.275
Compensation 62 − compensation 55		$74,320
B. 6 Percent Interest, 5 Percent General Wage Growth, 1 Percent Experience Growth, 3 Percent COLA		
Pension benefits	$25,706	$38,890
Total compensation	$271,522	$342,560
Pension/wage ratio	0.105	0.128
Compensation/productivity ratio	0.988	1.009
Compensation 62/compensation 55		1.262
Compensation 62 − compensation 55		$71,308
C. 11 Percent Interest, 10 Percent General Wage Growth, 1 Percent Experience Growth, No COLA		
Pension benefits	$8,939	$23,034
Total compensation	$272,238	$348,796
Pension/wage ratio	0.034	0.071
Compensation/productivity ratio	0.981	1.015
Compensation 62/compensation 55		1.281
Compensation 62 − compensation 55		$76,558
D. 11 Percent Interest, 10 Percent General Wage Growth, 1 Percent Experience Growth, 5.5 Percent COLA		
Pension benefits	$17,854	$31,626
Total compensation	$273,353	$347,735
Pension/wage ratio	0.070	0.100
Compensation/productivity ratio	0.985	1.012
Compensation 62/compensation 55		1.272
Compensation 62 − compensation 55		$74,382

Source: Authors' calculations.
Results are for the cohort hired in 1980; all dollar figures are in 1970 $s.

tions, not reported here, indicate that the thrust of this discussion is
not substantially affected by the presence of early-retirement incentives.)

The impact of inflation on pension incentives to keep working results from a number of forces. The net effect is that the degree of backloading increases with inflation. On the one hand, the ratio of the value of the pension for working seven more years increases from $32,162/17,286 = 1.86:1$, as seen in panel A, to $23,034/8,939 = 2.58:1$, as seen in panel C. On the other hand, the value of the pension falls with the higher interest rate, from $32,162 to $23,034 for those retiring at age 62 and from $17,286 to $8,939 for those retiring at age 55. The increased backloading results because benefits at age 62 fall to .72 of their initial value when the interest rate is increased but to .52 of their initial value at age 55. The incentive created by the pension, however, is the incremental reward for continued work. That pension reward declines slightly at the higher interest rate, from $32,162 - $17,286 = $14,876 at the 6 percent discount rate to $23,034 - $8,939 = $14,095 at the 11 percent rate. This occurs despite the effect on the base pension of the higher wage to be received at the 11 percent interest rate.

In addition, because the increase in the interest rate reduces the value of the pension to 52 percent and 72 percent of its value for those retiring at ages 55 and 62, respectively, a wage increase will have a direct effect on incentives. A 4 percent increase in the wage is needed to compensate for the 40 percent decline in the pension. Altogether, the increment for working seven more years is greater at the higher interest rate, increasing from $344,168 - $269,848 = $74,320 at 6 percent interest to $348,796 - $272,238 = $76,558 at 11 percent interest. The higher wage generates a second-order effect on the pension, which has been taken into account.

At the lower level of inflation, the pension COLA reduces by 4 percent the reward for working from early until normal retirement age. At higher inflation rates, the COLA reduces this reward by 2.8 percent. Thus, the COLA modestly reduces the incentive to remain with the firm from early to normal retirement age. To the extent that a higher COLA is granted to those who have been retired longer, the reward for working until normal retirement age would be further reduced. Clearly, an actuarial bonus of modest size is capable of offsetting the effects of a higher steady-state level of inflation. A COLA is not necessary to restore incentives to leave early eroded by a higher level of inflation.

INCENTIVES FOR MOBILITY AND PRODUCTIVITY

When the incentive not to leave the firm at an early age is examined in the context of the simulation model, we again find that the effects of inflation are of only modest importance. Vested terminated employees typically get a cost-of-living increase only as of their date of eligibility for early or normal retirement. Thus, the COLA has the same proportionate effect on the benefits of leavers and stayers. The simulation in table 8-10 provides some idea of the orders of magnitude. This example starts the COLA from the day of leaving the job, even if well before early retirement age, and for that reason overstates the effect of the COLA on the incentive for mobility. That is, in table 8-10 it is assumed that a worker who leaves after five years can take a benefit that is reduced on an actuarially fair basis from the benefit that is paid at normal retirement and that for such an early leaver the COLA adjustment will be made from the date of leaving the firm. In this simulation, for the same benefit formula, age of hire, and other factors as assumed previously, the reward for those who leave the firm at age 30 is compared with the reward for those who stay to retire at age 62. Despite the upward bias, the potential effect of pension COLAs on the incentives not to leave the firm proves to be very weak.

At an 11 percent rather than a 6 percent discount rate, the value of the pension for an individual who leaves the firm at age 30 is reduced from $660 to $106. At the 11 percent discount rate, the gain in the value of the pension from staying until age 62 is much lower than it is at the 6 percent discount rate, falling by almost a third with an increase in inflation, from $31,319 to $22,731. After the compensating difference in the wage, however, the net reward for staying until age 62 is almost unchanged, increasing from $299,940 to $302,683 with the increase in the interest rate. Although there is more backloading of the pension at the higher interest rate, the value of the pension declines with the higher interest rate and the wage is increased to compensate for the fall in the pension value, so that the net compensation for staying another thirty years is increased by only 1 percent at the higher inflation rate.

Analogously, the COLA makes very little difference in the reward for working an additional thirty years. For example, as can be seen by comparing panels A and B, at a 6 percent discount rate, the presence of a COLA reduces the reward for working another thirty years from $299,940 to $299,134, or by three-tenths of 1 percent. The COLA increases the value of the pension for those who leave at age 30 by $1,406 and the value of the pension for those who leave at age 62 by $6,829, but the compensating reduction in the wage has a greater effect on those who stay for a long time.

TABLE 8-10.   IMPLICATIONS OF INFLATION AND COLAS FOR PENSION
INCENTIVES TO REMAIN FROM FIVE YEARS AFTER HIRE AT 25 TO
NORMAL RETIREMENT AT 62

	Leave at 30	Leave at 62
A. 6 Percent Interest, 5 Percent General Wage Growth, 1 Percent Experience Growth, No COLA		
Pension benefits	$660	$31,979
Total compensation	$42,273	$342,213
Pension/wage ratio	0.016	0.103
Compensation/productivity ratio	0.929	1.008
Compensation 62/compensation 30		8.095
Compensation 62 − compensation 30		$299,940
B. 6 Percent Interest, 5 Percent General Wage Growth, 1 Percent Experience Growth, 3 Percent COLA		
Pension benefits	$2,062	$38,808
Total compensation	$42,711	$341,845
Pension/wage ratio	0.051	0.128
Compensation/productivity ratio	0.938	1.007
Compensation 62/compensation 30		8.004
Compensation 62 − compensation 30		$299,134
C. 11 Percent Interest, 10 Percent General Wage Growth, 1 Percent Experience Growth, No COLA		
Pension benefits	$106	$22,837
Total compensation	$43,133	$345,816
Pension/wage ratio	0.002	0.071
Compensation/productivity ratio	0.943	1.00
Compensation 62/compensation 30		8.017
Compensation 62 − compensation 30		$302,683
D. 11 Percent Interest, 10 Percent General Wage Growth, 1 Percent Experience Growth, 5.5 Percent COLA		
Pension benefits	$813	$31,483
Total compensation	$42,738	$346,168
Pension/wage ratio	0.019	0.100
Compensation/productivity ratio	0.934	1.008
Compensation 62/compensation 30		8.100
Compensation 62 − compensation 30		$303,430

Source: Authors' calculations.
Results are for the cohort hired in 1980.

FINDINGS USING ALTERNATIVE INTEREST, WAGE GROWTH
AND COLA ASSUMPTIONS

The empirical data on pension changes that we have analyzed span the period 1971–87. Over that period, the interest rate on Moody's AAA bonds averaged 10.1 percent, while compensation increased by 7.1 percent and the CPI increased by 6.7 percent (Economic Report of the President 1988, tables B68, B55, and B13, respectively). In view of these figures, it is of interest to investigate the sensitivity of the simulation results to alternative assumptions. Accordingly, we reran the model on the assumption that economy-wide productivity growth was three percentage points less than the interest rate. In addition, it was assumed that COLA increases were half the rate of wage growth.

Differences in compensation if workers remained until age 62 and if they left earlier appear in table 8-11. First we state results for the eight runs previously reported and then we report comparable outcomes under revised assumptions. As can be seen by comparing the differences in compensation between those cases in which the indicated COLA is offered and the comparable case in which there is no COLA, pension COLAs have a relatively small effect on the reward either for staying until normal retirement age, or for staying from five years after hire until one qualifies for normal retirement.

The analysis thus far has considered the effects of alternative steady-state discount rates on the incentives created by pensions to leave, shirk, and retire. The next and final exercise with the simulation model investigates the effects of pension COLAs in the face of varying rates of inflation and corresponding changes in discount rates. These simulations suggest that when account is taken of the redistribution to first-generation members of a pay-as-you-go system, the feedback effects from pension contributions to the wage, and the timing of any inflationary experiences, pension COLAs may be found either to exaggerate or to dampen the variance in lifetime compensation among generations resulting from varying inflation rates.[9]

In dealing with changes in the inflation rate, the period of adjustment becomes a crucial issue. The assets in the pension fund are all recorded in real terms, so that a once-and-for-all unforeseen change in the in-

9. To the extent that variation in inflation is expected to be symmetric around the steady-state value, the possibility that there will be random shocks to the inflation rate should have no major effects on incentives from pensions to retire, to move, or to shirk. Risk-averse individuals might undervalue the pension in these circumstances.

TABLE 8-11.   COMPENSATION INCREASES: WORK UNTIL 62 VERSUS
LEAVE AT THE INDICATED AGE, UNDER ALTERNATIVE ASSUMPTIONS

Assumptions	From Age 55 to Age 62	From Age 30 to Age 62
6% interest 5% wage growth No COLA	$74,320	$299,940
6% interest 5% wage growth 3% COLA	$71,308	$299,134
11% interest 10% wage growth No COLA	$76,558	$302,683
11% interest 10% wage growth 5.5% COLA	$74,382	$303,430
6% interest 3% wage growth No COLA	$31,966	$168,541
6% interest 3% wage growth 1.5% COLA	$31,203	$168,288
11% interest 8% wage growth No COLA	$34,498	$174,711
11% interest 8% wage growth 4% COLA	$33,702	$174,931

Source: Authors' calculations.

flation and discount rates are immediately reflected in the returns on assets. There is no evidence about the adjustment mechanism governing changes in pension contributions in response to changes in the steady-state inflation rate. The simulation model assumes that when a pension surplus develops, the contribution rate has a minimum value of zero. It assumes that when a deficit develops, the pension contribution rates can rise to total at most 25 percent of compensation. Thus, immediately after inflation accelerates, there is a surplus that may take six to eight years to dissipate. During that time workers are making no contributions to their plan. When the inflation rate declines, the contribution rate is increased so as to eliminate the deficit within a few years. Those on board during those years find their earnings reduced substantially. The

TABLE 8-12.   EFFECTS OF VARYING INFLATION RATES ON THE
COMPENSATION-PRODUCTIVITY RATIOS OF COHORTS, BY YEAR OF HIRE

	Inflation Rises, Then Falls (No COLA)	Inflation Falls, Then Rises (No COLA)	Inflation Rises, Then Falls (With COLA)	Inflation Falls, Then Rises (With COLA)
Average	0.999	1.001	1.004	1.007
Minimum	0.973	0.970	0.978	0.979
Maximum	1.031	1.027	1.030	1.039
Standard deviation	0.0129	0.0131	0.0139	0.0146
Standard deviation/ mean	0.0129	0.0131	0.0138	0.0145

Source: Authors' calculations.
COLAs are assumed to cover half the interest rate. Interest rates are either 6 percent or 11 percent, and wage growth is either 5 percent or 10 percent. Inflation changes in 2000 and again in 2020. The number of observations used in the simulation is 80.

resulting adjustment rate after a decline in the inflation rate is rapid and does not amortize over an extended period. Thus, observed cycles have wider amplitude and are of shorter duration than those that will be observed in the market.

In this simulation, the COLA is assumed not to be anticipated. That is, as is current practice, the worker has no legal right to a COLA, and the accounting scheme does not assume that a COLA increase will be made. (In our earlier simulations, which were based on steady-state assumptions, the COLA was assumed to be funded on a projected liability basis.) Table 8-12 summarizes the distribution of compensation-productivity ratios for each of the eighty cohorts hired from 1946 through 2025, under the assumption that the inflation rate, and thus the discount rate, varies because of unforeseen shocks. For these simulations, the firm is assumed to hire all employees at age 25 and to retire them at the normal age of 62. Thus, for each cohort, compensation and productivity are measured over the thirty-seven years of employment and the retirement period. In the first column, the inflation rate is assumed to begin at 6 percent, to increase to 11 percent from 2000 through 2020 (with the change not foreseen by the workers or the firm), and to fall again to 6 percent after 2020. For the second column, the sequence is reversed. The discount rate begins at 11 percent and falls to 6 percent in 2000, rising again to 11 percent in 2020. In columns 3 and 4, the sequence is repeated, but in each case there is a COLA that amounts to half the inflation rate.

Beginning with the scenario that underlies the descriptive statistics in column 1, an acceleration in inflation in the year 2000 reduces the real compensation of those who are retired at the time inflation accelerates and reduces the real value of the fixed, nominal pension. The cohort hired on January 1, 1947 at age 25 is the first one affected. Those in this cohort are retired for one year at the higher inflation rate, just before dying on their 80th birthday. The cohort hired in 1963 will work entirely at the lower interest rate and will retire just after inflation accelerates, so that they will receive their pensions entirely in a period of higher inflation. This unfortunate timing depresses the later cohort's compensation-productivity ratio to .973 (i.e., by 2.7 percent), or one year's compensation.

Among the gainers are those who work during a period of higher inflation, when their wages are increased to compensate for the expectation of a lower real pension, and then retire during a period of lower inflation. Other gainers are those who are contributing just after the inflation rate increases. Their contributions are reduced to zero until the surplus in the fund is exhausted.

The descriptive statistics for the four simulations suggest that pension COLAs do not necessarily dampen the variation in total income over workers' lifetimes. Mechanically, the COLA widens the variation in income-compensation ratios if it raises the ratios for those who, in the absence of a COLA, would have a compensation-productivity ratio that was greater than one. It also widens the variation if the COLA reduces the ratio of compensation to productivity for those who would have a ratio, in the absence of a COLA, of less than one.

Consider the changes experienced by some cohorts. Focus first on those on board when a pay-as-you-go COLA system starts up. If there is no COLA, in the sequence in which inflation rises and then falls, cohorts hired from 1946 through 1955 have replacement rates that are at or just below 1.0. When there is a COLA, these cohorts exhibit replacement rates that are one to two percentage points above 1.0. Thus, the cohort hired in 1950 has the same productivity in both sequences, pays about $400 more in contributions with a COLA, receives about $100 more in basic benefits, and receives $4,800 worth of COLA adjustments that it would not otherwise receive. When inflation falls and then rises, even stronger gains accrue to those hired from 1946 through 1974, again raising the intergenerational variation in benefit-compensation ratios.

For the sequence in which inflation rises and then falls, cohorts hired in the 1970s, who will retire seven years after inflation accelerates, have compensation-productivity ratios that are one-half to two percentage points above 1.0. With a COLA, these ratios are even higher. For those hired from 1980 to 2000, when the sequence is a rise and then a fall in inflation, the COLA reduces compensation-productivity ratios from one-half to two and a half points above 1.0, to ratios that are closer to 1.0. In these cases, the COLA reduces the variation in compensation-productivity ratios. For the scenario in which inflation falls and then rises, the COLA reduces the variation for cohorts hired in the 1980s, increasing ratios of compensation to productivity that are one to three percentage points below 1.0.

In the scenario of increasing and then falling inflation, the COLA raises the variation in compensation-productivity ratios among generations hired from 2005 to 2025. It does so by reducing replacement rates that were already below 1.0. Thus, for someone hired in 2010 who will retire in 2047, the contribution rate to the basic pension is about \$7,000 higher when there is a COLA than when there is no COLA, the basic benefit is about \$700 lower than when there is no COLA, and the COLA benefit itself amounts to \$5,700. Even without the COLA, the compensation-productivity ratio is below 1.0, so that when the COLA reduces the net value of the pension further for this cohort by requiring an incremental contribution that exceeds the incremental benefit, the variation in the compensation-productivity ratio increases.

In contrast, in the scenario in which the inflation rate falls and then rises, the effect of the COLA is to reduce the variation among cohorts hired from 2005 to 2025. It does so by reducing compensation-productivity ratios from a level that is one-half to two percentage points above 1.0 when there is no COLA and to lower ratios that nevertheless remain above 1.0 when there is a COLA.

Thus, the net effect of a COLA on the distribution of compensation-productivity ratios depends on the aggregate of results for separate cohorts that are affected differently by the introduction and funding of a COLA. The effect for each cohort depends on how the change in this ratio, brought about by the induced changes in benefits and contributions, is related to the basic compensation-productivity ratio in the absence of a COLA. Note also that those who are on board at the time of plan termination for a system that included a pay-as-you-go COLA will be adversely affected. While working, they will have made contributions under a pay-as-you-go system to support COLAs for those in earlier generations. But when their turn comes, there will be no flow of contributions to support their benefits. The statistics on intergenerational inequality reported in table 8-12 do not include those generations affected by plan termination, however.

To isolate the effects of start-up, it is useful to recalculate the descriptive statistics from table 8-13 for the cohorts who spend an entire thirty-seven years covered by the plan. For the fifty-five cohorts in the simulation covered for their full working lives, the effects of the pension COLA depend on the sequence of inflation shocks. On the one hand, even when those in the start-up phase are eliminated, when the sequence is a rising and then a falling inflation, the COLA increases the coefficient of variation of the ratio of compensation to productivity from 0.0120 to 0.0149. On the other hand, when the sequence is falling and then rising inflation, the coefficient of variation computed for the cohorts hired from 1970 through 2025 falls from 0.0140 when there is no COLA and to 0.0091 when there is a COLA.

In sum, pension COLAs do not necessarily reduce the variation in pension benefits. To be sure, a person who has just retired will experience lower variation in real income if he or she is covered by a COLA. And, under some scenarios, COLAs may have the effect of reducing the variation in lifetime real incomes among cohorts. But again, they may not. Careful analysis of the timing and funding of the scheme is required before one can reach any conclusions as to the importance of pension COLAs for reducing the risk to lifetime incomes from varying inflation rates.

POLICY IMPLICATIONS

We have offered some evidence about the behavioral motivations for pension COLAs and their role in the labor market, but much remains to be learned about the behavior that underlies the choice of pensions and pension COLAs. Until we are closer to having a plausible structural explanation and some estimates of key behavioral parameters, it would be injudicious to make strong statements about policy. Nevertheless, our analysis does not offer strong support in favor of expanding pension regulation to cover pension COLAs.

Changes in the price level over time have the effect of eroding the real value of a pension benefit that is fixed in nominal terms. At recently experienced inflation rates, a pension without COLA coverage may have only a fraction of the purchasing power near the end of the retirement period that it afforded immediately after retirement. When there is COLA coverage, a significant fraction of the total pension value may be accounted for by the COLA provision. Thus, we find empirically that pension COLAs are an important phenomenon. The relative importance of pension COLAs, and the fact that they are unfunded, certainly justifies closer examination of the economic behavior that underlies them.

We find no evidence that pension COLAs have played an important role in preserving incentives affecting worker turnover, retirement decisions, or shirking behavior. The effects of pension COLAs on the relevant incentives appear to be small, and alternative adjustments in the wage or pension benefit levels may provide superior ways to adjust to unforeseen inflation. Accordingly, policies regulating COLAs cannot be justified by a desire to increase the efficient operation of the labor market and related personnel policies. At the same time, there is no evidence that there will be severe consequences for productivity should the government decide to regulate or promote pension COLAs.

As long as compensating differentials are an important phenomenon, an economic rationale for mandating pension cost-of-living adjustments would have to show that workers misunderstand pension promises, that firms renege on these promises (especially if they are underfunded), that insurance is required against the effects of fluctuations in inflation over the cycle, and that the market is failing to provide such insurance. There is some evidence that raises questions about covered workers' understanding of their pensions (Mitchell 1988b; Gustman and Steinmeier 1989a), but this is insufficient to conclude that firms or individuals are so poorly informed that plan provisions should be determined outside the market. Moreover, workers must be convinced that pension COLAs will be forthcoming before compensating differentials will arise, and without compensating differentials competitive firms will be unable to offer cost-of-living adjustments to their workers. We do not yet know whether the fact that COLAs are ad hoc is evidence of rents or whether ad hoc COLAs are sufficiently valued that workers have accepted reductions in wages to pay for them.

So the question is, Where is the market failure? Partial pension insurance may be cost-effective (Feldstein 1983), so that firms have an incentive to provide it. The fear that firms will renege on an implicit contract would seem to provide only a weak justification for policies regulating pension COLAs and their funding. Current policy already permits a sharp discrepancy between the insured and projected liability from pensions and requires funding only for the accrued liability (Ippolito 1986). The liability from an unfunded pension COLA that has not yet been granted would seem to represent an obligation that is of an even lower order of priority. Finally, even if there is market failure that would justify mandating and closely regulating the provision and funding of pension COLAs, market adjustments in the wage and other provisions of the pension plan would make it extremely difficult to achieve any desired outcomes.

Summary

In this chapter we examined cost-of-living adjustments in pensions from the perspective of labor economics. Our aim was to describe pension COLAs and their effects on the level of pension wealth and the rate of accrual in pension wealth with continued work and to derive implications for the role of pension COLAs in the labor market and pension policy. Evidence from longitudinal microeconomic surveys of retirees' pension and annuity incomes suggests that pension COLAs were less important in the 1980s than in the 1970s. Nevertheless, they continued to offset about half the cost-of-living increases even in the latter period. In addition, we examined a longitudinal sample of pension COLA provisions from firms surveyed by the Wyatt Company over the period of 1968–88. We calculated the frequency and size of COLA increases and concluded that over the entire period retirees received pension increases in one-quarter of the years. This happened even though inflation rates fell in the second half of the period. The COLA increases were sizable: they represented 40 percent of the basic pension value over the twenty-year period. These increases were not uniform: those who had been retired longer received average annual raises of 2.2 percent between 1984 and 1988, while those who were retired for fewer than five years received increases averaging 1.1 percent per year. Moreover, conditional on years since retirement, the frequency and size of the COLA increases were lower, relative to cost-of-living increases, in the 1978–88 period than in the 1968–78 period.

To explore the effects of inflation and pension COLAs on incentives to retire, move, or shirk, we turned to a simulation analysis. That analysis suggests that pension COLA provisions are probably not motivated primarily by desires to preserve the pension incentives, as emphasized by the leading economic theories of pensions. The reason is that the pension COLAs have only a small effect on these incentives. We also found that pension COLAs do not necessarily reduce the variation in compensation among generations of employees, even in the face of sharp inflation shocks. Indeed, when account is taken not only of the pension benefits but also of the contributions to support the pension plan (and thus of the feedback effect on wages), pension COLAs under certain circumstances can exacerbate the variation in compensation among cohorts. Further analysis of the timing and funding of pension COLAs is required before one can determine the effects of inflation on compensation risk.

Finally, we conclude that there is no indication of market failure that would justify efforts to mandate or regulate pension COLAs. Nor is there evidence to suggest that regulating pension COLAs would have adverse side effects on worker productivity.

TABLE 8A. MEAN OF LOG PENSION BENEFIT CHANGES IN MICRO DATA SETS

	NLS[a] Men	NLS[a] Women	PSID[b]	RHS[a]	SCF[a]	Allen, Clark, Sumner (1986)	CPI
1971–72			0.038	{.028			.033
1972–73			0.030	{			.062
1973–74	{ 0.034[a]		0.018	{.032		.036	.110
1974–75	{		0.061	{	.041	.041	.091
1975–76	−0.009		0.048	{.051		.038	.058
1976–77	{ 0.036		0.035	{		.029	.065
1977–78	{		0.016	{.040		.045	.077
1978–79	{ 0.035		0.031	{		.029	.113
1979–80	{		0.044				.135
1980–81	0.037		0.042				.104
1981–82	{ 0.031		0.038				.061
1982–83	{	{0.099	0.025				.032
1983–84		{	0.013		{0.006		.043
1984–85		{0.025	0.025		{		.036
1985–86		{	0.015		{		.019
1986–87		0.002	0.023				.037

Source: Authors' calculations and Allen, Clark, and Sumner 1986.

To avoid the possibility that the pension was paid during only part of the initial year, in calculating pension changes, the pension observations for the first year of retirement are excluded.

[a]A change over a two- or three-year period is indicated when a number preceded by a bracket is followed by two or three brackets, vertically aligned, that are not followed by a number. Whatever number is followed by a sequence of brackets reports the percentage change over the full indicated period.

[b]With regard to the results for the PSID, the first two cells in the tables may contain observations of government pensions, since there is no way in the PSID to divide pensions into private versus government without reference to the job from which the pension came. Particularly for the early years, information about the pension job is not generally available.

TABLE 8B.   MEAN POSTRETIREMENT PENSION BENEFIT INCREASE AS A PERCENTAGE OF CURRENT BENEFITS, BY YEARS SINCE RETIREMENT AND YEAR OF BENEFIT INCREASE

Year of Increase	Years since Retirement			
	1–5	6–10	11–15	16–20
1969	1.9%			
1970	1.9			
1971	15.6			
1972	1.2			
1973	2.0			
1974	3.4	4.3%		
1975	2.6	3.1		
1976	2.9	3.6		
1977	2.3	2.4		
1978	4.7	5.5		
1979	4.3	5.1	6.4%	
1980	5.5	6.3	7.0	
1981	5.5	6.3	7.5	
1982	0.6	0.7	0.8	
1983	1.2	1.3	1.4	
1984	1.0	1.0	1.1	1.2%
1985	1.6	2.0	2.5	2.9
1986	1.6	1.9	2.2	2.6
1987	0.8	1.0	1.1	1.2
1988	1.7	2.2	2.6	3.1
Simple average, 1984–88	1.3	1.6	1.9	2.2

Source: Authors' calculations, based on Wyatt Company data.

PART III.
POLICY CHALLENGES OF AN AGING WORKFORCE

Chapter 9.
SOCIAL SECURITY AND OLDER WORKERS

Michael V. Leonesio

T HE WELL-DOCUMENTED post–World War II trend to earlier retirement in the United States can be viewed as a laudable achievement made possible by the nation's economic prosperity. Nonetheless, the reduction in the labor supply of older workers that this entails can have adverse consequences. First, to the degree that the social security program encourages full or partial retirement from the marketplace, the economy's pool of experienced labor is reduced and the nation's aggregate output is lower. Second, reductions in labor market activity by older workers decrease social security revenues and increase program expenditures, thereby disturbing the financial balance of the system. And third, reduced earnings can harm the economic well-being of the elderly by affecting both the size and the distribution of incomes. In light of the aging of the American population and workforce that is projected into the next century, there has been considerable public discussion about the extent to which government programs and policies discourage employment among older workers (see, for example, U.S. Department of Labor 1989).

Social security program rules have always embodied features that were likely to influence work and retirement decisions. A striking example is the original version of the retirement test, in which no earnings were to be permitted if benefits were to be paid that month. This severe

The author wishes to thank Benjamin Bridges, Jr., Gary Fields, Selig Lesnoy, Jan Olson, and John Straka for their helpful comments on earlier drafts of this paper. The views expressed are the author's and do not necessarily represent the position of the Social Security Administration or the U.S. Department of Health and Human Services.

restriction on work was quickly modified (in 1939 legislation, before it ever went into effect), and the limitation on earnings has been subsequently relaxed many times. More recently, the 1983 amendments to the Social Security Act contained various provisions that were intended to promote work. Congress voted for the following:

A gradual increase in the normal retirement age to 67. Beginning in 2000, the normal retirement age will be increased to 66 in 2009, and to 67 in 2027.

A gradual increase in the penalty for early retirement concurrent with increases in the normal retirement age. By 2027, retirement at age 62 will reduce the benefit amount by 30 percent of the primary insurance amount (PIA), rather than the current 20 percent.

A reduction in the retirement test reduction rate from one-half to one-third for beneficiaries aged 65 to 69, effective in 1990.

A gradual increase in the delayed retirement credit (DRC), from 3 percent to 8 percent. The DRC is scheduled to rise by .5 percent every other year, beginning in 1990, until it reaches 8 percent in 2008.

Continued increases in the annual exempt amount that can be earned under the retirement test. The exempt amount increases each year at the same rate as the increase in average wages.

In addition to changes that have already been enacted, other proposals that are intended to encourage work have been advanced. Among these are the following:

Eliminate the retirement test, or liberalize it further by either increasing the annual exempt amount beyond what is currently scheduled or lowering the benefit reduction rate.

Accelerate the timing of the scheduled increase in the DRC.

Further increase the normal retirement age or the early retirement age, or both.

Change benefit recomputation rules to give more weight to earnings in later years.

Eliminate the payroll tax for workers aged 65 and older.

Increase the income threshold at which benefits are subject to federal income taxation.

Some of these changes are clearly more likely to be enacted than others. For example, there are currently House, Senate, and administration proposals to increase the retirement test's annual earnings limit above currently scheduled amounts for persons aged 65 to 69, and some modest change would be no surprise. Other reforms are a more remote possibility.

How effective would these reforms be in inducing Americans to alter their retirement behavior? I recently reviewed approximately one hundred empirical retirement studies—most of which were written during the past decade—in an effort to discover what is known about the effect of social security on retirement decisions (Leonesio 1990b). On the basis of this research, it appears that changes in social security programs of the type and magnitude that are politically feasible in the foreseeable future are unlikely to produce large changes in retirement patterns. This chapter summarizes the evidence.

The discussion will be confined to the old-age and survivors insurance (OASI) components of social security and will omit any consideration of the disability insurance, medicare, and supplemental security income programs. Substantial attention is given to one particular feature of the OASI program that is often alleged to pose an employment barrier— the retirement test.

OASI AND THE DECISION TO RETIRE

The economic literature on the determinants of individual retirement decisions is both extensive and difficult to summarize. In addition to the problem of evaluating the relative credibility of the various studies, problems are created by the use of different models, different populations (for example, workers aged 62 to 65 versus workers aged 60 and older), and different definitions of what constitutes retirement.[1] Because there is no universally employed definition of the term, it is possible for different "retirement" studies to arrive at apparently conflicting conclusions about the importance of suspected causes because they are not actually studying the same phenomenon.

In a way, the research results are probably somewhat at odds with

1. Retirement has been said to occur when individuals leave their career jobs (even if they continue to work full time), withdraw from the labor force, significantly reduce their hours of work, work or earn less than some specified level, begin to receive a pension or social security benefits (or both), or declare themselves to be retired (Murray 1979; Ekerdt and DeViney 1990). In recent years there has been a shift in thinking away from viewing retirement as a discrete event toward viewing it as a more protracted process (Doeringer 1990).

186   *Michael V. Leonesio*

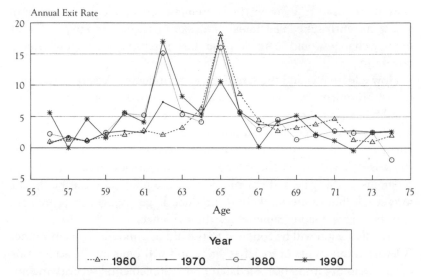

Source: 1960 data from Munnell 1977, table 4–3. Participation rates for later years are from unpublished data obtained from the U.S. Department of Labor.

FIGURE 9-1.   RETIREMENT RATES FOR MALES IN THE UNITED STATES, 1960–90

what one might expect on the basis of casual observation. After all, social security is the largest source of income for the retired population and certainly seems to play a very large role in the economic well-being of the aged. The post–World War II expansion of the social security system roughly coincides with the well-documented decline in the average retirement age of men and the sharp decline in the labor force participation rate of men aged 60 and older. Retirement at ages 62 and 65—social security's early and normal retirement ages—is popular, as can be seen in figure 9-1, which displays male retirement age patterns for 1960, 1970, 1980, and 1990. Each graph approximates the rates at which men of different ages left the labor force in those four years.[2]

In each of the four years represented in the figure, a pronounced peak occurs at age 65, the normal retirement age, which is the age at which

2. The retirement rate for age x is estimated by taking the difference in the labor force participation rate at age x with that for age $x - 1$, and dividing by the participation rate at age 55.

full social security retirement benefits are payable. Unlike the 1960 profile, however, the 1970, 1980, and 1990 graphs show a second peak at age 62. This is probably the result of the 1961 introduction of early retirement, permitting receipt of reduced retirement benefits at age 62. The data show that over the past three decades there has been a gradual, marked increase in the popularity of retirement at age 62. If the benefit reduction rate for retirement before age 65 is actuarially fair, which it roughly appears to be (Aaron 1982:62–63), and if individuals could borrow against future social security entitlements, then there should be no observed bunching of retirement at age 62. Individuals wanting to retire before age 62 could help finance this choice by establishing a retirement fund through private lenders, using their social security entitlements as collateral. That capital markets do not finance such an arrangement results in the peak at age 62 in the retirement age profile (Crawford and Lilien 1981). Most individuals with small amounts of liquid assets cannot afford to retire before age 62, when they first have access to their social security wealth. It is difficult to account for the double-peaked pattern in the 1970–90 graphs, or for the increased popularity of departure from the labor force at age 62, without assigning a central role to social security.

In surveys of retirees conducted during the first three decades of the existence of social security, respondents usually claimed that they retired either because their employers terminated their jobs, or because of health problems. The pronounced decline in labor force participation by men aged 62 and older during the 1960s and 1970s was associated with an increased incidence of voluntary departures from the labor force (Quinn, Burkhauser, and Myers 1990). Thus, according to Sally R. Sherman (1985), by the early 1980s, a majority of new male social security beneficiaries were indicating that retirement was self-initiated.

Retirement research proliferated during the 1970s and 1980s, stimulated in large part by the availability of a valuable new data source: the Social Security Administration's Retirement History Survey (RHS). This survey collected information on a nationally representative sample of more than eleven thousand men and unmarried women during six biannual interviews conducted during 1969–79. Respondents were aged 58 to 63 at the time of the initial interview. A large majority of the sample "retired" during the sample period, and the survey documents many of the attendant economic and personal circumstances. Much of what economists currently believe about retirement behavior in the United States derives from this database.

Most economic research now reflects the view that, for the most part, retirement is a choice made by workers who rationally weigh the personal advantages and disadvantages of continued labor force participation. Although the emphasis in economic models is certainly on the financial aspects of the decision, the research also addresses the coincidental impact of general economic conditions, personal characteristics (particularly age), health status, and individual attitudes toward work. In general, the findings support the view that earlier retirements have been largely voluntary, as workers have been increasingly able to afford to retire.

At the core of much of the economic analysis of retirement behavior is a *life-cycle* view of work, saving, and consumption. That is, individuals are assumed to be well-informed, far-sighted planners whose economic decisions represent integrated, long-term plans expected to generate adequate income to support a desired standard of living. Because the level of work activity that is anticipated in each future year is part of a long-range plan, any factor that ostensibly affects the incentive to work during one period can influence the amount of work planned for other periods as well. For example, a progressive tax on earned income might cause work to be shifted from high-earnings years to low-earnings years in order to lower lifetime tax liability. Viewed from a life-cycle perspective, decisions about leaving a career job, accepting a pension, applying for social security benefits, working in a postretirement job, and the like are all interdependent.

Within this life-cycle framework, the effects of social security on work are ambiguous; perhaps some persons are induced to retire earlier and others later. To the extent that the system forces people to save for their retirement and that the adjustment in benefit levels for delaying the onset of benefits is less than actuarially fair, *earlier* retirements are more likely to be encouraged. The material that follows summarizes the empirical evidence. In the interest of brevity, specific citations are limited to studies that are representative of the most persuasive scholarship; omission should not be taken to construe rejection or criticism.

Because social security benefits represent a substantial portion of retirement income for most Americans, their role in the retirement decision has been closely examined. Monthly benefit amounts influence both the timing of retirement and the choice of postretirement hours of work. Other things being equal, higher benefits are expected to promote earlier retirement, decrease the likelihood of working among retirees, and reduce the hours of work by labor force participants. Causation runs in the other direction as well, however, with the retirement decision affecting the value of the monthly benefit via three separate channels. First, at any time between the ages of 62 and 70, the actuarial adjustment and delayed retirement credit increase the amount of the monthly benefit when acceptance of benefits is postponed. Second, as long as annual earnings are greater than the smallest value included in the computation years for determining average indexed monthly earnings (AIME), postponing retirement will increase the primary insurance amount upon which the benefit amount is based.[3] Third, for some individuals, a delay in retirement can result in their accumulating the minimum number of quarters of covered employment to qualify for retirement benefits. Therefore, although in all three instances a delay in retirement would lead to increased monthly benefit amounts, higher benefit levels in and of themselves lower the probability of labor force participation.

Studies that use appropriate statistical procedures to account for the simultaneity between social security benefits and the timing of retirement usually find a negative relationship between benefit amounts and both retirement age and postretirement labor supply, although there is some variation in the estimated magnitude of the effects. Research on male retirement behavior has shown that increases in monthly benefit levels on the order of 10 to 20 percent have been associated with a decline in retirement age measured more in terms of weeks or a few months than many months or a few years. Defining retirement as a pronounced, permanent decline in annual earnings, Gary T. Burtless and Robert A. Moffitt (1984, 1985) find that a 20 percent benefit cut would cause the average male retirement age to increase by one or two months. Fields and Mitchell (1984) report about the same result: a 10 percent cut in monthly benefits would delay retirement (defined as leaving the originally observed job) by about a month. Similarly small effects associated with OASI benefit levels are reported by Richard V. Burkhauser (1980),

---

3. The primary insurance amount is the monthly amount payable to a retired worker who begins to receive benefits at age 65 and is calculated on the basis of the individual's earnings record.

Peter A. Diamond and Jerry A. Hausman (1984), Roger Gordon and Alan Blinder (1980), and Hausman and David A. Wise (1985).

While most economic models treat income streams as if they can be accurately foreseen, Burtless (1986) investigates the implications of changes in income that are *unexpected*, which was probably the case for most social security beneficiaries when large real increases in payments were approved by Congress in 1969 and 1972. Benefit increases of 10 percent above those that would have occurred under the existing rules were implemented in these years. Over a span of three years, real benefit levels rose approximately 20 percent beyond what would have been anticipated. The estimated effect was to reduce the average retirement age of men by just over one month (where retirement is defined as a discontinuous drop in annual hours worked). Had these income changes been fully anticipated, the long-term effect would have been to reduce the average retirement age by about two months.[4]

The effects of other social security features have been studied as well. On average, the influence of social security's normal retirement age (NRA) on the timing of retirement also appears to be modest. Gustman and Steinmeier (1985b) examine the effect of raising the NRA to 67 while increasing the penalty for early retirement at age 62 (to 30 percent of PIA). This is predicted to move the peak in the male retirement age distribution (self-assessed definition) from age 65 to age 67. It would be expected to increase the percentage of men working full time at ages 65 and 66 by about four to six percentage points and to lower the percentage working part time by one to two percentage points. This translates into an increase of about two months in the average retirement age. Gary S. Fields and Mitchell (1984) simulate the effect of raising the NRA to 68, leaving the actuarial adjustment rate for early retirement unchanged; that is, persons applying for benefits at age 62 would receive

4. B. Douglas Bernheim (1988) tested the accuracy with which expectations were formed about social security benefit amounts. He found that both men and women in the Retirement History Survey underestimated their benefits, indicating that the large real increases in social security benefit levels that occurred in the early 1970s were unanticipated, as suggested by Burtless. Individuals appear to think seriously about future benefits but do not forecast values very precisely. While they process the information that they have reasonably efficiently, many persons appear not to incorporate a great deal of relevant information available from the Social Security Administration. Note that the RHS data were collected well before the advent of the Personal Earnings and Benefit Estimate Statements (PEBES) that are now available on request. These statements inform individuals of their estimated social security benefits based on past and anticipated earnings.

60 percent of PIA. This policy change increased the average retirement age by 1.6 months, a little less than the magnitude of response predicted by Gustman and Steinmeier. Burtless and Moffitt (1984) conduct the same exercise and report an increase of 2.5 to 4.5 months.

Increasing the delayed retirement credit is thought to be one of the more effective ways of encouraging individuals to work after age 65. Here too the responses tend to be on the order of magnitude of a few months. Burtless and Moffitt (1984) predict that actuarially fair adjustments for delaying benefit acceptance would delay retirement by 4.5 months, on average. Gustman and Steinmeier (1985b) confirm this magnitude: full-time employment among men aged 65 to 66 would rise by four to six percentage points, while partial retirement would fall by about two percentage points. Fields and Mitchell (1984) indicate that increasing the DRC to 6.6 percent would delay retirement by about a week.

Although most studies conclude that the influence of social security on overall retirement patterns is modest, it is plausible that the program's financial incentives have very different effects on retirement decisions depending on other factors such as financial status, health, or job characteristics. James A. Kahn (1988) conjectures that, contrary to the assertions of Blinder, Gordon, and Wise (1980), work is not subsidized by the social security system for many older workers, particularly among those aged 62 to 64. In fact, work may be penalized to a greater extent among those who are observed retiring at earlier ages. When the distribution of male retirement ages (self-assessed) reported in the Retirement History Survey is plotted as in figure 9-1, the graph proves to be double-peaked, with the higher peak at ages 62 to 63. When the sample is divided into high-wealth and low-wealth subgroups, however, only the distribution for the low-wealth group is double-peaked, with a very pronounced spike at age 62. The distribution for the high-wealth group is single-peaked, at age 65. This is consistent with the view that the liquidity constraint is more powerful among those with fewer liquid assets.[5]

Kahn (1988) constructs social security wealth profiles using discount rates of 3 and 12 percent. The higher discount rate is consistent with the view that many workers face liquidity constraints in their life-cycle

---

5. Note, however, that this pattern can also be partially explained if low-wealth individuals have offers of jobs with lower wages and less agreeable job characteristics.

work and consumption plans. When using the lower rate, social security seems neither to encourage nor discourage work for persons aged 62 to 64. At the higher rate, it is a clear disincentive; social security wealth falls 2.5 to 5 percent for each additional year of work. The use of higher discount rates undermines Blinder, Gordon, and Wise's basic result (1980) that social security subsidizes work between the ages of 62 and 65.

Joseph F. Quinn (1977) investigates the relative impact of three sets of factors in explaining individual labor force participation decisions of men aged 58 to 63: personal and financial characteristics, local labor market conditions, and job attributes. Although health is found to be the single most influential variable—lowering the probability of participating by 20 percentage points—social security eligibility had a predictably negative effect. The influence of economic variables differed by health status. The effect of social security is eight times as large for those with poor health. Quinn (1978) also finds clear support for the view that people with jobs that have undesirable working conditions are more likely to retire. Persons with poor health are consistently more sensitive to job characteristics, especially those who are also eligible for social security retirement benefits. These results suggest that health status interacts with other retirement influences, particularly job characteristics and social security eligibility, in determining retirement status.

In one of the few studies of women's retirement behavior, Silvana Pozzebon and Mitchell (1989) find that the retirement decisions of married women appear to be relatively insensitive to financial incentives such as social security, a conclusion that is similarly drawn by Therese A. McCarty (1990). Working married women value retirement leisure highly, and there appears to be complementarity with their husbands' retirement leisure. In general, family considerations such as the husband's health status and income, as well as the difference between the husband's and wife's ages, appear to be the stronger influences.

Despite the shortcomings that are inherent in most empirical work, the retirement literature has evolved to the point where certain conclusions can be drawn about the role of social security. Viewed in total, the evidence indicates that the OASI program has contributed to the decline in the labor force participation of older men but that the direct financial effects appear to be modest. The social security system has contributed to the popularity of retirement at ages 62 and 65, as depicted in figure 9-1 but appears to be a minor force in the long post–World War II trend to retire at earlier ages.

THE RETIREMENT TEST

Perhaps no feature of the OASI program has attracted more sustained, vocal criticism over the years than the retirement (or earnings) test.[6] Critics argue that the test is discriminatory (it applies only to persons aged 62 to 69), that it discourages some beneficiaries from working at all, and that it causes others to reduce their hours of work to avoid a loss of benefits. Discussions about institutional barriers to increased labor market activity by older workers often single out this feature of the social security system (Herz and Rones 1989). There is certainly no shortage of anecdotal evidence about beneficiaries limiting their earnings to avoid loss of benefits (Christensen 1990).

The rationale for the retirement test is that retired-worker benefits are a form of social insurance and, as such, serve a purpose distinct from private pensions and annuities. The indemnified contingency under the Old-Age provisions is the loss of sufficient earned income in later years to support an adequate standard of living, not the specific condition of being old (Brown 1972). In recognition that some individuals will retain the capacity and desire to earn income in their later years, the retirement test has always been an integral feature of the retirement program. The test can be viewed as a means of targeting benefits at those persons likely to be in need of transfer income to replace lost earnings.

HOW THE TEST WORKS

Currently, the retirement test allows beneficiaries aged 62 to 69 to earn income up to a specified annual limit, the annual exempt amount, without loss of social security benefits. When earnings exceed this level, benefits are reduced $1 for every $3 earned over the limit for beneficiaries aged 65 to 69 and at a rate of $1 for every $2 for beneficiaries aged 62 to 64. Thus, for the older group, annual earnings in excess of the exempt amount are currently subject to a benefit reduction rate of 33 and 1/3 percent. The dollar amount of the limit depends on the worker's age; for persons aged 62 to 64, the 1992 figure was $7,440, and for those

---

6. A comprehensive review of economic evidence about the effects of the retirement test on older workers' labor supply can be found in Leonesio 1990a, from which material in this section is drawn.

aged 65 and older, it was $10,200. These amounts are increased yearly at the same rate as the increase in average wages.

At first glance, the effect of the retirement test on work effort appears to be clear-cut. Because the test lowers the financial reward for work when earnings exceed the exempt amount, it is tantamount to a tax on work and would seem, therefore, to discourage employment. Nonetheless, the actual impact of the test on labor supply could be modest for at least three reasons. First, other social security provisions that interact with the retirement test—such as the delayed retirement credit and automatic benefit recomputation—can substantially offset its effect. Second, the retirement test creates different work incentives depending on individual circumstances. For example, a worker whose desired annual earnings are several thousand dollars over the annual limit might reduce work effort to avoid loss of benefits, while a worker with earnings so high that benefits are fully withheld might work more to restore the lost income.[7] Third, in the course of calculating the amount by which the retirement test increases marginal tax rates for some workers, it is easy to forget the distinction between work incentives and the degree of responsiveness to those incentives. Although the retirement test might provide a disincentive to work in some situations, this alone is insufficient to conclude that the test causes an appreciable reduction in the overall work effort of older persons. It is necessary to know the extent to which behavior actually changes.

Before turning to the evidence about the work response to the retirement test, consider the first of these points. The actuarial adjustment (AA) for early retirement and the delayed retirement credit reduce the apparent penalty when current benefits are withheld because of the test. From age 62 to 64, the AA restores lost benefits at age 65 at an annual rate of 6.67 percent of the PIA, a rate that is considered to be actuarially fair on average. Insured persons aged 65 to 69 who lose benefits receive a delayed retirement credit, which works in approximately the same way as the actuarial adjustment. At its 1992 rate of 4 percent, the DRC falls considerably short of the 8 percent value that is thought to be about actuarially fair.

A numerical example should clarify how the DRC lowers the effective penalty rate of the earnings test. If a retired worker currently aged 65

---

7. That is, economists recognize that the retirement test can create both income and substitution effects that have opposing influences on work effort.

or older loses some but not all retirement benefits under the retirement test, an additional $300 of earnings results in a further reduction in benefits of $100. If the DRC were to raise future annual benefits by an actuarially fair amount (say, 8 percent), the present value of the additional $8 per year (8 percent of $100) is equal to the $100 in current benefits lost to the test. The actuarially fair DRC fully restores lost benefits, and the overall penalty rate is zero. In contrast, with the DRC at only 4 percent, future annual benefits rise by only $4, with a present value of $50 [(4.0/8.0) × $100]. With this amount of the retirement test penalty restored by the DRC, the effective tax rate is only 16.7 percent [($100 − $50)/$300], rather than the apparent 33 and ⅓ percent. Most current proposals to liberalize or eliminate the retirement test focus on the rules that apply to persons aged 65 and older. Further discussion here will assume that the test operates in the context of a less than actuarially fair DRC.

In addition to the DRC, automatic benefit recomputation (ABR) can lead to increased future benefit payments when current benefits are lost to the retirement test. As long as annual earnings are greater than the smallest indexed value included in the computation years for determining AIME, the ABR provision dictates that continued work will increase future values of the PIA. Thus, the apparent deterrent effect of the retirement test provision can be further offset for workers aged 65 and older by ABR, as well as by the DRC. Before the introduction of indexed earnings in the 1977 social security amendments, ABR was estimated to provide men turning age 65 in 1975 with an average wage subsidy of 54 percent (Blinder, Gordon, and Wise 1980). The switch to indexed earnings in the AIME formula no doubt substantially lowered the average subsidy rate.

EVIDENCE ON THE RETIREMENT TEST

A simple procedure for determining whether the retirement test deters work is to examine annual earnings patterns among social security beneficiaries to see whether unusually large numbers of workers report earnings that are at or near the annual earnings limit. This finding would be consistent with the view that retirees restrain earnings to avoid the retirement test penalty. I recently tabulated 1988 earnings data from the Social Security Administration's Continuous Work History Sample (CWHS) for persons aged 65 to 69 who were either old-age beneficiaries or fully insured nonbeneficiaries. Some of the results of this exercise are

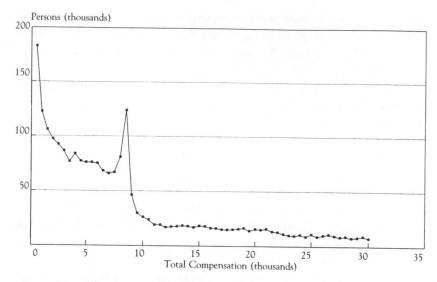

Source: Continuous Work History Sample.

FIGURE 9-2.   1988 EARNINGS PATTERNS OF U.S. RETIREES
(OASI beneficiaries and fully insured nonbeneficiary workers, aged 65–69)

displayed in figure 9-2; not depicted in the figure are the 5,651,500 persons with no reported earnings during the year, and the 333,200 who earned more than $30,000.

There is a clear tendency for workers to keep earnings at or below the retirement test's 1988 annual earnings limit of $8,400.[8] The group most likely to respond in the short run if the retirement test were eliminated is the approximately 200,000 workers with earnings at or near the annual limit (in the $7,500 to 8,500 range). These individuals have demonstrated that they want to work, and their earnings levels suggest that they may be sensitive to the annual limit and avoid the retirement test penalty by reducing their work hours. This group represents only about 2 percent of insured persons aged 65 to 69, however, a figure that necessarily limits the impact that their behavior could have on aggregate labor supply. Furthermore, it is not obvious that all earners in this range limit work activity because of the test. Finally, any increase

8. Despite the actuarial fairness (on average) of the actuarial adjustment, the distribution of earnings among beneficiaries aged 62 to 64 is similar in appearance, exhibiting a spike near their 1988 annual limit of $6,120.

in work effort forthcoming from this group would be contingent on their ability to adjust their work hours freely, an option that may not be 3available to all employees, or on their willingness to change jobs.

One would also expect other workers with reported earnings either below or above the annual limit to adjust their hours. Although some workers have only modest earnings aspirations and are not affected by the test, others might well respond to elimination or liberalization of the retirement test by switching to higher-paying jobs. Workers whose benefits are partially reduced by the retirement test—approximately 200,000—might either increase or decrease their hours of work, depending on whether they react primarily to the work stimulus of a higher rate of pay or to their enhanced ability to afford retirement leisure when retirement test-reduced benefits are restored. Giora Hanoch and Marjorie Honig (1983) find that the dominant effect is likely to be increased work effort in response to the higher take-home wage.

Some individuals are likely to reduce their labor supply in the short run. Beneficiaries with earnings so high that benefits are fully withheld—approximately 250,000—would have a clear incentive to work less. Eliminating the retirement test would increase their incomes, enhancing their ability to afford retirement leisure, but would leave their net wage unchanged at the margin. In addition, people currently eligible for retirement benefits but who do not claim them since their earnings are sufficiently high that most or all their benefits would be lost to the test would be likely to apply for benefits. These individuals would also be expected to behave in much the same way as current beneficiaries whose benefits are wholly offset.

The tendency for many beneficiaries to report earnings at or near the annual earnings limit, as depicted in figure 9-2, has been documented by many researchers (Gallaway 1965; Sander 1968; Burtless and Moffitt 1984; Vroman 1985; Lingg 1986; Packard 1990). Collectively, these studies support the view that through the years the retirement test has depressed the earnings of older workers, but the magnitude of this phenomenon appears to have declined over time as the test has been substantially liberalized. Wayne Vroman (1985) reports that as the earnings limit was increased annually from 1970–80, the noticeable cluster of workers with earnings just below the limit appeared to move upward accordingly, consistent with the view that workers were aware of the current exempt amount and continued to restrain earnings to avoid exceeding the limit. The clustering became less pronounced over the period, however. Vroman also notes that labor force reentry rates for retirees aged 65 to 71 appeared to be unresponsive to these changes in the earnings limit, even after unusually large increases in 1973 and 1978.

Periodic changes in earnings test rules and coverage have afforded some of the best opportunities for learning about the impact of the retirement test on labor supply. When key provisions of the test are changed, postchange behavior can be compared with that recorded during the prechange period. In 1983, the age at which OASI beneficiaries were exempt from the earnings test was lowered from 72 to 70. Michael D. Packard (1990) compares the labor force participation rates of 70- and 71-year-olds before and after 1983, looks for evidence of increases in earnings among those who choose to work, and checks for increased labor force reentry rates. He finds little change in the labor force participation rate of 70- and 71-year-olds when they were no longer subject to the retirement test. There is some evidence that the number of men and women returning to the labor force increased slightly in 1983 and 1984 but fell back to former rates in 1985, suggesting that eliminating the retirement test might have had some short-term effect on beneficiaries who were fully retired. A significant number of elderly workers increased their earnings from below to above the earnings limit when they were no longer subject to the test. This was especially true for men; the proportion increasing their earnings in this way more than doubled compared with the average for the five-year period before 1983.

Packard reports one curiosity: most of the reentrants reported earnings that were below the annual exempt amount and would not have lost benefits in any case, indicating a possible misperception of retirement test rules by retirees who want to work. Apparently many current and prospective beneficiaries are not well informed about the details of the retirement test provision, let alone the way it interacts with the DRC and ABR.[9] This raises a number of interesting questions about the

---

9. Packard (1985) examined responses to the 1982 New Beneficiary Survey, in which recent retirees were asked several questions about retirement test rules. Although 73 percent of retirees under the age 72 knew of the test, less than half the working retirees could identify the annual earnings limit accurately (within 5 percent of the true figure). Nonworking beneficiaries were substantially less knowledgeable than their working counterparts. In a study of thirty-six older workers in the New York City metropolitan area, many individuals reported part-time and self-employed jobs that were off the books (Christensen 1990). In most instances, they claimed that their earnings were not reported

accuracy of predicting the behavioral consequences of changing a provision that is poorly understood.[10]

Generally, studies that use aggregate labor supply measures such as participation rates or numbers of older workers indicate that the retirement test has little impact on the overall retirement picture. Nonetheless, it is possible that a minority of the elderly population is quite sensitive to the retirement test and that these individuals modify their desired work schedules appreciably. These retirement test–induced labor supply adjustments might be hard to detect given the relatively small number of people involved and the existence of other confounding influences. To accomplish this task requires more refined statistical analysis of detailed information on individuals' work histories, sources of income, and personal characteristics.

Anthony J. Pellechio (1978) authored one of the earliest attempts to estimate the effect of the retirement test on work and reports that repealing the test in 1972 would have resulted in an additional three hours of work per week for those beneficiaries who worked.[11] This result was derived from a period in which the retirement test was substantially more restrictive and when the DRC was only 1 percent and restored a smaller portion of the benefits lost to the retirement test.

Several researchers have examined the effect of the retirement test from a more explicit life-cycle planning perspective. That is, people are assumed to make decisions about all aspects of their lifetime work schedules as part of an integrated planning problem. Once these more complex decision rules have been estimated, it is possible to determine how various components of the lifetime labor supply would adjust to changes in key determinants. Burtless and Moffitt (1984, 1985) estimate the effect of the outright elimination of the retirement test for all age groups, including those aged 62 to 64. Only 10 percent of 62-year-old retirees would respond at all, but the average increase for this group is a substantial 10.6 hours per week. The size of the increase would decline

---

for fear of losing social security benefits, even though these earnings were typically less than $5,000 per year—well below the annual exempt amount in 1987 ($8,160).

10. Blinder, Gordon, and Wise (1980) suggest that work effort might be stimulated if social security provisions were better understood. Some individuals might be reducing their labor supply while thinking the restrictions on working are more severe than they are.

11. Increasing the annual exempt amount from $1,680 to $10,000 would raise annual hours by 57, while lowering the benefit reduction rate from 50 to 25 percent resulted in reducing annual hours by between 98 and 140, depending on the assumed exempt amount.

with age. The estimated change in the timing of retirement (defined as a pronounced decline in annual earnings) is small; for the average retiree with earnings above the limit, the retirement date would occur about three weeks earlier. Burtless and Moffitt conclude that eliminating the retirement test provision would have little effect on the overall retirement picture.

Gustman and Steinmeier (1991) simulate the labor supply response to changes in the retirement test and related provisions. Changes in the DRC are shown to dominate the effect of eliminating the retirement test. In any event, the predicted increase in aggregate male labor supply is relatively small. Simply increasing the DRC to 8 percent in 1990 expands the number of full-time male workers aged 65 to 69 by about 45,000, while eliminating the retirement test in the face of the gradual rise in the DRC scheduled under current law produces an increase of 17,000 full-time workers. A combined policy of eliminating the retirement test and immediately increasing the DRC to 8 percent increases the supply of full-time male workers by 47,000, only marginally larger than the response forthcoming from solely increasing the DRC.

Cordelia Reimers and Marjorie Honig (1990) look at whether the retirement test deters labor force reentry among men who have left a career job. They find that among white males, the probability of labor force reentry is negatively affected by the current value of monthly social security benefits. A 10 percent increase in monthly benefits lowers the probability of reentry by .037. The number of hours that individuals can work before reaching the retirement test's annual earnings limit also affects the probability of reentry. A 10 percent increase in the hours implied by the limit increases the probability of reentry by .20, even for persons under age 65.

Finally, an interesting piece of evidence comes from the Canadian experience (Tracy 1982). Canada's social security system abolished a fairly restrictive retirement test in 1975. At the time, the Canadian annual earnings limit was even lower than that in force for Americans (U.S.$1,868 versus U.S.$2,520), with the same benefit reduction rate of 50 cents on the dollar for earnings over the limit. The labor force participation rates of men aged 65 to 69 declined in four of the five years following repeal of the test. During the entire 1962–80 period, the single largest decline in participation (4.5 percentage points) occurred in the year immediately following elimination of the test. There has been no rigorous investigation of this information, in which other factors that may have been at work are taken into account, so conclusions must be viewed with some skepticism. Nonetheless, the episode provides some evidence that the expectation of a large increase in work activity in response to eliminating the retirement test might be unfulfilled.

In sum, economic research indicates that the social security retirement test plays a relatively small role in determining the aggregate labor supply of older workers. There appear to be several explanations for these findings. First, research suggests that retirement decisions are influenced by the availability and generosity of social security and private pensions, health status, job characteristics, wage offers, family circumstances, and personal preferences for work versus leisure time. These other contributing factors that encourage or enable retirement appear to be dominant. Second, other social security provisions, particularly the actuarial adjustment for early retirement, the delayed retirement credit, and the automatic benefit recomputation feature, significantly offset the apparent penalty of the test. Third, the retirement test has been substantially liberalized over the years, permitting beneficiaries to earn more money without loss of benefits. Although earlier, more stringent forms of the test may have posed significant work disincentives, the current rules are far less restrictive. Fourth, some beneficiaries are undoubtedly sensitive to the retirement test and respond by making important adjustments in their lifetime labor supply plans. Nonetheless, the relatively small size of this group limits any impact that their response can have when the aggregate behavior of many millions of people is measured. Finally, many workers have limited control over the number of hours they work and therefore may exhibit little reaction to changes in the retirement test in the short run.

CONCLUSIONS

Social security probably causes a reduction in the labor force activity of older Americans. This conclusion is consistent with two widely cited rationales for the existence of social security, both of which imply that the system promotes earlier retirement. As pointed out by John B. Hagens (1980), according to the *forced saving rationale*, individuals are often myopic and must be induced to save for their old age. If the program accomplishes this, individuals will enter their later years with greater personal wealth and will be able to afford more of all commodities, including their own leisure, so they will retire earlier. According to the *insurance rationale*, OASI provides insurance against the loss of earnings. The retirement date is uncertain when workers are young, and social security provides insurance for this risk. If retirement occurs late, workers might have more savings than they need to finance continuation of their normal lifestyles; however, early retirement can result in inadequate savings levels. The social security system can transfer resources from the former group to the latter if adjustments made to benefit payments in response to changes in the retirement date are less than actuarially fair. If late retirees effectively subsidize early retirees, the system encourages early retirement. Retirement neutrality has never been a primary goal of the OASI program, and it is inherently at odds with both the forced savings and insurance rationales.

Of course, it is possible that the conclusions about the influence of the OASI program on labor supply are in error and that somehow the economic studies have produced evidence that is a poor guide to what might be anticipated in the future. There are several reasons for hesitating to embrace these conclusions fully, particularly in predicting behavior in the 1990s and beyond.

1. Perusal of the historical evidence offers circumstantial evidence that the development of the social security system had an important impact on American retirement patterns. Roger L. Ransom and Richard Sutch (1988b) found that retirement rates among nonagricultural workers declined over the 1870–1930 period. In contrast, retirement rates for older men increased from 1940 until the mid–1980s. Although there are numerous possible causes for this turnaround apart from the advent of social security, the results from the microeconometric studies are— at least on the surface—somewhat at odds with this pattern.

2. Although the economic and statistical modeling displays impressive skills and industry on the part of the researchers, even the best retirement models ignore what would appear to be significant facets of the individual decision-making process and are consequently misspecified. The most sophisticated models bypass some or all factors such as uncertainty, liquidity constraints, replanning, the physical demands imposed by jobs, employer-imposed constraints on work choices, and unmeasured individual differences among workers. No single study attempts to address more than one or two of these phenomena. Only modest attention has been given to the way financial incentives might interact with other factors such as health status, the physical demands of jobs, and other nonmonetary influences. It is conceivable that better models

(that will certainly require better data) will attribute larger labor supply influence to the social security system.

3. Most of the influential economic studies have used data from a single source: the Retirement History Survey. Not only is this database becoming rather dated, but it documents the retirement behavior of a cohort whose life experiences may have shaped economic decisions and behavior in ways that are unlikely to be repeated in later generations. The RHS respondents were born during 1905–11, lived through the Depression and World War II in the early part of their adult lives, and benefited handsomely from the start-up phase of the social security system. Attitudes about work and saving represented in the RHS may well differ from those of later cohorts, and these differences may be reflected in the measured responsiveness of older workers to the incentives implicit in employment offers, social security, and private pension plans.

4. Nearly all empirical retirement studies have focused on the behavior of white male wage and salary workers. Only a few studies have examined the retirement decisions of women, minority groups, and self-employed workers. Very little research has looked at the joint retirement decisions made by couples.

5. Econometric investigations have treated private pension rules, asset levels, tastes, and other retirement factors as largely independent of the social security system, but social security—because of its size and visibility—may have established important guideposts to which personal preferences and other institutions have conformed. That is, there may be more endogeneity present in these models than has been explicitly addressed.

Most of the research reviewed in this chapter was conducted at a time when the labor force participation rates of older men had been falling for decades. This long-term decline apparently stopped in the mid–1980s, and men's rates have risen slightly during the ensuing six years. Whether this represents a temporary halt in a trend that will shortly resume or a historic turnaround is not yet evident. At this point, however, the U.S. Department of Labor is forecasting a 1.1 percentage point increase in the participation rate for men aged 55 to 64 during 1988–2000 (following a decline of 8 percentage points from 1976 to 1988; see Fullerton 1989).

The evidence argues against the view that there are politically acceptable changes in social security policy that are likely to result in a substantial increase in the labor force participation of older workers. Nonetheless, in their focus on monetary incentives, economic models might be missing a key element of social security's influence. That is, because it is the single largest source of retirement income, it may establish an important social norm. One aspect of policies such as an increase in the normal retirement age or elimination of the retirement test involves changes in financial incentives. Such changes also send strong messages about society's expectations concerning work and retirement. There can be little doubt that over the years social security and other institutions have consistently signaled that early retirement is desirable and well deserved.[12] Policies that clearly indicate that longer work lives are expected and will be rewarded may well generate larger work responses than changes in monetary incentives alone might suggest. At this time, there appears to be no solid evidence that this would be the case. Such a scenario must thus be regarded as speculative.

12. For example, Burtless and Moffitt (1984, 1985), Gustman and Steinmeier (1986), and Marshall B. Reinsdorf (1987) all find that individual preferences appear to change rapidly or to shift in favor of leisure at the time of retirement, a phenomenon that could in part be caused by social security's well-known early and normal retirement ages.

Chapter 10.
U.S. POLICY TOWARD WORKERS WITH HANDICAPS

Richard V. Burkhauser

THE ROAD TO DISABILITY begins with a health condition, but the transition into disability is influenced greatly by the social environment faced by people with handicaps. An important institutional component shaping this environment is the disability insurance provided by the government. Protection against income loss from a health condition that limits work is a core component of all modern social insurance systems. The structure of that protection and the circumstances under which it is offered vary across countries and over time, but universally such policies greatly determine the size and scope of the population with disabilities.

In this chapter I examine the twists and turns of two decades of U.S. policy toward people with handicaps. I then review new policies toward people with handicaps, as embodied in the Americans with Disabilities Act of 1990. Such policies have as their goal an increase in the employment rate of people with handicaps. I argue that early intervention through accommodation, when a health condition first begins to affect work, will increase the chances that a worker with handicaps will stay with a firm. I also argue, however, that the ADA is not a panacea and that it is unlikely to reach the doubly handicapped—those with a health condition that affects work who also have poor job skills. Finally, alternative work-oriented policies targeted at this group are outlined.

This paper was written while the author was a fellow in residence at the Netherlands Institute for Advanced Studies in the Humanities and Social Sciences in Wassenaar, the Netherlands.

POLICIES TOWARD THE HANDICAPPED
IN THE 1970S AND 1980S

Definitions of the populations with handicaps and disabilities vary. Here, those with a health condition that affects their ability to work are considered to have handicaps. The disabled are defined as people with handicaps that receive government disability transfer benefits.

After a health condition begins to limit work, some workers immediately leave their jobs and move onto the disability rolls. This is only one of many possible outcomes. The restrictions on work brought on by the health condition will influence this outcome, but so will the actions or inactions of employers and government. Thus, the work-related choices made by those with handicaps are limited not only by their health but by the social environment they face. The power of social institutions to influence their choices, and thus the size and composition of the disabled population is most graphically seen in cross-national comparisons.

CROSS-NATIONAL COMPARISON

The importance of public policy on disability is demonstrated in table 10-1, which shows the population per one thousand workers in the United States and three European countries who receive transfers from major disability programs. All four countries experienced substantial increases in their transfer prevalence rates in the 1970s, with the greatest increases in the Netherlands and the United States. The 1980s saw slower growth in all countries, with the United States and the Netherlands showing the greatest turnarounds.

By 1989, there were forty-three disability transfer recipients in the United States per one thousand workers. By comparison, the rate in Germany was almost 30 percent higher, the rate in Sweden more than 80 percent higher, and in the Netherlands more than 250 percent higher. It is hard to imagine how underlying health conditions alone could explain such enormous differences.

This is not to suggest that health does not play some role. Health conditions increase with age; so should the prevalence of disability transfers. This is borne out in table 10-1. Prevalence rates rise among the older population in all countries. Yet the startling differences across countries remain.

With the exception of the Netherlands, prevalence rates are modest

TABLE 10-1.   DISABILITY TRANSFER RECIPIENTS PER THOUSAND ACTIVE
LABOR FORCE PARTICIPANTS IN FOUR OECD COUNTRIES, 1970–89

Working-Age Population	1970	1975	1980	Percentage Change 1970s	1985	1989	Percentage Change 1980s
Aged 15–64							
United States	27	42	41	52	41	43	5
Germany	51	54	59	26	72	55	−7
Sweden	49	67	68	39	74	78	15
Netherlands	55	84	138	150	142	152	10
Aged 15–44							
United States	11	17	16	45	20	23	44
Germany	7	6	7	0	8	5	−29
Sweden	18	20	19	6	20	21	11
Netherlands	17	32	57	235	58	62	9
Aged 45–59							
United States	33	68	83	152	71	72	−11
Germany	75	64	84	12	103	75	−13
Sweden	66	95	99	50	108	116	17
Netherlands	113	179	294	160	305	339	15
Aged 60–64							
United States	153	265	285	85	254	250	−12
Germany	419	688	1,348	222	1,291	1,109	−18
Sweden	229	382	382	67	512	577	51
Netherlands	299	437	1,033	245	1,283	1,987	92

Source: Aarts, Burkhauser, and deJong 1992.

for those under age 45. For people of middle age—45 to 59—prevalence
rates rise in all countries; the United States and Germany have similar
low rates, Sweden a higher rate, and the Netherlands a rate nearly five
times that of the United States. Among the oldest working age group—
those age 60 to 64—the United States has the lowest rate by far. In
Germany, more people at this age received disability benefits than
worked, and in the Netherlands among those aged 60 to 64 twice as
many people received benefits as worked.

These results suggest that to understand the process to disability, it
is necessary to know both the medical and the social context in which
this process unfolds. One element of this process is the social insurance
system itself. The greater the share of wage earnings replaced by disability
benefits and the easier the access to them, the faster this transition will
take place. Burkhauser et al. (1992) reviewed the empirical evidence
on this proposition for the United States, and Leo Aarts and Philip
deJong (1992) examined it for the Netherlands.

But this is only one aspect of the process. Employer behavior also matters. Deteriorating health can affect job performance, but the rate of job exit can be slowed by employers' willingness to adjust the work environment to reduce or eliminate aspects of the job that interact with a health condition to reduce productivity. Burkhauser, J. S. Butler, and Yang Kim (1992) provide evidence of the importance of job accommodation to the tenure of men with handicaps.

Government policy has a more diverse role in the process to disability than is captured by disability insurance system rules. Government policy can retard the process by providing vocational rehabilitation to workers with handicaps so that they may either overcome their work impairments or learn job skills that make alternative employment possible. Governments can also provide subsidies to employers to hire or retain such workers or even provide them directly with jobs. In addition, government policy can mandate that employers accommodate people with handicaps or set quotas that require that jobs be provided for such workers.

Broader social policies by governments to counter unemployment or to regulate wages can also affect the process. It has long been observed that disability transfer rates are sensitive to general market conditions. During economic downturns, the distinction between unemployment caused by economic forces and unemployment caused by poor health are often blurred to provide assistance to those who are not working. This same blurring occurs with respect to retirement and disability policy in that those with health conditions are often given what amounts to early retirement benefits. Robert Haveman, Victor Halberstadt, and Burkhauser (1984) reviewed the disability policies of seven industrial countries during the 1970s in this regard. The net impact of these policies has been to influence the speed at which workers with handicaps move out of the workforce and onto the rolls of the disabled.

European policy has differed over time in its use of handicap policies. More than any of the other countries listed in table 10-1, the Netherlands has used transfers as the principal method of treating people with handicaps. In the 1970s and through much of the 1980s, full disability benefits—up to 70 percent of gross wage earnings—were provided for those with as little as a 15 percent loss in earnings capacity, if they were unemployed. This produced explosive growth in the population that was defined as disabled. Reductions in the generosity of the benefits and a tightening of the eligibility rules slowed growth considerably in the 1980s.

Sweden has a transfer structure similar to that of the Netherlands, but Sweden requires workers with handicaps first to seek rehabilitation. Only those who do not respond to treatment and return to work in the private sector or to a guaranteed government job are placed on the permanent disability rolls. This emphasis on work has kept disability prevalence rates low in Sweden despite its very high benefit levels. As can be seen in table 10-1, the one exception is among those over age 60. Beginning in the 1970s, older people with handicaps were no longer expected to work and became eligible for disability benefits if they were unemployed.

Germany has more stringent eligibility criteria—one must have suffered at least a 50 percent reduction in earnings capacity—and lower earnings replacement rates than the Netherlands. It also requires all firms with at least sixteen workers to employ one worker with a handicap per sixteen employees. This combination of less generous benefits and greater job protection accounts for the lower disability incidence rates in Germany.

Like Sweden, Germany has less restrictive eligibility rules for older workers with handicaps. Such workers can receive early-retirement benefits starting at age 60 if they are unemployed. The earliest retirement age for other men is 63. (Aarts, Burkhauser, and deJong 1992 provide a more detailed discussion of policy toward the handicapped in these countries in the 1980s.)

U.S. POLICY

Disability policy in the United States moved closer to that of the European countries discussed above during the early 1970s. Real social security retirement and disability benefits were raised by more than 50 percent during this period (Anderson, Burkhauser, and Quinn 1986). Eligibility rules for disability benefits were also relaxed by allowing "vocational characteristics" to enter into the evaluation process. Workers who were poorly educated, who worked in physically demanding jobs, or who were older were considered less likely to find employment if they had a handicap and, hence, were more likely to be granted benefits. While a strict definition of disability eligibility remained on the books—

TABLE 10-2.   PARTICIPANTS IN U.S. PROGRAMS FOR ADULTS WITH
HANDICAPS (AGES 18–64), 1970–90 (in thousands)

Type of Program	1970	1975	1980	1985	1990
A. Disability insurance	1,493	2,489	2,858	2,657	3,011
Percentage change[a]		67	15	−7	13
B. Supplemental security income	870[d,e]	1,678	1,692	1,851	2,418
Percentage change		93	1	9	31
C. Total disability pensions (A + B)	2,363	4,167	4,550	4,508	5,429
Percentage change		76	9	−1	20
Narrowly defined job program[b]	100	168	262	200[d]	200[d]
Percentage change		68	56	−76	0
D. Total job programs[c]	100	506	1,096	200[d]	200[d]
Percentage change		406	116	−82	0
E. Vocational rehabilitation	876	1,244	1,095	932	938
Percentage change		42	−12	−15	1
Total in all programs (C + D + E)	3,339	5,869	6,741	5,640	6,567
Percentage change		77	14	−16	16

Source: Burkhauser and Hirvonen 1989; U.S. Department of Education 1991; U.S.
Department of Health and Human Services, various years.

[a]Percentage change over previous five years.

[b]Jobs provided primarily to workers with physical or mental handicaps. This includes
those in sheltered workshops and CETA–public service employment (PSE) who are
defined as handicapped or disabled veterans.

[c]Also includes those with economic or social handicaps. This includes the entire
population of CETA-PSE as well as those in sheltered workshops.

[d]Estimate.

[e]In 1970, this included those adults aged 18 to 64 receiving Aid to the Blind and Aid
to the Permanently and Totally Disabled.

inability to perform any substantial gainful activity—in practice, a looser
definition was used.

In 1974, the supplemental security income program merged state
programs for the aged, blind, and disabled and also increased the benefits.
This means-tested program provides a guaranteed minimum income to
those who meet health criteria similar to those for social security disability insurance. As can be seen in table 10-2, these changes together
with a faltering economy resulted in a 76 percent increase in the disabled
population between 1970 and 1975.

Also at this time, the government directly intervened in the labor
market on behalf of people with handicaps. Beginning in 1973, workers
who were handicapped because of a health condition or because they

had poor work skills were offered government-supported jobs. By 1980, more than 1 million such jobs were provided under the Comprehensive Employment and Training Act (CETA) of 1973.

Adding jobs provided by this broader program to the more narrowly focused list of sheltered work jobs and vocational rehabilitation training in table 10-2, one can see the enormous increase in government commitment to people with handicaps that occurred in the 1970s. This combination of easier access to benefits and the provision of public service jobs and vocational training for those with social or medical handicaps moved the United States very close to a European-style system. But such policies were not to last.

The peak for disability transfers was attained in 1978, as first Jimmy Carter's administration and then Ronald Reagan's tightened eligibility criteria. In addition, all public service jobs were ended with the termination of CETA early in the Reagan administration. Hence, during the worst economic recession since the 1930s, U.S. workers with handicaps were faced with stricter disability eligibility rules than in the previous decade and no access to government-created jobs.

This retrenchment in government policy is seen in the 7 percent drop in the population receiving disability insurance and in the 16 percent drop in the population served by disability programs between 1980 and 1985. In 1984, the courts and then Congress limited the ability of the Social Security Administration to remove people from the disability transfer rolls (see Weaver 1986 for a fuller discussion). In the second half of the 1980s, the population served by the disability transfer program once again began to increase, with the greatest increases in the population in the supplemental security income program. Vocational rehabilitation clients also began to increase during this period after a decade-long drop.

ECONOMIC WELL-BEING OF THE HANDICAPPED

The twists and turns in American disability policy over the past two decades together with sharp business cycles have had a substantial effect on the economic well-being of the handicapped. Table 10-3 lists the relative wage earnings between 1967 and 1987 of working-age men with handicaps and the economic well-being (pretax income adjusted for family size) of their families relative to men without handicaps and their families.

These data, from the Current Population Survey, define the working-

TABLE 10-3.   ECONOMIC WELL-BEING OF MEN WITH HANDICAPS AND
THEIR FAMILIES RELATIVE TO MEN WITHOUT HANDICAPS AND THEIR
FAMILIES ACROSS EDUCATIONAL LEVELS, 1967–87

	1967	1972	1975	1979	1981	1983	1987
Wage Earnings of Men with Handicaps Relative to Men without Handicaps							
Overall	.66	.74	.66	.58	.51	.54	.49
High school dropout	.62	.67	.36	.46	.29	.32	.30
High school degree	.77	.75	.65	.62	.44	.57	.64
High school plus	.69	.85	.93	.70	.64	.71	.72
Family Economic Well-being of Men with Handicaps Relative to Men without Handicaps							
Overall	.74	.80	.80	.73	.66	.72	.75
High school dropout	.78	.81	.78	.75	.70	.72	.71
High school degree	.88	.84	.84	.76	.69	.74	.91
High school plus	.78	.83	.89	.79	.75	.83	.89

Source: Derived from tables in Burkhauser, Haveman, and Wolfe forthcoming.

age population with handicaps as those men aged 18 to 64 who are either
receiving transfer benefits from a health-related program or are not working or are not working full time because of a health condition (see Burkhauser, Haveman, and Wolfe forthcoming, for a fuller discussion).

The relative economic well-being of the families of men with handicaps rose substantially in the early 1970s despite a drop in their relative
wage earnings between 1972 and 1975. Increases in disability benefits
offset this drop, but further drops in wage earnings in the second half
of the 1970s and especially during the recession of the early 1980s
resulted in substantial drops in relative well-being. Thus, by 1981, male
workers with handicaps had only about half the earnings of male workers
without handicaps and two-thirds of their family income. The combination of the most serious economic downturn since the Great Depression and a significant cut in both the disability rolls and government-
provided jobs had a dramatic effect on the relative economic well-being
of people with handicaps.

It is not surprising that a poor economy would have a greater impact
on workers with handicaps than on other workers, but it was the view
of the Reagan administration that an economic policy that ensured a
fast and sustained recovery would in the long run be the best policy for
getting all Americans back to work, including those with handicaps.
Table 10-3 provides some support for this view but in a somewhat
surprising manner.

After the recession, the economic well-being of the families of men with handicaps improved relative to that of other men. By 1987, their economic well-being had risen to three-quarters that of the families of men without handicaps; it was thus at a level higher than the pre-recession year value of 1979 but still below the peak years of the early 1970s. Surprisingly, this was accomplished even though the relative wage earnings of men with handicaps did not, in general, recover from the recession.

One explanation for this surprising phenomenon is suggested in table 10-3, in which the relative wages and family economic well-being of male workers with handicaps and a given education are compared with those of men with the same education without handicaps. Such a dis-aggregration provides additional insight into the ability of economic recovery "to lift all boats." Thus, by 1987, not only had the average family income of men with a high school education or better who had handicaps fully recovered from the recession of the early 1980s but the relative economic well-being of this group was as high or higher than in the peak years of the 1970s. Further, this recovery occurred not only in the wages of the men with handicaps but also in the wages of other household members. Thus, recovery was a powerful force in improving the economic well-being of both these workers and their families.

For the doubly handicapped, those with health limitations and a poor education, there was no recovery. Poor education is certainly correlated with other poor employment characteristics, and for such fringe workers, neither their wage earnings nor their family's economic well-being lifted with the tide of economic recovery. Workers with handicaps but with good job skills have significantly reduced the difference between their economic circumstances and those of their educational counterparts without handicaps. But this has produced a population with handicaps whose employment and economic circumstances are now quite diverse. The doubly handicapped have been left behind not only by those without handicaps but by those with handicaps and good job skills.

POLICIES TOWARD THE HANDICAPPED IN THE 1990S AND BEYOND

The decline in the disability transfer population that began in 1978 ended in the mid–1980s, as Congress limited the power of the Social Security Administration to reexamine the eligibility of those already on the rolls. Since 1985, social security insurance and supplemental security income rolls have increased by 20 percent (see table 10-2).

Disability rates are likely to increase for two reasons in the next decades. As we saw in table 10-1, disability transfer incidence rates are sensitive to the age distribution, and as the baby-boom generation ages, health conditions will increase in this cohort. Hence, much of the financial pressures the baby-boom generation will put on the social security retirement program will be visited on the disability program at least one decade earlier. A second concern arises as an offshoot of the revisions in the social security retirement benefit rules, which will effectively reduce the retirement benefits paid at age 62 from 80 to 70 percent of what is currently received at normal retirement age. Disability payments are unaffected by this change except that it makes the value of being accepted onto the disability rolls greater relative to opting for early retirement. Both these forces will renew concerns about disability program costs in the coming decades. They will also renew interest in how workers with handicaps can be kept on the job.

THE AMERICANS WITH DISABILITIES ACT OF 1990

Keeping workers with health impairments on the job is the major goal of the most recent U.S. policy initiative concerning the handicapped. The Americans with Disabilities Act of 1990 requires employers to make reasonable accommodations to workers with handicaps unless this would cause an undue hardship on the operation of business. This policy thrust follows civil rights legislation of the 1960s in extending protection from employment discrimination to the handicapped. It will eventually extend the standards of discrimination set out in regulations implementing section 504 of the Rehabilitation Act of 1973 to all employers of fifteen or more workers (Burkhauser 1990; Weaver 1991).

WHO ARE THE DISABLED?

Unfortunately, little is known about whether employer accommodation is successful in keeping workers with health impairments on the job or about the ability of mandates to ensure such accommodation. To estimate the success of the act in accomplishing its goal of increasing the employment of people with handicaps, it is important to understand the characteristics of the population it is meant to help. Despite the now-familiar wheelchair as the symbol of people with handicaps and the high profile of people with sight- and hearing-impairments in the

TABLE 10-4. CHARACTERISTICS OF U.S. ADULT RECIPIENTS OF
DISABILITY INSURANCE AND SUPPLEMENTAL SECURITY INCOME
(AGES 18–64), 1989

Diagnostic Groups	All Beneficiaries[a]			Newly Enrolled[b]		
	< 50	50–64	All	< 50	50–64	All
Disability insurance						
Mental disorders	40.0	17.7	27.7	34.6	9.9	20.9
Circulatory diseases	6.3	25.4	18.2	8.5	25.0	17.6
Musculoskeletal diseases	12.4	22.9	18.9	12.7	20.0	16.8
Neoplasms	2.6	3.6	3.3	9.2	16.4	13.2
All others	38.7	30.4	31.9	35.0	28.7	31.5
Total	100.0	100.0	100.0	100.0	100.0	100.0
Total (millions)	1.10	1.77	2.87	.18	.23	.41
Total (percent)	38.4	61.6	100.0	43.9	56.1	100.0
Supplemental security income						
Mental disorders (other than retardation)	32.7	22.0	28.9			
Mental retardation	33.5	8.4	24.4			
Circulatory diseases	3.0	18.6	8.7			
Musculoskeletal diseases	3.7	16.8	8.5			
Neoplasms	1.1	2.4	1.7			
All others	26.0	31.8	27.8			
Total	100.0	100.0	100.0			
Total (millions)	1.26	.72	1.98			
Total (percentage)	63.6	36.4	100.0			

Source: Derived from tables in U.S. Department of Health and Human Services 1991, table 6.C.
[a]December 1989.
[b]1988.

battle for the ADA, only a small fraction of the population with handicaps is blind or deaf or uses a wheelchair.

As can be seen in table 10-4, the great majority of those currently on the disability insurance rolls suffer from one of four broad health conditions: mental disorders, circulatory diseases (predominantly heart problems), musculoskeletal diseases (predominantly arthritis), and neoplasms (cancer). Most did not have these handicaps for the majority of their work lives. In December 1989, approximately three out of five of those on the disability insurance rolls were between the ages of 50 and 64, and more than half the new beneficiaries in 1988 were in that age range. Almost half of all older beneficiaries suffer from a circulatory or musculoskeletal condition. Mental disorders are the most common condition for younger disabled: two of five beneficiaries under the age of 50 have a mental disorder.

The supplemental security income (SSI) population is much younger, and like the younger beneficiaries of disability insurance, those with mental disorders dominate. More than 60 percent of adult SSI recipients are under the age of 50, and the overwhelming majority suffer from either mental retardation or some other mental disorder.

Hence, one can think of the population served by disability transfers as composed of two groups. The first group consists of middle-age and older workers with substantial experience in the workforce who suffer from either the effects of a discrete medical event (e.g., heart attack) or the cumulative effects of a chronic condition (e.g., arthritis). These health conditions lead to work limitations that eventually mean the loss of their jobs and entry on the disability rolls. The second group is composed of younger mentally retarded persons who may or may not have much work experience and younger workers with a condition that affects their mental functioning. Such workers are much less likely to have work experience and are more likely than older workers to end up on the rolls for SSI.

TIMING OF POLICY INTERVENTION

Current recipients of disability transfer benefits will probably not return to work. Despite some efforts to encourage those on the rolls to reenter the workforce by extending the period of eligibility for medicare benefits, only a tiny percentage of those who go into these programs ever return to the workforce. John Bound (1989, 1991) showed that the prognosis is not all that much better for those who apply for disability benefits but are rejected. Using data from the 1978 Survey of the Disabled, he found that fewer than 30 percent of rejected applicants in the 1970s were employed in 1978 and only about two-fifths of them were working full time.

Such data suggest that once the transition process to disability has reached the point of either acceptance or rejection for a disability transfer program, a return to work is unlikely. By intervening much earlier in the process, however, work-oriented policies like the ADA may still prove effective in retarding this transition.

The legal process to disability can be a long one. Both those who succeed and those who fail to be put on the disability rolls have already traveled a long road. To be eligible for benefits, a worker must not have performed any substantial gainful activity for at least five months and must not be expected to do so for at least eleven months. But this is a minimum. The ultimate eligibility outcome can take several years to unfold as all possible appeals are exhausted. For workers with handicaps who "invest" in not working to improve their chances of program eligibility, a return to work may be quite unlikely even if they are ultimately rejected by the system (see Parsons 1991 for a fuller discussion). Yet deciding to remain on the job after a health condition first begins to affect performance may bear little resemblance to the decision to work of those who have long since left the job they held when their work impairment first began. The hope provided by ADA is that intervention at the point that a health condition first starts to affect job performance will delay job exit and application for disability benefits.

DOES ACCOMMODATION MATTER?

The 1978 Survey of the Disabled is the most recent economics-based national survey of the work experience of the health-impaired population. With these data, Burkhauser, Kim, and Theodore Pincus (1992) combined the subsample of the general population and the subsample of persons who applied for disability benefits to test the effect of accommodation on a worker's duration with a firm following the onset of a health condition that is beginning to affect work. Table 10-5 summarizes the results of this study.

The analysis was carried out on 1,430 men who were at least 20 years old but under the age of 60 at the time of the survey and employed when their health condition began to limit their work. The first row of table 10-5 shows the percentage of workers with handicaps whose employers helped them to stay on the job. The table shows that employers accommodated to workers long before the passage of the ADA. More than one worker in four was helped. Accommodation rates do not vary much across health conditions.

The next three columns show the marginal effect of accommodation on duration of employment. The first row comes from a hazard model that used the full sample and controlled for differences at onset in such economic variables as disability insurance replacement rates, education, job tenure, and experience in the workforce. General demographic variables were also controlled, including age, marital status, and race. All these variables were significant at the 5 percent level or better.

The results provide some evidence that accommodation can be important in prolonging the time a worker with handicaps stays on the job. On average, those who were not accommodated stayed a little more

TABLE 10-5. INCIDENCE AND EFFECT OF ACCOMMODATION

Main Health Condition	Sample Size	Percent Accommodated	Expected Duration in Years		
			Accommodated	Not Accommodated	Difference
Total	1430	26	5.0	2.3	2.7[a]
Heart attack	164	29	7.6	2.2	5.1[b]
Other heart problems	123	29	3.6	2.2	1.4[c]
Arthritis	97	29	5.0	2.5	2.5[c]
Back problem	133	23	3.2	1.7	1.5[c]
Emphysema	71	28	4.1	2.8	1.3
Nervous conditions	53	26	3.1	1.9	1.2

Source: Compilation of tables from Burkhauser, Kim, and Pincus 1992.
[a]Significant at the 1 percent level.
[b]Significant at the 5 percent level.
[c]Significant at the 10 percent level.

than two years. Those who were accommodated stayed an average of five years. This difference, which was significant at the 1 percent level, shows that accommodation more than doubles expected duration with the firm.

Sample size constraints prevent an analysis of the influence of accommodation for groups other than those representing the five largest health conditions, but even for these groups, the success of accommodation varies widely. Those who suffer heart attacks and receive accommodation have an increase in duration of more than five years, which is nearly twice the average increase. Those with other heart problems, arthritis, or back problems are influenced much less by accommodation. Those with emphysema and nervous conditions are not helped significantly. Small sample sizes may account for the lack of significance of these last two groups.

POWER OF POLICY INTERVENTION

These results suggest that accommodation can prolong work for people with handicaps. But the dimensions of this help must be put in perspective. The average age at onset of the health condition that limited work in the sample discussed above was 38. Shirley Smith (1985) reports that the average expected work life of a male that age is approximately twenty-two years. Hence, while accommodation more than doubles work life, it is not a panacea. The average duration for accommodated workers with handicaps is still likely to be only about 25 percent of average work life.

In addition, these results probably represent the upper limit of the effect of accommodation for at least two reasons. It is unlikely that employers randomly choose whom to accommodate. They are more likely to accommodate those whose chance of success per dollar spent on accommodation is highest. If successful, the ADA, which requires accommodation unless it places an undue burden on the firm, is likely to widen the scope of accommodation to handicapped workers with more serious conditions and with lower expected success rates.

A second, and potentially more important, concern is whether the law will in fact increase accommodation significantly, especially for those people with handicaps who have not been helped by economic recovery. The ADA's accommodation criteria are far from precise. It will take several years for the courts to decide the operational meaning of "reasonable" accommodation and "undue hardship." This is particularly true since most of the discussion of accommodation surrounding the passage of the ADA has been in physical terms. It is much more likely given the actual health conditions of the handicapped, especially those at older ages, that job flexibility will be a much more important accommodation.

Walter Oi (1991) has suggested that the job performance of workers with handicaps is more often constrained by their time and energy than by physical barriers. This is because the time and energy they expend in day-to-day maintenance is greater than that of workers without handicaps. Future court decisions on the reasonableness of accommodation through more flexible hours or even permanent part-time work are likely to be much more important in shaping the future workplace than are decisions on the reasonableness of physical changes.

As shown in table 10-3, economic recovery has lifted the families of well-educated men with handicaps to a level of well-being near that of their able-bodied counterparts. Recovery has also meant an upsurge in their wage earnings. It is the doubly handicapped that recovery has missed. This is the group most in need of government support either through transfers or jobs. Yet it is doubtful that this poor and poorly educated group will be able to use the sophisticated legal weapons provided by the ADA to secure accommodation. The much more likely scenario is that the ADA will be used by highly skilled workers with handicaps to negotiate with their employers.

TOWARD A POLICY FOR KEEPING PEOPLE WITH HANDICAPS EMPLOYED

Cross-national comparisons suggest that the goal of full employment for people with handicaps will be at least as difficult to meet as the older and still unattained goal of general full employment. The reform of the Dutch disability system includes accommodation provisions that go well beyond those in the United States. Since 1987, employers who provide accommodation and training to workers with handicaps receive direct government reimbursement. To date, few employers have taken advantage of these terms (see deJong, Herweijer, and deWildt 1990, for a discussion of these reforms). In Germany, employers are reimbursed for providing training to workers with handicaps, and a quota requires the employment of such workers. But noncompliance results in a small fine. During the 1980s, when unemployment rates were at a postwar high, quotas were less likely to be filled than during the better economic

TABLE 10-6.   LABOR FORCE PARTICIPATION RATES OF MALES AGED
55 TO 64 IN FOUR OECD COUNTRIES (in percents)

	1970	1975	1980	Percentage Change 1970s	1985	1989	Percentage Change 1980s
United States	81	75	71	− 12	67	67	− 6
Germany	80	68	66	− 18	57	57	− 14
Netherlands	81	72	63	− 22	47	47	− 25
Sweden	85	82	79	− 7	76	75	− 5

Source: International Labour Organisation 1970–90.

conditions of the 1970s and were much less likely to be filled in the private sector than in the government sector. Workers with handicaps who left their employers found it difficult to find other jobs. For instance, Bernd Frick (1990) reported that 90 percent of those included in the official count of workers with handicaps for purposes of the quota were already employed by their employer before being so designated.

Only in Sweden were the employment levels of those with handicaps maintained during the recession of the early 1980s. But this was almost exclusively because of government-supplied employment. And these jobs were primarily targeted at those under 60 years of age.

Table 10-6 shows that the United States has been more successful in keeping older working-age men in the labor force than either Germany or the Netherlands. In all three countries, about four out of five men aged 55 to 64 were in the labor force in 1970. While the labor force participation rates for men this age have fallen in all three countries over the past two decades, they fell least in the United States. Today the U.S. rates are 18 percent higher than Germany's and 43 percent higher than the Netherlands'. Only Sweden has had consistently higher labor force participation rates than the United States. But since 1980, the declines in these rates have been modest and almost identical in both countries. The economic recovery in the second half of the 1980s appears to have stopped the decline in all four countries, however.

This finding suggests that while it is possible to keep people with handicaps employed with government regulations and direct job creation, even in Europe it was done within limits and constrained by overall economic conditions. The economic cycle of recession and recovery remains a powerful force in the labor force participation of people with handicaps and older working-age men of all countries.

Unlike the 1970s, U.S. policy in the 1980s was quite different from that of the three European countries studied. Emphasis was put on developing a strong economy even at the expense of government commitment to people with handicaps through transfers and job creation. This policy was successful but only to a degree and has not helped the doubly handicapped.

The longest recovery of the postwar period has come to an end. If the 1990s are a period of stagnation, then it is likely that people with handicaps will be hurt relatively more than other workers, just as they were in the early 1980s. But a prolonged recovery from the recession of 1990–92 is likely to mean that for most people with handicaps, economic integration will continue to occur. For the doubly handicapped, however, no current policies are likely to bring economic integration.

Chronic budget deficits have precluded the discussion of new handicap policies, unless they were costless to the government. This constraint is in large part responsible for the passage of the ADA. But if the doubly handicapped are to be helped, it will come only through targeted government expenditures. It is unlikely that explicit quotas of the sort used in Germany will ever be a policy option in the United States. It is also unlikely that major job creation programs like those in Sweden will be used, given the lack of support for CETA. But even in the tight budget world of Washington, programs targeted at the doubly handicapped should be considered.

POLICIES FOR THE DOUBLY HANDICAPPED

If economic growth alone will not sustain the well-being of the doubly handicapped, if fiscal constraints limit income support measures, and if employment quotas and mandates such as those embodied in the ADA are likely to be ineffective, what remains? The answers lie in a new and more effective mix of direct transfers, job training, employment subsidies, and deregulation that will begin returning the doubly handicapped to the economic mainstream. It is to the design of such a strategy that public policy should now turn.

Programs that could begin to integrate the doubly handicapped into American society should include the following:

1. *Extension of the earned income tax credit.* The least obtrusive means of helping the doubly handicapped is by extending the earned income tax credit now available to workers in poor families with children to workers with handicaps who live in poor families. This would effectively

subsidize the kind of low-skills work that is within the abilities of many of the doubly handicapped, particularly the young mentally retarded. This credit could also give poor, older workers with handicaps who could perform part-time work additional income until they reach retirement age.

2. *Accommodation tax credits.* Employers in the European countries discussed above are reimbursed for accommodating workers with handicaps. This recognizes that the economic burden of accommodation need not fall on employers. Rather, if employing workers with handicaps is a social goal, society as a whole should finance its achievement.

3. *Jobs training for people with handicaps.* The Job Partnership Training Act of 1983 replaced CETA as the mechanism for putting the socially or medically handicapped into jobs. While the percentage of successfully placed trainees has been quite high in this program, it has been argued that the most difficult to place have been systematically excluded. Kathryn Anderson, Burkhauser, and Jennie Raymond (1992) provide some evidence of creaming in this program and show that people with handicaps are underrepresented in the trainee population. Changes in the reward structure for the councils that choose participants could lead to increased use of this program by people with handicaps. Increased funding for vocational rehabilitation targeted at the doubly handicapped would serve the same purpose.

4. *Regulatory changes.* More flexible work schedules may be the single greatest change that accommodation brings to the workplace. If so, it will go a long way toward positively restructuring the labor force for workers who are older or have handicaps and desire part-time work. More generally, Gustman and Steinmeier (1983) argue that constraints on part-time work are a major cause for retirement from full-time jobs. Joseph Quinn, Burkhauser, and Daniel Myers (1990) provide a detailed discussion of changes in pension and social security rules that would encourage part-time work by older workers.

5. *Changes in the Fringe Benefit Rules.* Employers who offer pension benefits to employees are required under ERISA to pay these benefits to part-time workers who fulfill a minimum requirement of service (1,000 hours per year or 20 hours per week for a year). This discourages firms from hiring part-time workers. Changing the rules so workers with handicaps who work part time receive an equivalent portion of these benefits would allow for more flexible work contracts and a greater willingness on the part of employers to accommodate workers in this way.

6. *Changes in health insurance provisions.* Workers with handicaps are likely to have greater expected health-care costs than workers without handicaps. Government subsidy of the added insurance costs of such workers would remove this barrier to employment. For workers with handicaps who are eligible for medicare, ending the requirement that their employer's insurance pick up the first dollar of health-care expenditures would also encourage their employment.

These policy suggestions are a sample of the kinds of changes in government policy that would increase the likelihood of employment for the doubly handicapped and increase their economic well-being. Because they would directly affect the government budget, however, these policies were not considered as alternatives to the ADA.

Over the last decade, government policy has been successful both in limiting the growth of the disabled population and in restoring the relative economic well-being of people with handicaps from recession-year lows. But even if economic growth dominates in the 1990s, its rewards are unlikely to be shared by the doubly handicapped. Nor is it likely that the accommodation mandated by the ADA will increase their chances of employment. It is now time to consider the most efficient method of reaching those whom economic growth has left behind.

Chapter 11.
THE FISCAL CHALLENGE OF AN AGING POPULATION

Gary Burtless

THE AVERAGE AGE OF Americans is rising. Low birth rates and increasing longevity have raised the median age by 4.5 years since 1970. These trends have not proved terribly burdensome so far. The proportion of the population that is past age 65 has grown, but the growth through the early 1990s has been modest. In 1960, there were 173 Americans aged 65 or older for every 1,000 who were between 20 and 64. Since 1960, the ratio has risen to 209 for every 1000.

To be sure, the cost of public programs for the retired elderly has placed greater fiscal pressure on governments at all levels. But most of the increase in program costs is explained by the introduction of expensive new programs, such as medicare and medicaid, or the liberalization of old ones, such as social security. The increase in the fraction of the population older than 65 does not account for much of the increased spending.

Moreover, the growth in the aged dependency ratio has been matched by an even sharper drop in the youth dependency ratio—the number of people less than age 20 divided by the number aged 20 to 64. The fiscal burden of providing for a larger number of retired elderly has been offset to some degree by the lessened burden of providing for children.

Over the next two decades the aged dependency ratio will change very little, while the youth dependency ratio will continue to fall. When the baby-boom generation begins to retire, starting around 2010, how-

I gratefully acknowledge the research assistance of Suzanne Smith and the helpful suggestions of Ronald Ehrenberg, Alice Rivlin, and participants at the Cornell Conference on the Aging Workforce. The views expressed are the author's alone and should not be ascribed to the staff or trustees of the Brookings Institution.

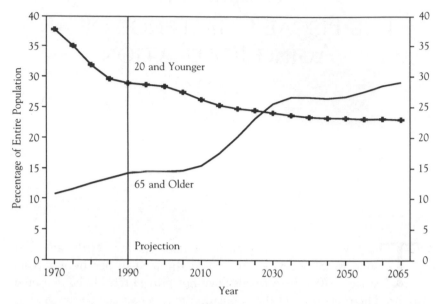

FIGURE 11-1.   PERCENTAGE OF POPULATION OLDER THAN 65 AND
YOUNGER THAN 20

ever, the aged dependency rate will climb sharply. Under the Social
Security Administration's intermediate demographic forecast, this rate
is projected to jump from 220 per 1,000 in 2010 to 379 per 1,000 in
2035 (see figure 11–1).

These demographic changes will place heavy pressure on government
budgets because a large proportion of retirees' consumption is financed
through public spending. Even if benefits are not raised above their
current levels, the rising proportion of the population that is old and
the shrinking fraction that remains at work will push up tax burdens on
active workers. This prospect has aroused anxiety and even alarm among
some observers, who doubt that future workers will tolerate sharply
higher taxes.

This chapter examines the fiscal implications of the aging of the U.S.
population. In the next section I offer a forecast of the budgetary effects
of population aging and describe the principal sources of sharply higher
public spending. I also assess the capacity and willingness of the nation
to pay for programs that will benefit the elderly after the baby-boom
generation retires. The following section examines the possibility that

future benefits can be reduced by restricting the rate of improvement in benefit generosity.

I then consider whether the additional burdens of the programs can and should be ameliorated by changes in fiscal policy *before* the baby-boom generation retires. This question is currently the subject of heated debate, both inside and outside the government. Some politicians and economists argue that the government should anticipate the future burdens of having a larger retired population by boosting the nation's saving rate today, either by reducing government deficits or building up large public sector surpluses. Because of the high political cost of pursuing this strategy, many observers are dubious that it could or should be implemented. In the conclusion, I examine the debate over fiscal policy within the context of recent developments in national saving.

COSTS OF AN AGING POPULATION

The impact of population aging on government budgets is large and economically significant because old people derive so much of their income from public transfer programs. Social security benefits account for about 60 percent of the cash income received by poor families with an aged family member. These transfers constitute more than one-quarter of the income received by nonpoor families with an aged family member and an even higher percentage of the income of older people who live alone (U.S. Congress 1986). The medical insurance protection provided by medicare also represents a sizable contribution to the well-being of the elderly. The cost of providing medicare benefits to old people is one-half the cost of paying them social security pensions (U.S. Congress 1991). In addition to social security and medicare, the elderly receive benefits under a variety of other federal, state, and local programs, including railroad retirement, veterans' programs, medicaid, food stamps, supplemental security income, and subsidized public housing.

The cost of these programs is large and growing. The congressional budget office estimates that federal spending on the elderly amounted to $356 billion in 1990, or about $11,290 per person aged 65 and older. This spending comprises more than 28 percent of all federal spending and nearly half the spending outside of defense and interest on the public debt (U.S. Congress 1991). These percentages have risen rapidly over the past twenty-five years. As recently as 1965, less than 16 percent of federal outlays were devoted to programs for the elderly.

Federal spending on the elderly has grown for two reasons. The number of elderly rose, and spending per elderly person rose, too. But whereas the number of old people rose by two-thirds between 1965 and 1990, federal spending rose nearly fivefold. Spending per person older than 65 nearly tripled, rising from $3,860 to $11,290 in inflation-adjusted 1990 dollars.

The future course of public spending for the elderly depends on the rate of growth in the elderly population, which can be predicted with some confidence, and the rate of change in spending per old person, which is much harder to predict. It is highly unlikely that future spending trends will mirror those of the past quarter-century, a period that saw the liberalization of social security pensions and the introduction of medicare and medicaid. As programs for the elderly have absorbed a growing percentage of federal dollars, it has become much more difficult to justify (or afford) continued liberalization in benefit levels. In fact, the 1977 and 1983 amendments to the Social Security Act significantly scaled back OASDI pension levels for future generations of retirees, and cost controls in the hospital insurance program reduced the rate of increase in medicare spending during the second half of the 1980s.

The most detailed projections of future spending on programs for the elderly are those prepared for OASDI and HI by the actuaries of the social security and medicare programs.[1] The long-range projections rest on detailed assumptions about the size and age of the beneficiary population, average benefit rates, and taxable payrolls. In estimating the number of future beneficiaries and taxable workers, actuaries rely on three sets of demographic assumptions, yielding optimistic, intermediate, and pessimistic forecasts of the long-range solvency of the programs. Figure 11-1 is based on the intermediate demographic assumptions contained in the 1991 annual report of the OASDI trustees.

Figure 11-2 shows historical and projected outlays on social security and medicare under the intermediate assumptions in the 1991 annual reports. Annual outlays are measured as a percentage of contemporaneous gross national product, which is forecast in the OASDI annual report. The U.S. government does not publish a long-range forecast of

---

1. OASDI, commonly referred to as social security, is the old-age, survivors, and disability insurance program. HI, popularly known as part A of medicare, is the hospital insurance program. Less detailed forecasts are prepared for the supplemental medical insurance program (SMI), also known as medicare part B. See Board of Trustees of the Federal OASDI Trust Funds 1991, Board of Trustees of the Federal HI Trust Fund 1991, and Board of Trustees of the Federal SMI Trust Fund 1991.

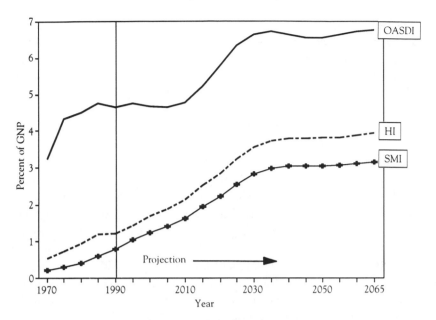

FIGURE 11-2. OUTLAYS ON SOCIAL SECURITY AND MEDICARE

spending on medicare part B, the SMI program. To derive my forecast, I assume that SMI spending will continue to rise relative to spending on HI until it reaches 80 percent of HI outlays. Thereafter, SMI spending is projected to rise at the same rate as spending on HI.

The trend in projected spending in the OASDI program mirrors the trend in the future dependency ratio. The share of GNP that will be spent on social security pensions will remain almost unchanged over the next two decades. It will jump by about two percentage points of GNP (40 percent) within the twenty-five-year span between 2010 and 2035 and then stabilize.

Medicare spending follows a very different pattern. Outlays will continue to grow between now and 2010, primarily because of the expected rapid increase in medical care costs. Even though the medicare-insured population will grow no faster than the population collecting social security pensions, medicare spending per beneficiary will grow much faster. If the dependency ratio remained unchanged, medicare spending would ultimately grow approximately as fast as medical care costs. Since these costs are rising at twice the rate of general price inflation, a higher proportion of national income must be devoted to insuring the medical expenses of the aged and disabled. Thus, over the next two decades, the rising fiscal burden of medicare will be due principally to medical care cost inflation, not to population aging. After 2010, medicare outlays will also rise as the relative size of the insured population starts to climb. The reason so little acceleration of medicare burdens is visible after 2010 is that the HI actuary assumes medical care inflation will eventually tend to fall toward the rate of general price inflation. After 2030, the forecast implies that medicare outlays will absorb a slowly growing proportion of GNP.

To derive estimates of spending on other programs for the elderly, I tabulated outlays for a set of such programs during the past twenty years.[2] Spending in these programs has risen slightly faster than the growth of spending on social security and medicare combined. In 1990, outlays on these programs represented slightly less than 23 percent of combined spending on social security and medicare. In the future, I assume spending on the programs will amount to exactly 23 percent of combined social security and Medicare outlays. Under this assumption, it is straightforward to project combined spending on all programs for the elderly.

My estimates of past and future government outlays on the elderly are shown in figure 11-3.[3] Between 1975 and 1990, total spending on programs for the aged increased by 1.6 percentage points of GNP, or roughly one-quarter. If current projections of future social security and medicare costs are accurate, spending increases during the next two decades will be somewhat slower but will accelerate after 2010. Between 1990 and 2035, the percentage of national output that will be absorbed in public spending on the elderly will double, rising from 8.2 percent to 16.5 percent of GNP. By way of comparison, total government spending—including spending by state and local governments—represented 32.7 percent of GNP in 1990. If other elements of government spending remain unchanged, the jump in spending on the elderly will boost overall

2. The programs I included are railroad retirement, federal civilian retirement, military retirement, old-age benefits for coal miners, supplemental security income, veterans' pensions, medicaid, and a portion of food stamps. See U.S. Congress 1991:1343. Unlike the estimates produced by the Ways and Means Committee staff of the House of Representatives, my estimates include state and local spending on medicaid.

3. The estimated costs include *all* spending on social security and medicare, including that portion spent on people under 65. Most beneficiaries under 65 are comparatively old, since they are older disabled workers or early retirees in the OASDI program.

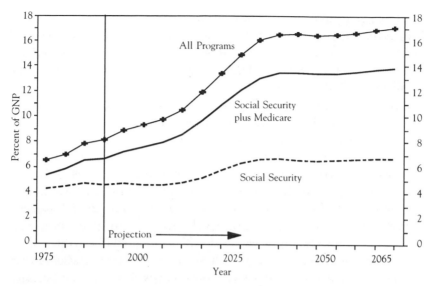

FIGURE 11-3. OUTLAYS ON PROGRAMS FOR THE ELDERLY AS A
PERCENTAGE OF GNP

government spending above 40 percent of GNP by 2035, a rise of more
than one-quarter above the prevailing level in the 1980s.

Readers should be cautious in interpreting the numbers shown in
figures 11-2 and 11-3. The estimates are based primarily on the intermediate spending and national income projections of the Social Security
Administration, and these projections are very uncertain beyond the
next five or ten years. Consider, for example, the seventy-five-year
projections that would have been made by a prudent actuary in 1915.
In the three-quarters of a century that followed, the United States
entered two world wars, the Great Depression, and an unprecedented
cold war. The nation experienced wide swings in fertility, immigration,
inflation, interest rates, and productivity. Even a casual consideration
of this history should persuade readers that the actuaries' crystal ball
might be a bit cloudy.

The actuaries' intermediate projection suggests that by 2035 social
security spending will amount to 6.7 percent of national income. The
Social Security Administration also prepares an optimistic and a pes
simistic forecast. The optimistic forecast is based on the assumption that
future fertility rates will be high, mortality rates will fall only slightly,

and real economic growth will be very strong. The pessimistic forecast is based on the opposite set of assumptions. Under the optimistic forecast, social security spending could be as low as 5.7 percent of GNP by 2035. Under the pessimistic forecast, spending could be as high as 7.9 percent of GNP.

The uncertainty surrounding the medicare estimates is much wider than the uncertainty around social security projections, because future medical care costs and utilization are much harder to predict than future real wages. Under an optimistic set of assumptions about future national income and medicare spending trends, total spending on programs for the elderly might reach only 11.5 percent of GNP by 2035. Under the pessimistic set of assumptions, total spending could reach 25.2 percent of GNP, more than three times the level of spending in 1990. Obviously, this band of uncertainty is very wide. Readers should bear this uncertainty in mind while reading the rest of this chapter. I assume that future spending will reach a level consistent with the Social Security Administration's intermediate projections. That is, total spending on programs for the elderly is assumed to reach 16.5 percent of GNP by 2035.

TOLERANCE FOR INCREASES IN SPENDING

It is natural to ask whether the increases in spending just described will be politically manageable or economically sustainable. One way to think about this question is to consider actual changes in the level of public spending over the past several decades. Table 11-1 shows government spending and its major components over the postwar period, with expenditure measured as a percentage of U.S. gross national product. In the four decades after 1950, total government spending absorbed an additional ten percentage points of national income. More than six percentage points of this increase was consumed by added spending on social security and medicare.

In spite of the high, rising, and conspicuous price tags of the two programs, neither suffers from any lack of popularity among the voting public. Public opinion polls routinely show that medicare and social security are the most popular programs administered by the federal government. In 1986, after a funding crisis that required highly publicized increases in the social security payroll tax, an overwhelming share (82 percent) of American adults expressed satisfaction with the taxes they paid to support the program. This level of support is astonishing in view

TABLE 11-1.   GOVERNMENT SPENDING AS A PERCENTAGE OF U.S.
NATIONAL INCOME (GNP), 1947–90

Fiscal Year	Total Expenditure	Defense and International	Social Security and Medicare	Net Interest	All Other	Total Revenue
1947	20.1%	8.3%	0.2%	1.9%	9.7%	22.6%
1950	22.7	6.9	0.3	1.8	13.6	21.0
1955	24.6	11.6	1.1	1.3	10.6	23.4
1960	25.8	10.1	2.2	1.4	12.0	25.9
1965	25.9	8.3	2.5	1.2	13.8	25.8
1970	29.2	8.7	3.7	1.3	15.6	29.3
1975	31.8	6.1	5.1	1.2	19.2	28.7
1980	30.7	5.5	5.7	1.4	18.2	28.9
1985	32.4	6.8	6.5	2.5	16.7	28.6
1990	32.7	5.8	6.5	2.6	17.8	29.4

Source: U.S. Office of Management and Budget, *Budget of the United States Government*, 1992.

of the fact that the payroll tax rate had been raised on eleven separate occasions in the previous two decades, causing it to be almost doubled between 1965 and 1986. Amazing majorities of adults actually favor *raising* benefits under both the social security and medicare programs. Contrary to the common-sense intuitions of many who oppose the programs, social security and medicare are popular across the entire age spectrum. The percentage that supports the current level of taxes is exactly as high among 18- to 34-year-olds as it is among 50- to 64-year-olds. The level of support among people 65 and older is only slightly higher than the support among people under 65 (Cook 1990).

Public support for taxes that pay for social security and medicare is not matched by a willingness to pay for other obligations of government. Since 1970, public spending has edged up from 29 percent to 33 percent of national output, but government revenues have hardly changed at all, fluctuating around 29 percent of GNP. The resulting imbalance of government outlays and revenues resulted in soaring public debt, especially in the 1980s, and a growing obligation to fund interest payments on the debt.

The evidence in table 11-1 contains mixed signals about the willingness of the public to pay for added spending on the elderly. Actual spending on social security and medicare rose 6.2 percent of GNP between 1950 and 1990, about the same increase that will be required over a comparable period after 2010. Most of the money to pay for the programs is derived from a highly visible, earmarked tax on workers' wages. In spite of steady and large increases in the tax, the programs remain hugely popular, even among workers who pay the tax. Such evidence suggests that the tax increases needed to pay projected benefits in the next century will probably be forthcoming.

The evidence on overall government revenues is less promising. After rising about as fast as government outlays from the end of World War II until the early 1970s, government revenues have stopped growing, suggesting that voters or their representatives may be unwilling to tolerate taxes much above 30 percent of national income. If this is true, it is difficult to believe that spending on the elderly could rise as much as predicted in figure 11-3. Because of the growing burden of interest payments, it is doubtful that the current level of government deficits could be sustained indefinitely; a substantial increase in the deficit over a thirty- or forty-year period seems unimaginable. If the deficit cannot rise enough to finance added spending on the elderly, an obvious alternative is to reduce spending on other noninterest obligations, although it is not clear which obligations might be reduced.

In spite of their resistance to taxes, voters and legislators have been willing to raise taxes enough to pay for the added costs of selected programs. Federal social insurance taxes have risen fast enough to cover the increased costs of social insurance programs. State and local taxes have risen enough to pay for increased state and local obligations. Legislators have been notably reluctant, however, to raise federal taxes enough to pay for federal spending other than for social insurance—for defense, interest on the public debt, or other federal obligations. Federal legislators may one day discover that voters can be persuaded to pay for nonsocial insurance obligations of the federal government only if taxes are specifically earmarked for popular programs, including defense, education, and national parks. In any event, voters have revealed a strong willingness to pay taxes earmarked for social insurance programs. Since these are the programs that primarily sustain the consumption of the elderly, it is conceivable that public spending on the elderly can continue to grow, even if other forms of federal public spending are tightly constrained. We should also remember that older voters will be more numerous in the future, implying that their political influence will grow as well.

Another way to think about the increase in public spending needed

TABLE 11-2.   GOVERNMENT EXPENDITURE AND ITS COMPONENTS AS A
PERCENTAGE OF NATIONAL OUTPUT (GDP) IN SIX OECD COUNTRIES

Country (Year)	Total Expenditures	Defense	Pensions	Net Interest	All Other
United States (1987)	36.9%	6.6%	7.0%	5.0%	18.3%
Japan (1988)	32.9	0.9	6.2	4.3	21.5
Germany (1987)	46.9	2.7	11.5	2.8	29.9
France (1986)	51.6	3.1	13.9	2.9	31.7
United Kingdom (1986)	45.5	4.9	6.8	4.5	29.3
Sweden (1987)	59.3	2.6	11.3	6.5	38.9

Source: OECD.

to pay for an aging U.S. population is to compare it with the level of
spending in other advanced industrialized countries. Table 11-2 contains
OECD estimates of government outlays in six industrialized countries,
measured as a percentage of gross domestic product. Because the OECD
measures government spending somewhat differently than does the U.S.
Office of Management and Budget, the figures for the United States in
Tables 11-1 and 11-2 do not necessarily correspond. The OECD attempted to measure government expenditures in a consistent way in the
six countries included in table 11-2, however, so comparisons across
countries should be meaningful.

Of the countries considered in the table, only Japan has a government
sector smaller than that of the United States. The four European countries currently maintain a government sector that is larger than the one
that would be required in the United States to fund current spending
as well as all future additional spending on programs that benefit the
U.S. elderly. For example, the projections shown in figure 11-3 imply
that the share of U.S. GDP that is devoted to programs for the elderly
will rise by about 8.5 percentage points between 1990 and 2035. The
United Kingdom maintains a government sector that is 8.7 percentage
points larger than that of the United States; the German public sector
is 10 percentage points larger; and the French and Swedish public sectors
are at least 14 percentage points larger. Public spending on pensions
consumes 6.6 percent of GDP in the United States but almost 14 percent
of GDP in France and more than 11 percent of GDP in Germany and
Sweden.

Although public spending is sharply higher in most other advanced
industrialized countries than it is in the United States, some public

spending abroad pays for services that must be privately financed in this country. Private health-care spending comprises 6.6 percent of national income in the United States, for example, but less than 2 percent of national income in Japan, Germany, and France and less than 1 percent of national income in the United Kingdom and Sweden (U.S. Bureau of the Census 1990). The gap in public spending between the United States and western European countries thus tends to exaggerate the difference between the two continents. The burden of paying for public services plus health care is more similar on the two continents than is the burden of paying for public services alone.

Even accounting for this difference between the continents, however, total spending in the United States is considerably lower than it is in most well-to-do European countries. Public spending on the American elderly can clearly rise substantially before we match the spending levels of some other countries with similar standards of living. Even when we attain the peak spending levels predicted in figure 11-3, we will still spend less of our national income on public programs than many of our major trading partners do today. The evidence in table 11-2 clearly suggests that the spending levels forecast for the United States in figure 11-3 are economically sustainable.

CURTAILMENT OF BENEFITS

An alternative to higher public spending on the elderly is curtailment of publicly financed benefits, through either tighter restrictions on program eligibility or reductions in average benefit entitlements. To weigh the effects of these alternatives, it is useful to decompose the expected increase in future spending into two separate components, one that is due to the pure effect of population aging and the other that is attributable to changes in the relative generosity of program benefits. To derive estimates of these two components, it is necessary to establish some baselines for comparison. The baselines I have chosen are the population age structure and the prevailing benefit level in effect in 1990.

To measure the influence of changes in expected benefit generosity over time, I predict future spending levels based on the assumption that the number of beneficiaries relative to the number of active workers will remain unchanged from the ratio observed in 1990. Increases in program spending above the level observed in 1990, evaluated as a percentage of GNP, represent a simple measure of the influence of changes in program generosity.

To measure the pure effects of population aging on program spending, I use a similar procedure, though in reverse. Rather than hold the age structure fixed over time, I hold benefit generosity constant at the level observed in 1990. I calculate benefit generosity by measuring the ratio of average benefits to output per worker. Average benefits are calculated as total program spending divided by the average number of program beneficiaries. Output per worker is calculated as GNP divided by average total employment during a year. Some readers might prefer a calculation in which average *real* benefits are held constant at their 1990 level. Instead, I essentially hold constant the ratio of average benefits to average annual compensation. This procedure is preferable for two reasons. First, it does not link my estimate quite so closely to the Social Security Administration's forecast of future productivity trends, which ultimately determine the future course of real benefit levels. And second, my definition of program generosity corresponds closely to the widely understood concept of the wage replacement rate. If replacement rates remain constant over time, my definition would imply that program generosity remains unchanged.[4]

MEDICARE

Figure 11-4 shows my estimates of future medicare spending under the three sets of assumptions. The solid bold line shows combined spending on medicare parts A and B under the assumptions contained in the HI and SMI trustees' 1991 annual reports. Combined spending in the two programs is predicted to rise from about 2 percent of GNP in 1990 to nearly 7 percent of GNP by 2040. The lower broken line shows the effect of expected increases in benefit generosity. That is, it shows the predicted course of spending if the population age structure remains unchanged after 1990.

Until 2005, virtually all the rise in medicare spending is due to in-

4. My definition does not correspond to the wage replacement rate as it is typically calculated by the Social Security Administration, however. The SSA definition generally includes only social security–covered wages in the denominator, that is, in the measure of wages that are replaced. By contrast, my definition of the denominator includes all output per worker. Output per worker typically rises at the same rate as average compensation per worker, not average covered wages per worker. The difference between the two can be significant if a substantial and changing fraction of compensation is excluded from the taxable wage base.

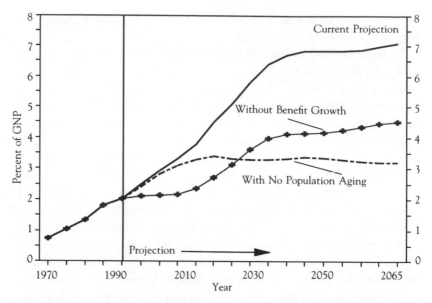

FIGURE 11-4.   OUTLAYS ON MEDICARE, WITH AND WITHOUT
POPULATION AGING AND BENEFIT GROWTH

creasing generosity. After 2015, gains in benefit generosity are assumed
to cease altogether. Nonetheless, benefits are about two-thirds higher
by 2015 than they would be if benefit levels remained unchanged. If
the nation could curb the rate of increase in medicare benefit generosity,
it would avoid more than 70 percent of the increase in medicare spending
that will occur between 1990 and 2015. After 2015, none of the increase
in medicare spending is caused by changing benefit generosity. The
increase is entirely due to changes in the population age structure. By
the year 2040, for example, total medicare spending is projected to be
4.8 percentage points higher than its level in 1990—6.8 percentage
points of GNP versus 2 percentage points in the earlier year. Only 1.3
percentage points of this increase—about one-quarter—is due to increases in benefit generosity. The remainder is due to population aging.
Moreover, "benefit generosity" has a special meaning in this context.
The increase in spending per beneficiary is due primarily to an increase
in the cost of medical care, only part of which represents true improvement in the quality of care. The remainder is associated with pure price
increases for essentially unchanged medical procedures.

Even if only one-quarter of the medicare spending increase in 2040 is attributable to increased program generosity, the resulting increase in spending amounts to 1.3 percent of GNP, a higher percentage of GNP than was consumed by *total* spending on medicare as recently as the late 1970s. If these costs can be avoided, possibly through rigorous cost containment, it is well worth the effort to do so.

The influence of population aging is represented by the cross-hatched line in the middle of figure 11-4. This line shows medicare spending under the assumption that average benefits after 1990 will rise at precisely the same rate as output per worker. These estimates suggest that program outlays will more than double between 1990 and 2040, even if a cost-containment program should succeed in holding medicare benefits unchanged at their 1990 level.

The only way to reduce spending below the level indicated by the cross-hatched line is to restrict benefits to a narrower class of the elderly, through a means test, for example. Such a restriction would reduce the budgetary cost of providing medical insurance to the elderly, though I am skeptical that it would reduce the economic cost of insurance. Older people who are excluded from public benefits through a means test would presumably obtain insurance and medical care on their own. The cost of their care will not show up in government budgets, but nearly all of it will still represent a claim on future national income. This burden of population aging cannot be avoided simply by removing older people from public insurance rolls. There is thus an important distinction between cost containment—which reduces the economic resources used up in providing medical care—and eligibility curtailment—which removes the costs of some medical care from public budgets and places them instead in private household or business budgets.

SOCIAL SECURITY PENSIONS

The effects of population aging and changes in benefit generosity on social security spending are displayed in figure 11-5. The solid bold line represents projected OASDI spending under the intermediate assumptions of the 1991 trustees' annual report. The broken line at the bottom represents spending if the age structure of the population remains unchanged after 1990. Surprisingly, the latter line actually *declines* after 1995, falling a little more than 6 percent per decade until 2040. Average benefits are thus expected to *shrink* relative to output per worker, partially offsetting the influence of population aging.

A careful reading of the OASDI trustees' report reveals two reasons

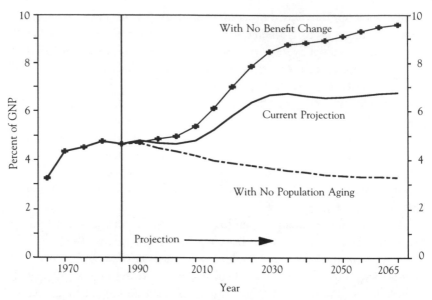

FIGURE 11-5.   OUTLAYS ON OASDI, WITH AND WITHOUT POPULATION
AGING AND BENEFIT GROWTH

for the decline. One explanation is the decision of the president and
Congress to cut benefits. The 1977 social security amendments actually
reduced benefits for workers reaching age 65 in 1982 and later years
below the level received by earlier cohorts of retirees. The 1983 amendments modestly reduced real benefits still further and, in addition, raised
the normal retirement age starting early in the next century. When this
reform is fully implemented in the third decade of the next century,
benefits for 65-year-old retirees will be 15 percent lower (relative to past
covered earnings) than the benefits received by a 65-year-old retiree
today.

A second explanation for the decline in benefit generosity is the
continuing erosion in the taxable wage base of social security. Workers
with earnings substantially above the maximum covered wage are receiving a growing percentage of wages. In addition, a rising fraction of
all compensation is received in the form of untaxed fringe benefits, such
as employer contributions to health and retirement plans. If part of
employee compensation is excluded from the wage base, it cannot influence the level of future social security benefits, which are determined
by past covered earnings. Even if social security benefits rose at the same

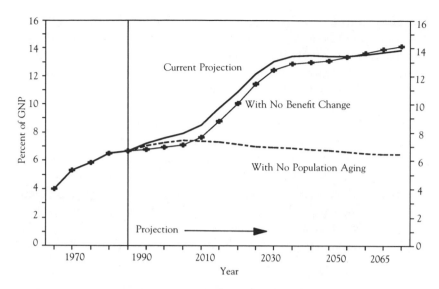

FIGURE 11-6.   OUTLAYS ON OASDI AND MEDICARE, WITH AND
WITHOUT POPULATION AGING AND BENEFIT GROWTH

pace as covered earnings, benefits would rise more slowly than average
compensation.

The upper cross-hatched line shows projected social security spending
under the assumption that benefit generosity will remain unchanged at
its 1990 level. This line shows the pure influence of population aging
on OASDI spending. For the reasons just mentioned, outlays would be
substantially higher were benefit generosity to remain unchanged at
today's level. By 2040, OASDI spending would consume an additional
2.2 percentage points of GNP—8.8 percent of GNP rather than 6.6
percent. One important lesson in figure 11-5 is that political and economic developments have already or soon will reduce the budgetary
burden of future social security benefits.

Figure 11-6 shows the effect of population aging and changes in benefit
generosity on social security and medicare spending combined. Once
again, the solid bold line represents the actual level of spending projected
in the 1981 trustees' annual reports, while the broken line reflects combined spending if the population age structure remains unchanged after
1990. The figure plainly shows that virtually all the long-term increase
in public spending on the elderly is due to the graying of the U.S.

population. In the next few decades, some of the projected increase in spending could be avoided if medicare cost increases were held down. By 2040, however, very little of the spending increase could be avoided. Actual spending is projected to rise 6.8 percentage points of GNP between 1990 and 2040. If social security and medicare benefit generosity were held in check, outlays would rise 6.3 percentage points. In the long run, decreases in social security benefit generosity will just about offset expected increases in medicare generosity. An overwhelming share of the increase in combined outlays is due to the pure effect of population aging. It is not due to increases in the combined generosity of social security and medicare benefits. We can avoid a major part of these additional costs only through further reductions in OASDI payment levels or through cost containment in medicare, which would bring the benefit generosity level substantially *below* that enjoyed by recipients in 1990.

BUDGET POLICY IN THE SHORT RUN

The expected future costs of programs for the elderly are high but economically manageable. It is less clear whether the costs are politically tolerable. U.S. voters have balked at paying taxes much above 30 percent of GNP, yet such tax levels will be needed if the full expected costs of programs for the aged are to be financed out of current tax revenues. The analysis in the previous section suggests that rigorous cost containment in medicare could help the nation avoid some of the projected future costs of programs for the elderly. But in the long run, the only way a substantial part of these costs can be avoided is through combined reductions in social security and medicare benefits that will make these programs much less generous than they are today.

One strategy to ameliorate the effect of cost increases is to undertake policies that will raise future GNP. In each of the figures and tables discussed thus far, the economic burden of programs for the elderly has been represented as a percentage of GNP or, equivalently, as a percentage of output per worker employed. While such analysis makes good sense in certain applications, it has an important limitation. The workers who are taxed to support public spending are not indifferent about the level of their real output. If 38 percent of their earnings must ultimately be paid as taxes to finance public spending, it makes a great deal of difference whether their hourly wage is $10 or $20. A 38 percent tax will be more affordable to the better-paid worker. To be sure, a lower tax rate is preferable whether wages are $10 or $20 an hour. But if the higher tax is unavoidable, it would certainly be better to pay it out of a higher wage.

In a book I wrote with two colleagues, we argued that it is possible to raise future incomes over the next several decades through prudent changes in fiscal policy (Aaron, Bosworth, and Burtless 1989). The operating surpluses in social security and medicare provide a convenient vehicle for achieving the desired change in policy. In particular, if the surpluses actually contribute to higher national saving over the next several decades, they could boost the size of the U.S. capital stock and help raise future national income.

The mechanism of this effect is quite straightforward. Both social security and medicare hospital insurance collect more payroll taxes each year than they need to pay current retirees. The annual excess of revenues over outlays is placed in separate OASI, DI, and HI trust funds as reserves. By law, these reserves must be invested in securities guaranteed as to principal and interest by the federal government. In practice, they are used to purchase special securities issued by the U.S. Treasury, where they earn an interest rate equivalent to that on medium-term government bonds.

In theory, this transaction reduces the need of the federal government to borrow from the public. Private businesses and households, left with more of their own savings to invest, are induced to invest a greater amount of their savings in private businesses rather than in government bonds. The resulting increase in private investment in this country raises the size of the domestic capital stock and gradually raises the potential GNP of the United States. Alternatively, the freed-up savings could be invested abroad, where they would earn the rate of return available overseas. In either case, the future incomes of Americans are raised.

Even though social security and medicare payments will someday absorb a higher fraction of U.S. incomes, the size of the future economic pie can be enlarged so there will be more income to be shared between future workers and retirees. Workers will receive higher incomes to the extent that increases in the capital stock are translated into higher productivity and wages. Retirees will receive higher incomes too, because their public and private retirement benefits are usually linked to their real earnings during their last few years on the job. In the short and intermediate runs, the real incomes of retirees will not rise as fast as the incomes of workers because real wage gains of current workers

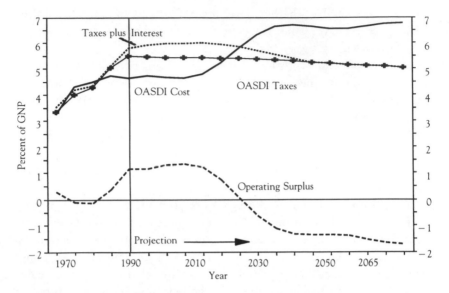

FIGURE 11-7.   OASDI OUTLAYS, TAX REVENUES, AND
OPERATING SURPLUSES

do not directly affect the pension entitlements of current retirees. For
that reason, a more rapid growth in worker productivity and real wages
actually reduces the share of wages that must be set aside to pay for
current retirement benefits. Not only does faster growth increase the
size of the pie; it also reduces slightly the share of the pie that is consumed
by retirees.

The theoretical effects of saving the social security and medicare
surpluses would have only academic interest if the size of these surpluses
were small. They are not. The surpluses are large enough to make a
noticeable difference in the size of the U.S. capital stock. Figures 11-7
and 11-8 show the future financial status of social security under the
1991 intermediate demographic and economic assumptions. Projected
tax receipts, interest earnings, benefit payments, and trust fund reserves
are measured as percentages of contemporaneous GNP. Over the next
twenty years, outlays fall as a share of GNP, and for several decades
they will remain below revenues. With the rapid growth of reserves,
interest on the trust funds becomes a major source of revenue, rising to
about 10 percent of total receipts during the second half of the next
decade. At their peak, the annual surpluses in social security will amount
to nearly 1.5 percent of GNP and the total trust fund reserve will

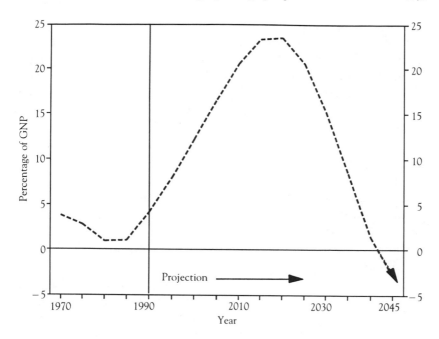

FIGURE 11-8. OASDI TRUST FUND AS A PERCENTAGE OF GNP

represent almost one-quarter of GNP. After 2020, however, the growing proportion of retirees in the population will result in an increase in benefit payments above OASDI income. The trust fund will begin to decline. The operations of the social security trust fund will reduce rather than raise national saving unless benefits are curtailed or tax rates increased.

For the next three decades, however, the social security program represents a large potential source of saving. The accumulating reserves in the system can raise the incomes and reduce the burden on future workers of paying for the retirement benefits that must be financed when the huge baby-boom generation retires. But the burden on future generations can be reduced only if the growing social security surpluses actually produce an increase in national saving and investment. For this to occur, the country will need a different budget policy than the one it has followed over the past decade. In particular, it will need to reduce the large and growing deficits in the non–social security budget accounts.

The net effect of the surpluses on government saving can be inferred from the first and last columns in table 11-1. Even though the social security surplus amounted to more than 1 percent of GNP in 1990, the overall deficit in government accounts exceeded 3 percent of GNP. The table provides no evidence that growing social insurance surpluses have reduced government dissaving in the past decade. Instead, government deficits have soared. Rather than adding to national saving, the surpluses are simply being used to finance the current operations of the federal government.

In our book (Aaron, Bosworth, and Burtless 1989), my colleagues and I propose two fundamental changes in fiscal policy. First, we recommend that the federal government attempt to achieve small or negligible deficits in the non–social security, nonmedicare portion of the budget. Better fiscal policy could be achieved if budget targets were set so as to exclude the surpluses in social security and medicare. The surpluses in these programs could then accomplish the desired result, namely, a boost in national saving.

Second, we urge that the tax or benefit schedules in social security be adjusted periodically to keep the program in close actuarial balance. The actuarial balance of the program is determined based on a comparison of the expected benefit payout and the income rates of the program over the next seventy-five years. The OASDI program is considered to be in close actuarial balance if the expected income of the trust fund, exclusive of interest, is within 5 percent of expected outlays, where both income and outlays are discounted back to the present. When the income resources available to the fund fall below 95 percent of expected outlays over the seventy-five-year horizon, we suggest that payroll taxes be raised immediately or benefits reduced so as to restore the program to exact actuarial balance.

This proposal, if implemented, would have the effect of raising social security and medicare surpluses over the entire seventy-five-year planning horizon. The social security program was restored to close actuarial balance by the amendments of 1983. It remained in close balance for the next five years under the Social Security Administration's intermediate demographic and economic assumptions. The program is no longer in close actuarial balance. Under our proposal, taxes should be raised or benefits reduced, either now or within the next several years. Whether taxes are raised or benefits reduced, the surplus in social security will rise.

In simulations reported in our book, we found that our proposal would increase the peak size of the OASDI trust fund reserve by about one-quarter, measured as a percentage of national income. The net effect of the proposal on the wider economy would be substantial. As a result of increased investment, the capital stock, labor productivity, and real wages all would rise. National income rises slightly more than 4 percent by 2020, in addition to the income change that would otherwise have taken place. Consumption declines initially because national saving can only be raised at the expense of current consumption. Within ten years, however, per capita consumption is higher than it would be if current fiscal policy were maintained.

The most important finding in our study concerned the size of the gain in net national consumption, after subtracting out the extra portion of national income that must be provided to a larger retired population. If fiscal policy is maintained so that social security surpluses increase national saving, the extra future consumption made possible by the increase in the capital stock exceeds the increased burden of social security that is associated with population aging. In other words, a high-saving fiscal policy will produce enough extra income so that the net incomes of future workers will not be reduced by the presence of a large retired population. This conclusion would have had to have been modified if we had included the extra burden associated with medicare and other programs for the elderly. But the basic message of the study would have been the same. Increases in national saving today of approximately the size of our proposed social insurance surpluses can eliminate or substantially reduce the effect of population aging on the net incomes of future workers.

The policy recommendations just described are controversial. They are unwelcome to politicians and current taxpayers because they involve short-term sacrifice. Moreover, the people who stand to gain the most are future workers who do not vote.

The recommendations have been subject to deep economic criticism as well. David Cutler and his colleagues (1990) have argued that decreased fertility and population aging are not reasons by themselves for increasing national saving. These economists argue that other things being equal, the optimal policy response to recent and anticipated demographic changes is almost certainly a *reduction* rather than an increase in the national saving rate. Hence, they conclude that demographic trends provide no compelling reason either to increase the size of the social security surpluses or to reduce the level of non–social security deficits.

The reasoning behind this conclusion is straightforward. The immediate effect of recent demographic changes is to lower the dependency rate and reduce the anticipated rate of labor force growth. As noted earlier, the increase in the aged dependency ratio will occur long after a sharp drop in the youth dependency ratio. The slower rate of labor force growth implies that the nation does not need to save such a high proportion of current production to train and equip new workers. The capital-labor ratio can be maintained with a smaller annual flow of new investment, thus freeing up some previous saving for current consumption. In the next couple of decades, this effect of the demographic swing is the dominant one. When the baby-boom generation retires in the next century, consumption levels will have to fall. Cutler and his colleagues argue, however, that it would be suboptimal to attempt to offset future declines in consumption by making sacrifices in consumption today.

While the reasoning behind this conclusion is sound, the authors restrict their analysis to an economy in which only one important feature of the environment has changed—the fertility rate. In the United States and other industrialized economies, several other important changes also occurred within a ten- or fifteen-year span. Fertility declined, the productivity growth rate fell sharply, and public and private saving rates plummeted. The fertility decline by itself may not provide a good justification for increased government saving, but the other changes do.

My colleagues and I investigated the impact of higher government saving under alternative assumptions about future productivity growth. In performing this analysis, we considered two alternative fiscal policies. Under the first, we assumed that social security would return to pay-as-you-go funding. Under that policy, the large operating surpluses in social security would be eliminated within the next two years. We also assumed, optimistically, that the overall federal deficit—including the surpluses in social security and medicare—will be gradually reduced over the next few years until the deficit is close to its historical norm (about 1.5 percent of GNP).

The second fiscal policy involved advanced funding of social security, as already described. Under this policy, social security reserves would rise over the next ten years at the same rate as currently projected by the chief actuary of the Social Security Administration. But reserves would climb even faster than the current projection starting in the late 1990s, as a result of a payroll tax hike. The tax increase is needed to keep social security in close actuarial balance. Under this assumption, we examined the effect of raising the amount of net government saving by the amount of annual accumulations in the social security trust fund.

In the very short run, the two financing policies do not have very different effects on the economy. The pay-as-you-go policy involves lower taxes, because the payroll tax can be reduced about two percentage points in the 1990s while still collecting enough revenues to pay for expected social security outlays. Thus, pay-as-you-go financing raises the after-tax incomes of American households and businesses in the short run. In the intermediate and longer runs, however, the two policies lead to major differences in the size of the capital stock, in worker productivity, and in average incomes.

I now consider the implications of these two fiscal policies under two assumptions about future productivity growth. Under one assumption, productivity growth will be fairly rapid—about as rapid as it has been, on average, since 1950. Under the more pessimistic assumption, productivity growth will remain as low as it has been since 1973, when it collapsed in the United States.

The effects of these two productivity growth assumptions and two fiscal policies on the after-tax earnings of workers are shown in table 11-3. The detailed calculations are based on the intermediate demographic and economic assumptions adopted by the OASDI trustees in their 1986 annual report. (Those assumptions have subsequently been changed, but the changes have no practical effect on our conclusions.) The first two columns show how fast after-tax wages will rise if total-factor productivity growth occurs at the rate of productivity improvement since 1950. I subtract only OASDI payroll taxes in making this calculation, not income taxes or payroll taxes for medicare. As noted earlier, I also adjusted the OASDI payroll tax to reflect the fact that the rate must be raised at irregular intervals if the social security program is to be kept in close actuarial balance.

The second pair of columns shows how fast after-tax wages will rise if productivity growth continues at the anemic pace the nation has experienced since 1973, a rate that is more than 70 percent below the rate assumed in the first two columns. Wage growth will clearly be much slower if productivity growth continues to be this low. For purposes of comparison, after-payroll-tax compensation per hour rose 27 percent per decade in the first three decades after World War II.

The table shows that wage growth can be significantly improved if a

Gary Burtless

TABLE 11-3. GROWTH OF AFTER-TAX REAL WAGES UNDER
ALTERNATIVE ASSUMPTIONS ABOUT SOCIAL SECURITY FINANCING
POLICY AND PRODUCTIVITY GROWTH

Year	Productivity Growth of 1.4 Percent		Productivity Growth of 0.4 Percent	
	Pay-as-You-Go Financing[a] (1)	Advance Funding[b] (2)	Pay-as-You-Go Financing[a] (3)	Advance Funding[b] (4)
1990	12%	10%	5%	3%
2000	35	35	13	15
2010	65	70	21	26
2020	99	111	27	38
2030	141	159	33	46

Source: Aaron, Bosworth, and Burtless, 1989:92.
After-tax real wage is compensation per hour, including fringe benefits, after subtracting the social security (but not medicare) payroll tax. The table shows percentage rise
in compensation above its level in 1985.
[a]Social security surplus is virtually eliminated after reserves reach 100 percent of annual
outlays; OASDI payroll tax is adjusted to keep social security income equal to outlays.
[b]Social security surplus is added to national saving—the federal government does not
spend it on other operations; OASDI payroll tax is adjusted to keep social security program
solvent in the long run.

social security surplus is accumulated and if it is saved rather than spent
on non–social security federal government operations. Columns 1 and
3 show wage growth under pay-as-you-go social security financing; columns 2 and 4 show wage growth with advance funding when the surplus
is added to national saving. After-tax wage growth is always faster in
the intermediate and long runs if a surplus is accumulated and saved.

For the surplus to be saved, sacrifices in consumption are necessary
in the short run. For example, if a $60 billion social security surplus
were to be saved, the federal deficit would need to be reduced by $60
billion below the level that would occur in the absence of the surplus.
This involves reductions in government spending and increases in federal
taxes that in combination amount to $60 billion.

The estimates in the table are helpful in deciding whether these short-
term consumption sacrifices are desirable. If productivity grows rapidly—
at 1.4 percent a year—net wages would grow 12 percent faster between
1985 and 2020 under the high-saving fiscal policy (111 percent versus
just 99 percent). But if productivity continues to be sluggish, net wages
would grow 41 percent faster under the high-saving policy.

Another way of looking at the same figures may be illuminating.

Under an optimistic assumption about future productivity growth, the wages of workers in 2020 will be about twice as high as those earned by workers in 1985, regardless of the funding mechanism for social security or the fiscal policy adopted. Under a pessimistic assumption, earnings will be only one-third higher. The earnings gain could be substantially affected, however, by the financing and fiscal policies adopted over the next three decades. If productivity growth is going to be high, there is little reason to worry about future workers. Their living standards will be much higher than our own, regardless of the sacrifices in consumption we make today. If productivity growth will be slow, sacrifices today could make a significant difference in raising the living standards of future workers and reducing the burden on them of paying for higher social security benefits.

Productivity rates in the recent past look much more like those assumed in columns 3 and 4 than those assumed in columns 1 and 2. Hence, the policy of accumulating a large reserve fund and adding it to national savings appears relatively much more attractive today than it did before 1973.

CONCLUSION

The nation could have enjoyed the same economic advantages in the past if it had adopted partial advance funding of social security and medicare and if it had used the resulting surpluses to add to national saving. What are the special advantages of this policy in the 1990s?

National saving collapsed in the 1980s. Federal deficits reached levels that were previously attained on a sustained basis only during wars or depressions. The private saving rate slumped nearly three percentage points of national income. From World War II to 1980, the net saving rate in the United States averaged 8 percent of national income. Today the rate is just 2 percent.

The slump in private saving and the sharp rise in federal government dissaving explain why many economists believe that deficits should be reduced to restore the overall saving rate to a level closer to the historical norm. Economists' views on this issue have also been affected by the dramatic declines in productivity growth and population growth that have occurred over the past two decades. If average productivity and the size of the working-age population are growing rapidly, it is less burdensome for workers to finance the retirement benefits of a given generation of retirees. Pensions and medical care for the aged will be paid out of rapidly rising real earnings. The share of earnings that must be set aside for retirement benefits can be kept relatively low. We can anticipate that when productivity and population growth decline, as they have over the past two decades, a rising share of earnings will eventually have to be set aside to finance the consumption of the elderly.

Taken in combination, the trends described in this chapter imply that future workers will be asked to sacrifice a growing share of their earnings to pay for benefits aimed at the aged and disabled. The rising burden of these benefits, which would appear manageable if earnings and productivity were rising strongly, will seem grossly inequitable if earnings are stagnant or declining. To be fair to future generations, we should ask current workers to shoulder a larger part of the burden of paying for their own retirement benefits. This strategy is not only equitable to future workers, it can also raise the productive capacity of the nation.

REFERENCES

Aaron, Henry J.
1982   *Economic Effects of Social Security.* Washington, D.C.: Brookings Institution.

Aaron, Henry J., Barry P. Bosworth, and Gary Burtless
1989   *Can America Afford to Grow Old? Paying for Social Security.* Washington, D.C.: Brookings Institution.

Aarts, Leo, Richard Burkhauser, and Philip deJong
1992   "The Dutch Disease: Lessons for U.S. Disability Policy." *Regulation* 15 (2): 75–86.

Aarts, Leo, and Philip deJong
1992   *Economic Aspects of Disability Behavior:* Amsterdam: North-Holland.

Allen, Steven G., Robert L. Clark, and Ann A. McDermed
1992   "Post-Retirement Benefit Increases in the 1980's." In *Trends in Pensions 1992,* ed. John A. Turner and Daniel J. Beller, 319–40. Washington, D.C.: Government Printing Office.

Forth-   "Pensions, Bonding, and Lifetime Jobs." *Journal of Human Resources.*
coming

Allen, Steven G., Robert L. Clark, and Daniel Sumner
1986   "Post-Retirement Adjustments of Pensions." *Journal of Human Resources* 21 (1): 118–37.

Anderson, Kathryn, Richard Burkhauser, and Joseph F. Quinn
1986   "Do Retirement Dreams Come True? The Effect of Unanticipated Events on Retirement Plans." *Industrial and Labor Relations Review* 39 (4): 518–26.

Anderson, Kathryn, Richard Burkhauser, and Jennie Raymond
1992   "Reality or Illusion: The Importance of Creaming on Job Placement Rates in Job Training Partnership Act Programs." *Metropolitan Studies Program Income Security Policy Paper no. 2. Maxwell School, Syracuse University.

Anker, Richard
1983 "Female Labour Force Participation in Developing Countries: A Critique of Current Definitions and Data Collection Methods." *International Labour Review* 122 (6): 709.
Aoki, Masahiko
1989 *Information, Incentives and Bargaining in the Japanese Economy.* New York: Cambridge University Press.
Association of Employment Development for Senior Citizens
1980 *Teinen Hakusho* (White Paper on Mandatory Retirement).
1985 Tokyo.
1988 *Teinen Tōtatsusha nado no 60 Sai Zenhanki ni okeru Shūgyō to Seikatsu* (Work and Life for Mandatory Retirees Ages 60–64). Tokyo.
1991 *Kōreishakai Tōkei Yōran* (Aging Society Statistical Handbook). Tokyo.
Barringer, Melissa W., George T. Milkovich, and Olivia S. Mitchell
1991 "Predicting Employee Health Insurance Selection in a Flexible Benefits Environment." CAHRS-ILR-Cornell Working Paper. Cornell University.
Bartel, Ann, and George Borjas
1981 "Wage Growth and Job Turnover: An Empirical Analysis." In *Studies in Labor Markets*, ed. Sherwin Rosen, 65–90. Chicago: University of Chicago Press.
Berkowitz, Monroe
1988 "Functioning Ability and Job Performance as Workers Age." In *The Older Worker*, ed. Michael E. Borus, Herbert S. Parnes, Steven H. Sandell, and Bert Seidman, 87–114. Industrial Relations Research Association Series. Madison, Wis.: Industrial Relations Research Association.
Bernheim, B. Douglas
1988 "Social Security Benefits: An Empirical Study of Expectations and Realizations." In *Issues in Contemporary Retirement*, ed. Rita Ricardo-Campbell and Edward P. Lazear, 312–50. Stanford, Calif.: Hoover Institution Press.
Blinder, Alan S., Roger Gordon, and Donald E. Wise
1980 "Reconsidering the Work Disincentive Effects of Social Security." *National Tax Journal* 33 (4): 431–42.
Board of Trustees, Federal Hospital Insurance Trust Fund
1991 *The 1991 Annual Report of the Board of Trustees of the Federal Hospital Insurance Trust Fund.* Washington, D.C.
Board of Trustees, Federal Old-Age and Survivors Insurance and Disability Insurance Trust Funds
1991 *The 1991 Annual Report of the Board of Trustees of the Federal Old-Age Insurance and Disability Insurance Trust Funds.* Washington, D.C.
Board of Trustees, Federal Supplementary Medical Insurance Trust Fund
1991 *The 1991 Annual Report of the Board of Trustees of the Federal Supplementary Medical Insurance Trust Fund.* Washington, D.C.

Bodie, Zvi
1990   "Pensions as Retirement Income Insurance." *Journal of Economic Literature* 28 (1): 28–49.
Bound, John
1989   "The Health and Earnings of Rejected Disability Insurance Applicants." *American Economic Review* 79 (3): 482–503.
1991   "The Health and Earnings of Rejected Disability Insurance Applicants: Reply." *American Economic Review* 81 (5): 1427–34.
Brown, J. Douglas
1972   *An American Philosophy of Social Security.* Princeton: Princeton University Press.
Bulow, Jeremy I.
1982   "What Are Corporate Pension Liabilities?" *Quarterly Journal of Economics* 97 (3): 435–52.
Bumpass, Larry
1990   "What's Happening to the Family? Interactions between Demographic and Institutional Change." *Demography* 27 (4): 483–98.
Burdett, Kenneth
1978   "A Theory of Employee Job Search and Quit Rates." *American Economic Review* 68 (1): 212–20.
Burdett, Kenneth, and Dale T. Mortenson
1980   "Search, Layoffs, and Labor Market Equilibrium." *Journal of Political Economy* 88 (4): 652–72.
Burkhauser, Richard V.
1980   "The Early Acceptance of Social Security: An Asset Maximization Approach." *Industrial and Labor Relations Review* 33 (4): 484–92.
1990   "Morality on the Cheap: The Americans with Disability Act." *Regulation* 3 (2): 47–56.
Burkhauser, Richard V., J. S. Butler, and Yang Kim
1992   "The Importance of Employer Accommodation on the Job Duration of Disabled Workers: A Hazard Model Approach." Syracuse University Working Paper.
Burkhauser, Richard V., J. S. Butler, Yang Kim, and George Slotsve
1992   "Modeling the Timing of the Application for Disability Insurance as a Retirement Decision: A Hazard Model Approach Using Choice-Based Sampling." Metropolitan Studies Program Income Security Policy Paper no. 3. Maxwell School, Syracuse University.
Burkhauser, Richard V., Robert Haveman, and Barbara Wolfe
Forth-   "How People with Disabilities Fare When Public Policies Change."
coming   *Journal of Policy Analysis and Management.*
Burkhauser, Richard V., and Petri Hirvonen
1989   "United States Disability Policy in a Time of Economic Crisis. A Comparison with Sweden and the Federal Republic of Germany." *Milbank Quarterly* 67 (suppl. 2, pt. 1): 166–94.
Burkhauser, Richard V., Yang Kim, and Theodore Pincus
1992   "How Employer Accommodation Influences the Job Duration of

Workers with Acute or Chronic Health Conditions." Syracuse University Working Paper.

Burkhauser, Richard V., and Joseph F. Quinn
1990   "Economic Incentives and the Labor Force Participation of Older Workers." In *Research in Labor Economics*, vol. 11, ed. Laurie Bassi and David Crawford, 159–80. Greenwich, Conn.: JAI Press.

Burtless, Gary T.
1986   "Social Security, Unanticipated Benefit Increases, and the Timing of Retirement." *Review of Economic Studies* 53 (5): 781–805.

Burtless, Gary T., and Robert A. Moffitt
1984   "The Effect of Social Security Benefits on the Labor Supply of the Aged." In *Retirement and Economic Behavior*, ed. Henry J. Aaron and Gary Burtless, 135–74. Washington, D.C.: Brookings Institution.
1985   "The Joint Choice of Retirement Age and Postretirement Hours of Work." *Journal of Labor Economics* 3 (2): 209–36.

Cantrell, Stephen, and Robert L. Clark
1982   "Individual Mobility, Population Growth and Labor Force Participation. *Demography* 19 (1): 147–60.

Carliner, Geoffrey
1982   "The Wages of Older Men." *Journal of Human Resources* 17 (1): 25–38.

Caves, Richard, and Masu Uekusa
1976   "Industrial Organization." In *Asia's New Giant: How the Japanese Economy Works*, ed. H. Patrick and Henry Rosovsky, 459–523. Washington, D.C.: Brookings Institution.

Chang, Hyun-Joon
1985   "Age and the Length of Unemployment Spells: A Structural Hazard Analysis." Ph.D. diss., Cornell University.

Christensen, Kathleen
1990   "Bridges over Troubled Water: How Older Workers View the Labor Market." In *Bridges to Retirement*, ed. Peter B. Doeringer, 175–207. Ithaca, N.Y.: ILR Press.

Clark, Robert L.
1991   *Retirement Systems in Japan*, Homewood, Ill.: Dow Jones-Irwin.
1992   "Population Aging and Retirement Policy: An International Perspective." In *Demography and Retirement: The 21st Century*, ed. Anna Marie Rappaport and Sylvester Schieber. Philadelphia: University of Pennsylvania Press.

Clark, Robert L., and Richard Anker
1989a   "International Comparisons of Labor Force Participation of the Elderly." Department of Economics Working Paper no. 142. North Carolina State University, Raleigh.
1989b   "Labour Force Participation Rates of Older Persons: An International Comparison." Population and Labour Policies Programme Working Paper no. 171. International Labour Office, Geneva.

1990   "Labour Force Participation Rates of Older Persons: An International
         Comparison." *International Labour Review* 129 (2): 255–72.
1991   "Cross-National Analysis of Labor Force Participation of Older Men
         and Women." Department of Economics Working Paper. North Car-
         olina State University, Raleigh.
1992   "Recent Trends in Labor Force Participation of Older Persons." Work-
         ing Paper No. 56, Labor Market Analysis and Employment Planning.
         May.
Clark, Robert L., and Naohiro Ogawa
1992a   "The Effect of Mandatory Retirement on Earnings Profiles in Japan."
         Industrial and Labor Relations Review 45 (2): 258–66.
1992b   "Employment Tenure and Earnings Profiles in Japan and the
         United States: Comment." *American Economic Review* 82 (1):
         336–45.
Cook, Fay Lomax
1990   "Congress and the Public: Convergent and Divergent Opinions on
         Social Security." In *Social Security and the Budget*, ed. Henry J. Aaron,
         79–107. New York: University Press of America.
Crawford, Vincent P., and David Lilien
1981   "Social Security and the Retirement Decision." *Quarterly Journal of
         Economics* 96 (3): 505–29.
Cutler, David M., James M. Poterba, Louise M. Scheiner, and Lawrence H.
Summers
1990   "An Aging Society: Opportunity or Challenge?" *Brookings Papers on
         Economic Activity* 1990 (1): 1–73.
deJong, Philip, Michael Herweijer, and Jaap deWildt
1990   *Form and Reform of the Dutch Social Security System*. Deventer, Neth-
         erlands: Kluwer Law and Taxation Publishers.
Dekle, Robert
1990   "Do the Japanese Elderly Reduce Their Total Wealth? A New Look
         with Different Data." *Journal of the Japanese and International Economies*
         4: 309–17.
Devine, Theresa J.
1988   "Arrivals versus Acceptance: The Source of Variation in Reemploy-
         ment Rates across Demographic Groups." Working Paper. Pennsyl-
         vania State University.
Devine, Theresa J., and Nicholas Kiefer
1991   *Empirical Labor Economics: The Search Approach*. New York: Oxford
         University Press.
Diamond, Peter A., and Jerry A. Hausman
1984   "Individual Retirement and Savings Behavior." *Journal of Public Eco-
         nomics* 23 (1–2): 81–114.
Doeringer, Peter B.
1990   *Bridges to Retirement: Older Workers in a Changing Labor Market*. Ithaca:
         ILR Press.

Dowd, Bryan, and Roger Feldman
1985   "Biased Selection in Twin Cities Health Plans." *Advances in Health Economics and Health Services Research* 6: 253–71.
Dowd, Bryan, Roger Feldman, Steven Cassou, and Michael Finch
1991   "Health Plan Choice and the Utilization of Health Care Services." *Review of Economics and Statistics* 73: 85–93.
Durand, John D.
1975   *The Labor Force in Economic Development.* Princeton: Princeton University Press.
Easterlin, Richard A.
1980   *Birth and Fortune: The Impact of Numbers on Personal Welfare.* New York: Basic Books.
Economic Report of the President
1988   Washington, D.C.: Government Printing Office.
Ehrenberg, Ronald G., and George H. Jakubson
1988   *Advance Notice Provisions in Plant Closing Legislation.* Kalamazoo, Mich.: W. E. Upjohn Institute for Employment Research.
Ekerdt, David J., and Stanley DeViney
1990   "On Defining Persons as Retired." *Journal of Aging Studies* 4 (3): 211–29.
Espenshade, Thomas J.
1985   "Marriage Trends in America: Estimates, Implications, and Causes." *Population and Development Review* 11 (2): 193–246.
Feldman, Roger, Michael Finch, Bryan Dowd, and Steven Cassou
1989   "The Demand for Employment-Based Health Insurance Plans." *Journal of Human Resources* 24 (1): 115–42.
Feldstein, Martin
1983   "Should Private Pensions Be Indexed?" In *Financial Aspects of the United States Pension System*, ed. Zvi Bodie and John B. Shoven, 211–30. Chicago: University of Chicago Press.
Feldstein, Paul
1988   *Health Care Economics.* New York: Wiley.
Fields, Gary S., and Olivia S. Mitchell
1984   *Retirement, Pensions, and Social Security.* Cambridge: MIT Press.
Flaim, Paul O., and Howard N. Fullerton
1976   "New Labor Force Projections to 1990." *Monthly Labor Review* 99 (Dec.): 3–13.
1978   "Labor Force Projections to 1990: Three Possible Paths." *Monthly Labor Review* 101 (Dec.): 25–35.
Frick, Bernd
1990   "Interne Arbeitsmärkte und betriebliche Schwerbehindertenbeschäftigung: Theoretische Analysen und empirische Befunde." Ph.D. diss., Trier University.
Friedman, Bernard
1974   "Risk Aversion and Consumer Choice of Health Insurance Option." *Review of Economics and Statistics* 56 (2): 209–14.

Fujita, Yoshitaka
1984   *Employee Benefits and Industrial Relations*. Japanese Industrial Relations
       Series no. 12. Tokyo: Japan Institute of Labour.
Fullerton, Howard N.
1982   "How Accurate Were Projections of the 1980 Labor Force?" *Monthly
       Labor Review* 105 (July): 15–21.
1988   "An Evaluation of Labor Force Projections to 1985." *Monthly Labor
       Review* 111 (Nov.): 7–17.
1989   "New Labor Force Projections, Spanning 1988 to 2000." *Monthly
       Labor Review* 112 (Nov.): 3–12.
Fullerton, Howard N., and John Tschetter
1983   "The 1995 Labor Force: A Second Look." *Monthly Labor Review* 106
       (Nov.): 3–10.
Gallaway, Lowell E.
1965   "The Retirement Decision: An Exploratory Essay." Research Report
       no. 9. Division of Research and Statistics, Social Security
       Administration.
Gibbons, Robert, and Lawrence Katz
1992   "Does Unmeasured Ability Explain Inter-Industry Wage Differences?"
       Review of Economic Studies 59 (3): 515–35.
Goldin, Claudia
1990   *Understanding the Gender Gap: An Economic History of American
       Women*. New York and Oxford: Oxford University Press.
Goldscheider, Frances K.
1990   "The Aging of the Gender Revolution: What Do We Know and What
       Do We Need to Know." *Research on Aging* 12 (4): 531–45.
Goldscheider, Frances K., and Linda J. Waite
1991   *New Families, No Families? The Transformation of the American Home*.
       Berkeley: University of California Press.
Gordon, Andrew
1985   *The Evolution of Labor Relations in Japan: Heavy Industry*. Cambridge:
       Harvard University Press.
Gordon, Roger, and Alan Blinder
1980   "Market Wages, Reservation Wages, and Retirement Decisions."
       Journal of Public Economics 14 (2): 277–308.
Gronau, Reuben
1971   "Information and Frictional Unemployment." *American Economic Re-
       view* 61 (3, pt. 1): 290–301.
Gustman, Alan L., and Olivia S. Mitchell
1992   "Pensions and Labor Market Activity: Behavior and Data Require-
       ments." In *Pensions and the U.S. Economy: The Need for Good Data*,
       ed. Zvi Bodie and Alicia Munnell, 39–87. Philadelphia: University
       of Pennsylvania Press.
Gustman Alan L., and Thomas L. Steinmeier
1983   "Minimum Hours Constraints and Retirement Behavior." *Contem-
       porary Policy Issues* 3 (2): 77–91.

1985a   "The Effect of Partial Retirement on the Wage Profiles of Older Workers." *Industrial Relations* 24 (2): 257–65.

1985b   "The 1983 Social Security Reforms and Labor Supply Adjustments of Older Individuals in the Long Run." *Journal of Labor Economics* 3 (2): 237–53.

1987   "Pensions, Efficiency Wages and Job Mobility." NBER Working Paper no. 2426. National Bureau of Economic Research, Cambridge, Mass.

1989a   "An Analysis of Pension Benefit Formulas, Pension Wealth and Incentives from Pensions." In *Research in Labor Economics*, vol. 10, ed. Ronald G. Ehrenberg, 33–106. Greenwich, Conn.: JAI Press.

1989b   "Evaluating Pension Policies in a Model with Endogenous Contributions." NBER Working Paper no. 3085. National Bureau of Economic Research, Cambridge, Mass.

1991   "Changing the Social Security Rules for Work after 65." *Industrial and Labor Relations Review* 44 (4): 733–45.

1992   "The Stampede toward Defined Contribution Pension Plans: Fact or Fiction?" *Industrial Relations* 31 (2): 361–69.

Forth-   "Pension Portability and Labor Mobility: Evidence from the Survey
coming   of Income and Program Participation." *Journal of Public Economics*.

Hagens, John B.
1980   "Social Security and Retirement." ORS Working Paper no. 17. Office of Research and Statistics, Office of Policy, Social Security Administration.

Hall, Robert E.
1982   "The Importance of Lifetime Jobs in the U.S. Economy." *American Economic Review* 72 (4): 716–24.

Hamermesh, Daniel S.
1984   "The Human Capital Losses of Displaced Workers." *Poverty Institute Working Paper*, DP 753–84 (July).

Hanoch, Giora, and Marjorie Honig
1983   "Retirement, Wages, and Labor Supply of the Elderly." *Journal of Labor Economics* 1 (2): 131–51.

Hashimoto, Masanori
1990   *The Japanese Labor Market in a Comparative Perspective with the United States*. Kalamazoo, Mich.: W. E. Upjohn Institute for Employment Research.

Hausman, Jerry A., and David A. Wise
1985   "Social Security, Health Status, and Retirement." In *Pensions, Labor, and Individual Choice*, ed. D. A. Wise, 159–191. Chicago: University of Chicago Press.

Haveman, Robert, Victor Halberstadt, and Richard Burkhauser
1984   *Public Policy toward Disabled Workers: A Cross-National Comparison of Economic Impacts*. Ithaca: Cornell University Press.

Heckman, James J.
1979   "Sample Bias as a Specification Error." *Econometrica* 47 (1): 153–62.

Herz, Diane E., and Philip L. Rones

1989 "Institutional Barriers to the Employment of Older Workers." *Monthly Labor Review* 112 (April): 14–21.

Hewitt Associates
1989 *Flexible Compensation Programs and Practices.* Lincolnshire, Ill.

Hoefer, Michael D.
1991 "Immigration Limits and Projected Immigration for Fiscal Years 1990– 97." Table. Statistics Division, U.S. Immigration and Naturalization Service.

Holmer, Martin
1984 "Tax Policy and the Demand for Health Insurance." *Journal of Health Economics* 3 (3): 203–21.

Hutchens, Robert M.
1986 "Delayed Payment Contracts and a Firm's Propensity to Hire Older Workers." *Journal of Labor Economics* 4 (4): 439–57.
1988 "Do Job Opportunities Decline with Age?" *Industrial and Labor Relations Review* 42 (1): 89–99.
1989 "Seniority, Wages and Productivity: A Turbulent Decade." *Journal of Economic Perspectives* 3 (4): 49–64.

International Labour Organisation
1970–90 *Yearbook of Labour Statistics.* Geneva.

Ippolito, Richard A.
1986 *Pensions, Economics and Public Policy.* Homewood, Ill.: Dow Jones-Irwin.
1990 "Toward Explaining Earlier Retirement after 1970." *Industrial and Labor Relations Review* 43 (5): 556–69.

Japan Ministry of Labor
1988a *Kōnenreisha Shūgyō no Jittai* (Older Persons Survey). Tokyo.
1988b *Rōdō Hakusho* (Handbook of Labor Statistics). Tokyo.
1990 *Rōdō Tōkei Yōran* (White Paper on Labor). Tokyo.

Japan Ministry of Welfare
Annual *Shakai Hoshō Nenpō* (Yearbook of Social Insurance). Tokyo.
1987 *Jigyō Nenpō* (Annual Operations Report). Tokyo.
1988

Japan Office of the Prime Minister
1970 *Population Census of Japan.* Tokyo.
1985
Various *Labor Force Survey.* Tokyo.
years

Johnston, William B., and Arnold H. Packer
1987 *Workforce 2000.* Indianapolis: Hudson Institute.

Juba, David A., Judith R. Lave, and Jonathan Shaddy
1980 "An Analysis of the Choice of Health Benefits Plans." *Inquiry* 17 (1): 62–71.

Kahn, James A.
1988 "Social Security, Liquidity, and Early Retirement." *Journal of Public Economics* 35 (1): 97–117.

Kawakita, Takashi
1989   "Elderly Workers in Japan." *Japan Labor Bulletin*, June, 6–8.
Keyfitz, Nathan
1973   "Individual Mobility in a Stationary Population." *Population Studies*
          27: 335–52.
Kotlikoff, Laurence J., and Daniel E. Smith
1983   *Pensions in the American Economy*. Chicago: University of Chicago
          Press.
Kotlikoff, Laurence J., and David A. Wise.
1985   "Labor Compensation and the Structure of Private Pension Plans:
          Evidence for Contractual Versus Spot Labor Markets." In *Pensions,
          Labor, and Individual Choice*, ed. David A. Wise, 55–85. Chicago:
          University of Chicago Press.
1987   "The Incentive Effects of Private Pension Plans." In *Issues in Pension
          Economics*, ed. Zvi Bodie, John B. Shoven, and David A. Wise, 283–
          336. Chicago: University of Chicago Press.
Lazear, Edward P.
1979   "Why Is There Mandatory Retirement?" *Journal of Political Economy*
          87 (6): 1261–84.
1981   "Agency, Earnings Profiles, Productivity, and Hours Restrictions."
          American Economic Review 71 (4): 606–20.
1983   "Pensions as Severance Pay." In *Financial Aspects of the United States
          Pension System*, ed. Zvi Bodie, and John B. Shoven, 57–85. Chicago:
          University of Chicago Press.
Leonesio, Michael V.
1990a   "The Effects of the Social Security Earnings Test on the Labor- Market
          Activity of Older Americans: A Review of the Evidence." *Social Se-
          curity Bulletin* 53 (5): 2–21.
1990b   "Economic Retirement Studies: An Annotated Bibliography." ORS
          Working Paper no. 45. Office of Research and Statistics, Office of
          Policy, Social Security Administration.
Levine, Phillip B., and Olivia S. Mitchell
1992   "Expected Changes in the Workforce and Implications for Labor Mar-
          kets." In *Demography and Retirement: The 21st Century*, ed. Anna
          Marie Rappaport and Sylvester Schieber. Philadelphia: University of
          Pennsylvania Press.
Lingg, Barbara A.
1986   "Beneficiaries Affected by the Annual Earnings Test in 1982." *Social
          Security Bulletin* 49 (5): 25–32.
McCarty, Therese A.
1990   "The Effect of Social Security on Married Women's Labor Force Par-
          ticipation." *National Tax Journal* 43 (1): 95–110.
McGuire, Thomas G.
1981   "Price and Membership in a Prepaid Group Medical Practice." *Medical
          Care* 19 (2): 172–83.

Maddala, G. S.
1983   *Limited-Dependent and Qualitative Variables in Econometrics.* New York: Cambridge University Press.
Marquis, M. Susan, and Martin R. Holmer
1986   "Choice under Uncertainty and the Demand for Health Insurance." Rand Note N-2516-HHS. Rand Corp., Santa Monica, Calif.
Meisenheimer, Joseph R. and William J. Wiatrowski
1989   "Flexible Benefits Plans: Employees Who Have a Choice." *Monthly Labor Review* 112 (December): 17–23.
Merrill, Jeffrey, Catherine Jackson, and James Reuter
1985   "Factors That Affect the HMO Enrollment Decision: A Tale of Two Cities." *Inquiry* 22 (4): 388–95.
Mirkin, Barry A.
1987   "Early Retirement as a Labor Force Policy." *Monthly Labor Review* 110 (March): 19–33.
Mitchell, Olivia S.
1982   "Fringe Benefits and Labor Mobility." *Journal of Human Resources* 17 (2): 286–98.
1988a   "The Relation of Age to Workplace Injury." *Monthly Labor Review* 111 (July): 8-13.
1988b   "Worker Knowledge of Pension Provisions." *Journal of Labor Economics* 6 (1): 21–39.
1992   "Trends in Pension Benefit Formulas and Retirement Provisions." In *Trends in Pensions 1992*, ed. John A. Turner and Daniel J. Beller, 177–216. Washington, D.C.: Government Printing Office.
Mitchell, Olivia S., and Emily Andrews
1981   "Scale Economies in Private Multi-Employer Pension Systems." *Industrial and Labor Relations Review* 34 (5): 522–30.
Moffitt, Robert A.
1987   "Life-Cycle Labor Supply and Social Security: A Time Series Analysis." In *Work, Health and Income among the Elderly*, ed. Gary Burtless, 183–219. Washington, D.C.: Brookings Institution.
Mortensen, Dale T.
1986   "Job Search and Labor Market Analysis." In *Handbook of Labor Economics*, ed. Orley Ashenfelter and Richard Layard, 849–919. New York: North-Holland.
Motokawa, Akira, and Ryuji Mori
1981   "Kōnenreisha no Shūgyō ritsu Henka ni Kansuru Yōin Bunseki" (Factor Analysis of Changes in the Participation Rate of Older People). *Rōdō Geppō* 33 (5): 4–21.
Munnell, Alicia H.
1977   *The Future of Social Security.* Washington, D.C.: Brookings Institution.
Murray, Janet
1979   "Subjective Retirement." *Social Security Bulletin* 42 (11): 1–7.

Nagano, Hitoshi
1990   *Kigyō Grūpunai Jinzai Idō no Kenkyū* (Studies on Personnel Movement within Corporate Groups). Tokyo: Taka Shuppan.
Narendranathan, Wiji, and Stephen Nickell
1985   "Modelling the Process of Job Search." *Journal of Econometrics* 28 (1): 29–49.
Nikkeiren (Japan Federation of Employers' Association)
1990   "60 Saidai Zenkisō Saikoyō Seido no Jitsurei" (Case Studies of Reemployment Systems for Ages 60–64). *Chingin Jitsumu* (Nov.): 21–32.
Oi, Walter
1962   "Labor as a Quasi-Fixed Factor." *Journal of Political Economy* 70 (6): 538–55.
1991   "Disability and a Workforce-Welfare Dilemma." In *Disability and Work: Incentives, Rights, and Opportunities*, ed. Carolyn Weaver, 31–45. Washington D.C.: American Enterprise Institute.
Olshansky, S. Jay, Bruce A. Carnes, and Christine Cassel
1990   "In Search of Methuselah: Estimating the Upper Limits to Human Longevity." *Science* 250: 634–40.
O'Neill, June
1990   "Women and Wages." *American Enterprise*, Nov.–Dec., 25–33.
Otake, Fumio
1991   "Isan Dōki to Kōreisha no Chochiku—Rōdō Kyōkyū" (The Bequest Motive and the Savings and Labor Supply of Older Persons). *Keizai Kenkyū* 42 (1): 21–30.
Packard, Michael D.
1985   "Knowledge of the Earnings Test." Unpublished manuscript. Office of Research and Statistics, Social Security Administration.
1990   "The Effects of Removing 70- and 71-Year-Olds from Coverage under the Social Security Earnings Test." ORS Working Paper no. 44. Office of Research and Statistics, Social Security Administration.
Parnes, Herbert, and Gilbert Nestel
1981   "The Retirement Experience." In *Work and Retirement: A Longitudinal Study of Men*, ed. Herbert Parnes, 155–97. Cambridge: MIT Press.
Parsons, Donald
1991   "The Health and Earnings of Rejected Disability Insurance Applicants: Comment." *American Economic Review*: 81 (5): 1419–26.
Pellechio, Anthony J.
1978   "The Social Security Earnings Test, Labor Supply Distortions and Foregone Payroll Tax Revenue." NBER Working Paper no. 272. National Bureau of Economic Research, Cambridge, Mass.
Piontkowski, Dyan, and Lewis H. Butler
1980   "Selection of Health Insurance by an Employee Group in Northern California." *American Journal of Public Health* 70 (3): 274–76.
Pozzebon, Silvana, and Olivia S. Mitchell
1989   "Married Women's Retirement Behavior." *Journal of Population Economics* 2 (1): 39–53.

Preston, Samuel H.
1992 "Demographic Change in the United States, 1970–2050." In *Demography and Retirement: The 21st Century*, ed. Anna Marie Rappaport and Sylvester Schieber. Philadelphia: University of Pennsylvania Press.

Quinn, Joseph F.
1977 "Microeconomic Determinants of Early Retirement: A Cross-Sectional View of White Married Men." *Journal of Human Resources* 12 (3): 329–46.
1978 "Job Characteristics and Early Retirement." *Industrial Relations* 17 (3): 315–23.
1987 Comment on "Life-Cycle Labor Supply and Social Security: A Time Series Analysis." In *Work, Health and Income among the Elderly*, ed. Gary Burtless, 220–28. Washington, D.C.: Brookings Institution.
1992 Comment on "Expected Changes in the Workforce and Implications for Labor Markets." In *Demography and Retirement: The 21st Century*, ed. Anna Marie Rappaport and Sylvester Schieber. Philadelphia: University of Pennsylvania Press.

Quinn, Joseph F., Richard V. Burkhauser, and Daniel A. Myers
1990 *Passing the Torch: The Influence of Economic Incentives on Work and Retirement*. Kalamazoo, Mich.: W. E. Upjohn Institute for Employment Research.

Ransom, Roger L., and Richard Sutch
1988a "The Labor of Older Americans: Retirement of Men on and off the Job." *Journal of Economic History* 46 (March): 1–30.
1988b "The Decline of Retirement in the Years before Social Security: U.S Retirement Patterns, 1870–1940." In *Issues in Contemporary Retirement*, ed. Rita Ricardo-Campbell and Edward P. Lazear, 3–37. Stanford, Calif.: Hoover Institution Press.

Rebick, Marcus
1990 "Japanese Labor Markets and Institutions under Slower Growth: Essays on the Period 1970–1989." Ph.D. diss., Harvard University.

Reimers, Cordelia, and Marjorie Honig
1990 "The Perceived Budget Constraint under Social Security: Evidence from Re-entry Behavior." Department of Economics Working Paper. Hunter College, New York.

Reinsdorf, Marshall B.
1987 "Implications of Structural Retirement Models." Bureau of Statistics Working Paper no. 162. U.S. Department of Labor.

Riche, Martha Farnsworth
1990a *The Shape of the American Marketplace*. Ithaca: American Demographics Press.
1990b "The Boomerang Age." *American Demographics* 12 (5): 24–28ff.
1991 "Minority Majority." *American Demographics* 13 (10): 26–34.

Ruhm, Christopher J.
1990 "Career Jobs, Bridge Employment, and Retirement." In *Bridges to*

Retirement: Older Workers in a Changing Labor Market, ed. Peter B. Doeringer, 92–107. Ithaca: ILR Press.

Salop, Steven, and Joanne Salop
1976   "Self-Selection and Turnover in the Labor Market." *Quarterly Journal of Economics* 91 (4): 619–28.

Sander, Kenneth G.
1968   "The Retirement Test: Its Effect on Older Workers' Earnings." *Social Security Bulletin* 31 (6): 3–6.

Seike, Atsushi
1985   "Kōreisha Shūgyō no Sūsei to Kōteki Nenkin" (Trends of Older Worker Employment and Public Pensions). *Nihon Rōdō Kyōkai Zassi* (June): 9–16.
1989   "The Effect of the Employee Pension on the Labor Supply of the Japanese Elderly." Paper presented at the JCER-NBER Joint Conference on Aging, Tokyo, Sept. 9.

Self
1990   *The New Diversity: Self Magazine Reports on American Women.* New York: Condé Nast.

Shapiro, David, and Steven Sandell
1985   "Age Discrimination in Wages and Displaced Older Men." *Southern Economic Journal* 52 (1): 90–102.

Sheppard, Harold L., Louis Ferman, and Seymour Faber
1960   *Too Old to Work, Too Young to Retire.* Washington, D.C.: U.S. Special Committee on Unemployment Problems.

Sherman, Sally R.
1985   "Reported Reasons Retired Workers Left Their Last Job: Findings from the New Beneficiary Survey." *Social Security Bulletin* 48 (3): 22–30.

Sindelar, Jody L.
1982   "Differential Use of Medical Care by Sex." *Journal of Political Economy* 90 (5): 1003–19.

Smith, Shirley
1985   "Revised Worklife Tables Reflecting 1979–1981 Experiences." *Monthly Labor Review* 108 (December): 23–30.

Smitka, Michael
1991   *Competitive Ties: Subcontracting in the Japanese Automotive Industry.* New York: Columbia University Press.

Speare, Alden
1987   "The Role of Immigration in U.S. Population Distribution." Paper presented at the annual meeting of the Population Association of America, Chicago, April 30–May 2.

Taubman, Paul J., and Sherwin Rosen
1982   "Healthiness, Education, and Marital Status." In *Economic Aspects of Health*, ed. Victor R. Fuchs, 121–40. Chicago: University of Chicago Press.

Tracy, Martin B.
1982   "The Earnings Test and Work Patterns in Four Nations." Final Report to the Office of International Policy, Social Security Administration.

Tzeng, Mei-Shenn, and Robert D. Mare
1990   "Labor Market and Socioeconomic Effects on Marital Stability, 1966–
        1987." Paper presented at the annual meeting of the Population As-
        sociation of America, Toronto, May 3–5.
United Nations
1988   *World Demographic Estimates and Projections, 1950–2025.* New York.
1989   *World Population Prospects, 1988.* New York: United Nations.
1991   "Global Population Estimates and Projections: 1990." Diskette.
U.S. Bureau of the Census
1957   *Illustrative Projections of the Population of the United States, by Age and
        Sex, 1960 to 1980.* Current Population Reports, ser. P–25, no. 187.
        Washington, D.C.: Government Printing Office.
1984   *Projections of the Population of the United States, by Age, Sex, and Race:
        1988 to 2080.* Current Population Reports, ser. P–25, no. 952. Wash-
        ington, D.C.: Government Printing Office.
1986   *Projections of the Hispanic Population: 1983 to 2080.* Current Population
        Reports, ser. P–25, no. 995. Washington, D.C.: Government Print-
        ing Office.
1989   *Projections of the Population of the United States, by Age, Sex, and Race:
        1988 to 2080.* Current Population Reports, ser. P–25, no. 1018.
        Washington, D.C.: Government Printing Office.
1990   *Statistical Abstract of the United States, 1990.* Washington, D.C.: Gov-
        ernment Printing Office.
1991a   *Money Income and Poverty Status in the United States: 1988–89.* Current
        Population Reports, ser. P–60, no. 172. Washington, D.C.: Govern-
        ment Printing Office.
1991b   "Census Bureau Releases Refined Estimates from Post-Enumeration
        Survey of 1990 Census Coverage." Press Release CB91–221. June 13.
1991c   "1990 Census Profile (3): Metropolitan Areas and Cities." Brief.
U.S. Congress. House. Committee on Ways and Means
1986   *Background Material and Data on Programs within the Jurisdiction of the
        Committee on Ways and Means.* Washington, D.C.: Government
        Printing Office.
1991   *1991 Green Book: Background Material and Data on Programs within the
        Jurisdiction of the Committee on Ways and Means.* Washington, D.C.:
        Government Printing Office.
U.S. Department of Commerce. Bureau of Economic Analysis
1985   *BEA Regional Projections.* Washington, D.C.: Government Printing
        Office.
U.S. Department of Education
1991   *Caseload Statistics: State Vocational Rehabilitation Agencies, Fiscal Year
        1991.* Washington, D.C.: Rehabilitation Services Administration,
        Office of Special Education and Rehabilitative Services.
U.S. Department of Health and Human Services. Social Security Admin-
        istration
1983   *Economic Projections for OASDI Cost Estimates, 1983.* Actuarial Study
        no. 90. Washington, D.C.: Government Printing Office.

Various   *Social Security Bulletin. Annual Statistical Supplement.* Washington,
years   D.C.: Government Printing Office.
U.S. Department of Labor
Various   *Employee Benefits in Medium and Large Size Firms.* Washington, D.C.:
years   Government Printing Office.
1961   *Employment and Earnings.* January. Washington, D.C.: Government
          Printing Office.
1965   *The Older American Worker.* Report of the Secretary of Labor to the
          Congress under Section 715 of the Civil Rights Act of 1964. Wash-
          ington, D.C.: Government Printing Office.
1989   "Older Worker Task Force: Key Policy Issues for the Future." Report
          of the Secretary of Labor.
1991   *Employment and Earnings.* January. Washington, D.C.: Government
          Printing Office.
U.S. National Center for Health Statistics. Public Health Service.
1991a   *Monthly Vital Statistics Report,* vol. 39, no. 12. Washington, D. C.:
          Government Printing Office.
1991b   *Advance Report of Final Marriage Statistics, 1988,* vol. 40, no. 4
          (suppl.). Washington, D.C.: Government Printing Office.
1991c   *Advance Report of Final Natality Statistics, 1989,* vol. 40, no. 8 (suppl.).
          Washington, D.C.: Government Printing Office.
Vroman, Wayne
1985   "Some Economic Effects of the Social Security Retirement Test." In
          Research in Labor Economics, vol. 7, ed. Ronald G. Ehrenberg, 31–
          89. Greenwich, Conn.: JAI Press.
Weaver, Carolyn
1986   "Social Security Disability Policy in the 1980s and Beyond." In *Dis-
          ability and the Labor Market: Economic Problems, Policies, and Programs,*
          ed. Monroe Berkowitz and Ann Hill, 29–63. Ithaca: ILR Press.
1991   *Disability and Work: Incentives, Rights, and Opportunities.* Washington,
          D.C.: American Enterprise Institute.
Welch, W. P.
1986   "The Elasticity of Demand for Health Maintenance Organizations."
          Journal of Human Resources 21 (2): 252–66.
Welch, W. P., and Richard G. Frank
1986   "The Predictors of HMO Enrollee Populations: Results from a Na-
          tional Sample." *Inquiry* 23 (1): 16–22.
Wilensky, Gail, and Louis Rossiter
1986   "Patient Self-Selection in HMOs." *Health Affairs* 5 (1): 66–80.
Wyatt Company
Various   *A Survey of Retirement, Thrift and Profit Sharing Plans Covering Salaried
years   Employees of 50 Large U.S. Industrial Companies.* Annual survey.
Yamada, Tetsuji
1990   "The Labor Force Participation of Elderly Males in Japan." *Journal of
          the Japanese and International Economies* 4 (1): 1–23.

CONTRIBUTORS

MELISSA W. BARRINGER is an assistant professor of management at the University of Massachusetts at Amherst. She specializes in employee compensation and is currently working on research projects on flexible benefits plans and international compensation. Barringer earned her Ph.D. in human resource studies from Cornell University.

RICHARD V. BURKHAUSER is a professor of economics and a research associate in the Metropolitan Studies Program at Syracuse University. He received his Ph.D. in economics from the University of Chicago. He has published widely on issues related to disability and retirement policy. His books include *Public Policy toward Disabled Workers: A Cross-National Comparison of Economic Impacts*, with Robert H. Haveman and Victor Halberstadt, and, most recently, *Passing the Torch: The Influence of Economic Incentives on Work and Retirement*, with Joseph F. Quinn and Daniel A. Myers.

GARY BURTLESS is a senior fellow in the Economics Studies Program at the Brookings Institution in Washington, D.C. His previous positions included policy posts at the U.S. Department of Labor and the U.S. Department of Health, Education and Welfare. He has written several books on labor market and aging policy, including *Can America Afford to Grow Old?* He received his Ph.D. in economics from MIT.

ROBERT L. CLARK has been on the faculty of North Carolina State University since 1975 and was appointed interim head of the Division of Economics and Business in 1990. He also is a senior fellow at the Center for the Study of Aging and Human Development at Duke University and a senior research fellow at the Center for Demographic Studies, also at Duke. Clark earned his Ph.D. in economics from Duke University.

ALAN L. GUSTMAN is the Loren M. Berry Professor of Economics at Dartmouth College and a research associate at the National Bureau of Economic Research. Other professional affiliations include the technical review board of the Bureau of Labor Statistics National Longitudinal Survey, chair of the Working Group on Labor Force Participation and Pensions for the University of Michigan Survey Research Center and the National Institute on Aging, Health and Retirement Survey, and the National Academy of Social Insurance. He has published widely on the economics of retirement and pensions. He received his Ph.D. in economics from the University of Michigan.

ROBERT M. HUTCHENS is a professor of labor economics at the School of Industrial and Labor Relations at Cornell University. Hutchens received his Ph.D. in economics from the University of Wisconsin in 1976. A specialist in labor economics, public finance, and econometrics, he has written several papers on the economics of government transfer programs, with an emphasis on unemployment insurance and aid to families with dependent children. In 1980–81, he was a policy fellow at the Brookings Institution, devoting part of his time to the Department of Health and Human Services. His current research encompasses not only government transfer programs but also long-term implicit contracts and the market for older workers.

MICHAEL V. LEONESIO is an economist in the Division of Economic Research in the Office of Research and Statistics of the Social Security Administration. His research interests concern the relationship between social security programs and labor market activity. He received his Ph.D. in labor economics from Cornell University. His recent publications include studies on the effects of the social security earnings test on labor supply and research on in-kind transfers.

PHILLIP B. LEVINE is an assistant professor of economics at Wellesley College. He recently completed a Ph.D. in economics at Princeton University after pursuing graduate work in labor economics at Cornell University. His research interests include unemployment and unemployment insurance, women in the labor market, and the effects of demographic change in labor markets.

OLIVIA S. MITCHELL is a professor of labor economics at Cornell University's School of Industrial and Labor Relations and a research associate with the National Bureau of Economic Research. She specializes in the labor market impact of the baby boom, employee benefits, and social insurance programs. Mitchell also directs the Labor Force Demographics Program for the Institute for Labor Market Policy at Cornell University, works with Cornell's Center for Advanced Human Resource Studies, and is associate editor of the *Industrial and Labor Relations Review*. Mitchell received her Ph.D in economics from the University of Wisconsin at Madison.

MARCUS REBICK is an assistant professor of labor economics at Cornell University's School of Industrial and Labor Relations. His research interests focus on international and comparative labor economics, especially United States–Japan comparisons. He received his Ph.D. in economics from Harvard University.

MARTHA FARNSWORTH RICHE is the director of policy studies at the Population Reference Bureau (PRB), a private, not-for-profit organization that specializes in providing information about Americans' changing demographic, social, and economic characteristics. Before joining PRB, Riche was a founding editor of

American Demographics magazine, a Dow Jones monthly that interprets consumer trends for business. The author of numerous articles in business and economic journals, Riche is regularly quoted as an expert by the national media and appears often on television and radio. She received her Ph.D. from Georgetown University.

THOMAS L. STEINMEIER is a professor of economics at Texas Tech University. Other professional affiliations include the University of Michigan's Survey Research Center, and National Institute on Aging, Health and Retirement Survey, and chair of the Working Group on Non-Household Record Linkages. He has published widely on the economics of retirement and disability. He received his Ph.D. in economics from Yale University.

INDEX

Aaron, Henry J., 187, 243, 246
Aarts, Leo, 207, 209
Actuarial adjustment: of benefits under
  social security, 194, 196
Africa: aging in, 8, 58–60, 62–63;
  labor force participation in, 57–77
Age: demand for health insurance by,
  125–46; disability and, 217;
  discrimination, 10, 82, 115, 193;
  influence on social security, 237–40;
  in Japan, 104; structure, 27, 225;
  trends in distribution of, 4–8, 27–
  29, 32. See also Population
Age Discrimination in Employment
  Act (ADEA), 48
Allen, Steven C., 65, 148, 153, 154,
  155
Americans with Disabilities Act
  (ADA), 13, 205–24
Anderson, Kathryn, 209, 223
Anker, Richard, 68
Asia: aging in, 8, 62–63; labor force
  participation in, 57–77; population
  by country of origin, 30–31
Asian-Americans: population of, 29–
  30
Association of Employment
  Development for Senior Citizens,
  111, 116
AT&T, 150
Automatic Benefit Recomputation
  (ABR): under social security, 194,
  198
Average indexed monthly earnings
  (AIME), 189, 195

Baby boom: in Europe, 58–60;
  generation, 22, 23–25, 27, 35, 225–
  26; in Japan, 58–60; in the United
  States, 4, 7. See also Cohort;
  Demographic transition; Population
Baby bust: in Europe, 58–60;
  generation, 22–23; in Japan, 58–60;
  in North America, 58–60
Barriers for older workers, 81–102,
  185, 193. See also Labor market;
  Retirement
Barringer, Melissa W., 11, 132n, 139
Bartel, Ann, 81
Benefits: for the disabled, 223; health
  insurance, 125–46; pension, 147–80;
  social security, 49–54, 106, 185–
  204. See also Insurance
Berkowitz, Monroe, 48n
Bernheim, B. Douglas, 190n
Black population, 5, 30–31
Blind, the, 214–15; aid to, 210. See
  also Handicaps
Blinder, Alan S., 191, 192, 194, 199n
Blue Cross/Blue Shield, 125. See also
  Health insurance
Board of Trustees of the Federal HI
  Trust Fund, 228
Board of Trustees of the Federal
  OASDI Trust Fund, 228
Board of Trustees of the Federal SMI
  Trust Fund, 228
Bodie, Zvi, 161
Bound, John, 216
BP America, 151
Bridge jobs, 6. See also Retirement